**THE
DISCOVERY
OF SOCIETY**

D$3.95

Daniel Nelson

102 Clark St,

THE DISCOVERY OF SOCIETY

RANDALL COLLINS
University of California, San Diego

AND

MICHAEL MAKOWSKY
San Francisco Extension Center
University of California, Berkeley

RANDOM HOUSE
New York

ISBN: 0-394-31051-9

Library of Congress Catalog Card Number: 77-165789

Manufactured in the United States of America

Composed by Cherry Hill Composition, Pennsauken, New Jersey
Printed and bound by Kingsport Press, Kingsport, Tennessee

987654

TO
HERBERT BLUMER
AND
LEO LOWENTHAL

PREFACE

As an introduction to sociology, *The Discovery of Society* offers accounts of the lives of pioneers in the field within the perspective of the cultures in which those sociologists lived. Since idea systems do not spring magically into existence, it is important to understand the circumstances that conditioned the emergence of social theories that have profoundly affected the ways in which we view our world.

Throughout this book we emphasize the necessity of joining mere speculation with empirical observation, remembering that theory without research is blind and research without theory is empty. Our primary hope, however, is that students will take from this book a knowledge that sociology is more than a science in process of formulation—it is also a branch of humane learning.

There are many who must be thanked. Joseph Gusfield and Alvin Gouldner kindly read and commented on parts of the manuscript. Hans Gerth, Leo Lowenthal, and Herbert Marcuse provided reminiscences on particular points. None of these can be held responsible for our errors. This perhaps cannot be said about our various teachers. Ideas never spring up full-blown in any individual mind; they grow in long chains of passage from teachers to students. We are fortunate in the legacies we have received from our teachers in several universities, including

Joseph Ben-David, Reinhard Bendix, Robert Bierstedt, Herbert Blumer, Kingsley Davis, Wolfram Eberhard, Leo Lowenthal, and Talcott Parsons. The presence of Erving Goffman at the University of California at Berkeley in the mid-1960s was also unmistakable, although neither of us has been a formal student of his. Other influences came with the atmosphere of that memorable community.

CONTENTS

**THE
DISCOVERY
OF SOCIETY**

INTRODUCTION: SOCIOLOGY AND ILLUSION

We all conceive of ourselves as experts on society. In fact, however, the social world is a mystery—a mystery deepened by our lack of awareness of it. Society is our immediate, everyday reality, yet we understand no more of it merely by virtue of living it than we understand of physiology by virtue of our inescapable presence as living bodies. The history of sociology has been a long and arduous effort to become aware of things hidden or taken for granted: Things we did not know existed—other societies in distant place and times, whose ways of life make us wonder about the naturalness of our own. Things we know of only distortedly—the experiences of social classes and cultures other than our own; the realities of remote sectors of our own social structure, from that inside the police patrol car to those behind the closed doors of the politician and the priest. Things right around us unreflectingly accepted—the network of invisible rules and institutions that govern our behavior and populate our thought, seemingly as immutable as the physical landscape but in reality as flimsy as a children's pantomime. Most obscure of all, our own feelings, actions, thoughts, and self-images —the tacit bargains that we make and remake with friends, lovers, acquaintances, and strangers and the paths we steer amid emotions, habits, and beliefs. All of these things are beneath the usual threshold of our awareness.

We think of ourselves as rational, choice-making masters of our actions if not of our destinies; in reality, we know little about the reasons for either. And if the social world is shrouded from us today, it becomes even more illusory the further back we go into our history. It is only a few hundred years back in European history to an era when authority of kings and aristocracies was legitimized by the supernatural, when unexpected behavior from our fellows was explained as witchcraft and seizures of the devil, and foreign lands were populated not merely by blood-thirsty Communists or the terrible Turk but by werewolves and cyclopses. "History is a nightmare from which I am trying to awake!" James Joyce declared. Sociology has been part of that very slow awakening.

The social world as we know it and have known it is mostly illusion. Yet, if we were all completely deluded, there would be no point in trying to investigate and explain, and this writing as well as any other would be worthless. The existence of illusions is not incompatible with the existence of facts and of the principles of logic. But facts and logic are inextricably mixed with concepts and theories, and for the study of society the concepts and theories are ones that we daily act upon as well as use to explain how things are and why.

Sociology is not an impossible science, but it is a very difficult one. It has progressed by disengaging the web of everyday belief, not all at once, but little by little as one taken-for-granted assumption after another is questioned and replaced. As was once said of philosophy, sociology is like rebuilding a boat, plank by plank, while floating on it in the middle of the ocean. The history of sociology is a progression of world views, each an advance on some other in that it asks some previously unasked question, avoids some previous confusion, or incorporates some previously unobserved fact. Each world view, including our own, has its illusions; waving the banner of science is no more absolute a guarantee of truth than any other. Nevertheless, there has been a series of major breakthroughs in understanding, including some quite recent ones, and we can be confident now that we are on the right path.

THE SOURCES OF ILLUSION

At the center of the web that clouds our vision is the fact that our knowledge is both subjective and objective. "Facts" are things that independent observers can agree upon; but we must look for facts in order to see them, and what we look for depends on our concepts and theories. What questions we can answer depends on what questions we ask. But the form of the question cannot be the only determinant of the answer, or else our knowledge would never go beyond the subjective point of view of the particular questioner. Any completely subjective viewpoint undermines its own validity, since there is no reason for anyone else to accept it. If there are no objective standards, then the man who claims that there are no such standards can never prove his claim to be true.

There is a realm of objectivity, then, based on shared observations and the exigencies of logical communication. We do not know, however, whether any particular theory or even any particular belief about the facts is true. The problem of separating illusions from reality has been an especially difficult one for sociology, since it begins in the midst of the social world of everyday ideas and ideologies. Until we begin to notice phenomena and ask questions about them, we cannot start to check our theories against the facts or even to check our assumed facts against careful observations. It took many centuries of controversy about ideological and practical issues before some men realized that their ordinary ideas might not be accurate and hence were in need of logical ordering and empirical testing. Even after there arose a community of men dedicated to this purpose, much of the raw material of human illusion remained mixed in with the more solid part of sociological knowledge. Progress has come not because sociologists were convinced that a particular theory was right, but because the scholarly community generated a cutting edge of objectivity out of their own controversies and research efforts that has moved them onward in the right direction.

We cannot usually notice something unless we have a name for it. This is true of the physical world—the botanist notices dozens of species of plants where the layman sees only a field—and it is especially important for understanding society. No one has ever seen a "society," although we have all seen the people who belong to one; no one has ever seen an organization, but only its members, the buildings and equipment that belong to it, and its name or emblem written on signs and pieces of paper. We live in a social world of symbols: of symbolic entities such as "property"—land that would "belong" to no one except by a social convention, a set of rules as to how various people must behave toward it and what words they must use in talking about it—and of symbolic acts such as "marriage"—a recorded ceremony that enables middle-class Americans to recognize the otherwise indiscernible difference between a couple illicitly living together and a "respectable" family. These symbols are by no means obvious if one has never thought about them. The fish apparently does not notice the water until he is out of it. The idea of a *society*, as distinct from the *state*, did not develop until the commercial and industrial changes of the eighteenth century and the French Revolution woke men up to the recognition that there were two different forms of social institutions, each going its own way. One hundred years later, thinkers such as George Herbert Mead came to recognize the symbolic nature of society and thus provided us with concepts with which to analyze the operations of this world that we have so long taken for granted.

Much of sociology has developed by uncovering facts that we had not previously known, either because they were remote from ordinary experience or because they had been deliberately ignored. The earliest efforts at sociology were inspired by the discoveries of the explorers of the Orient, the Americas, Africa, and the South Seas: The familiar ways of life of Europe could no longer be unreflectingly accepted as the natural order of God, but had to be explained along with the ways of the newly discovered peoples. The first efforts in this direction were naïve and consisted mainly of doctrines of progress, which accounted for the European differentness simply as social advance over other cultures. Such theorizing, nevertheless, began a tradition of thought concerned with explaining society. It was an early thinker on social evolution, Auguste Comte, who first gave sociology its name and thus helped to create that "invisible college" of thinkers who have ever since asked questions about society.

Many facts, to be sure, could have been discovered without the voyages of Captain Cook. But the voyage to the other side of town is harder to make than a trip around the world, and a voyage of discovery in one's own home is the hardest of all. Conventional biases against looking for or recognizing facts that touch on one's own life have been greater impediments to sociological understanding than the lack of facts themselves. These same biases that have kept most of social reality obscure have prevented us from seeing that they are biases. Not the least important aspect of an illusion is the fact that one believes it to be the truth. The great sociologists have contributed to the sociology of knowledge as an intrinsic part of their work. They have broken through illusions by analyzing the ways in which the conditions of social life determine the contents of our consciousness. The history of sociology has been a progressive sophistication about our own thought, uncovering sources of bias that we did not know existed.

The uncovering began with Karl Marx, the first great thinker to see life from the standpoint of the common working man. Marx did not discover social classes, of course; ancient and medieval law as well as social thought spoke openly of the various ranks of society, which indeed everyone knew about from daily experience. Ideological denial of stratification is an innovation of modern America. What Marx discovered was that our own thought is a product of our social circumstances and that much of what we believe to be reality is but a reflection of our socially determined interests. Marx may have defined "interests" too narrowly in economic terms, but there is no doubt of the validity of this general principle. Marx was not the first to notice that governments tell lies or that newspapers, writers of books, and individuals in conversation put forward alleged facts and explanations that are actually selected and distorted according to the interests of their formulators. Much of the thought of the Enlightenment is epitomized by Voltaire's effort to unmask the absurdity of supernatural explanations of human events. Marx went beyond Voltaire when he pointed out how the socially conservative thought of the Church was only to be expected from the leaders of a wealthy, landowning institution whose higher ranks were filled from the aristocracy and whose leaders, like Cardinals Mazarin and Richelieu, often served in the government of the king.

Marx's dictum "Religion is the opiate of the masses" is a puzzle in its own terms, however: If ideas reflect material interests, how could the lower classes hold ideas that did not reflect their own interests? It took Max Weber's analysis of the relation between ideas and power and Emile Durkheim's recognition of the effects of ritual on solidarity to provide the keys to this paradox. But the opening wedge first driven by Marx has never been retracted, even though there is a constant danger that our ideas will be molded in keeping with the prevailing political orthodoxy.

We know now that ideas are upheld as conventions within particular social groups and that the ideas of the group tend to take the form that will most enhance its status and advance its interests. We know that people associate closely only with persons of similar outlook and that individuals modify their ideas to fit the groups they join. And we also know how it is possible for men to have some freedom from ideological bias by institutionalizing a *competition* of ideas, especially among men whose interests are based on their achievements within the collective enterprise of science or scholarship.

Marx's recognition of ideological bias in social ideas is not a counsel of despair. The bias cannot be wished away, but it can be gradually pushed back by continuous effort to examine our own and others' ideas for their adequacy in explaining the full range of facts about society. This is not to say that biases cannot be found in modern social science. They are deeply embedded, especially in the areas of politics, deviance, and stratification. But we can have some faith that the search for the most powerful explanatory theory will lead us away from ideological distortion, whether from the right, the left, or the center.

One result of Marx's unveiling of ideology has been a distinction (first emphasized by Max Weber) between depictions of reality and evaluations of it, between "facts" (here used broadly to refer both to empirical data and to theories summarizing and explaining the data) and "values." This seems obvious enough: It is one thing to find out what the state of affairs is in the world, another thing to decide whether we think it is good or bad, just or unjust, beautiful or ugly. This distinction is important because most of our thought about the social world is evaluative: We are more interested in finding wrongdoers to condemn and heroes to praise than in explaining what happens or even in ascertaining the facts. Just after World War II it was popular to point to the "big lie" techniques of propaganda as a sign of totalitarian regimes and to stereotypes and distortions as the warning signs of extremist political thought. A closer acquaintance with serious sociology would have shown that such distinctions are naïve: that all governments try to manipulate their own legitimacy, that all politics deals in slogans and ideology, and that the popular world view is made up of stereotypes. If we are to expose the authoritarian and the brutal, deeds are much better indicators than words.

The distinction between facts and values thus has a twofold usefulness: It warns us to note which statements are saying something about reality and which are only assuming something about that reality in order to arouse our feelings about the good or evil of it, and it points us to the hard discipline of separating out and testing a body of knowledge whose validity does not depend merely on our moral point of view.

In the history of sociology the struggle against value biases is far from won. Indeed, controversy currently rages over this very issue. There is a strong tendency, especially among younger sociologists whose personal sympathies are vehemently on the side of persecuted racial minorities of America and the oppressed peasants of Southeast Asia and Latin America, to declare that all sociology must be value-biased and hence that the only choice is the moral one: Which side are you on? In support of this position, it is pointed out that academic social scientists have claimed to be value-neutral and yet have created theories that extol the virtues of American democracy, minimize the plight of oppressed groups, and rationalize military support for brutal dictatorships in Vietnam and elsewhere. But the lesson is not clearly drawn. Propaganda for the left is no more valuable *intellectually* than propaganda for the right or the center, whatever one may think of its *moral* virtue.

The distinction between facts and values remains crucial, even in this context. If we do not make an effort to uphold the ideal of intellectual objectivity in assessing theories and facts, no valid knowledge is possible—even the sort of knowledge that practical and activist men claim to have about the problems of the world. If objectivity is not maintained, both serious theory and intelligently guided action will be impossible. A successful explanatory theory is universally acceptable as knowledge; but in the realm of value judgments, every man's basic values are as good as any other man's, and no logical argument can force him to change his mind. This means that *applied* sociology will be much more diverse than *pure* sociology; and it is for applied sociology that the arguments of radical sociologists hold true: It comes down to a moral question of in whose interests you choose to apply it. The attack on some of the older sociologists, then, is a legitimate attack only on their applied work; their pure sociology, on the other hand, can be judged only by the standards of scholarly objectivity, comprehensiveness, and consistency, and if mistakes are made here, they can be corrected by the normal processes of the advance of research. If some of these men have misleadingly claimed value-neutrality in an effort to make others accept the conclusions of the applied work they carried out in the interests of cold-war politics, the blame cannot fall on the doctrine that distinguishes between facts and values, but on the misuse these men have made of that doctrine. In the end the fact-value distinction remains absolutely crucial, and not only for the development of objective sociological theory; whatever our values may be, only by taking a position of detachment are we able to see society realistically enough to be able to act on it with any insight into our chances of success.

The fact-value distinction is important to keep in mind in the following chapters. We have attempted throughout to present the successive developments of sociological theory and to assess their objective validity as theories. Since most of them are far from complete in terms of formalizing the logic of their arguments and testing their factual predictions, our judgments on them must reflect the balance of existing evidence and the most promising prospects for future elaboration. But all of this is an attempt to move forward within the realm of objective sociological knowledge. We have also tried from time to time to state some applications of these theories to particular practical issues of today. It should be clear that these applications are made from a particular point of view and in that sense cannot make a claim on others to agree with us unless they happen to share our particular sets of values. These values are heavily on the side of maximizing personal liberty and are slanted toward the point of view of those coerced by systems of power. There are of course many other points of view from which theory could be applied; we have given little attention to practical questions as seen from the viewpoints of military officers, politicians, businessmen, administrators, or dominant classes and status groups. For the pure side of sociological knowledge presented here, we would like to claim as much objectivity as the considerable progress of the sociological enterprise allows. For our practical applications, we claim no more than that an effort has been made to see the world accurately as it bears on our particular values.

The fate of Karl Marx's insights warns us of how arduous the path to sociological understanding is. The fact that one man, even a famous one, makes an advance is no guarantee that other social thinkers will maintain it. Marx's thought had little impact on the respectable thinkers of his day. It lived on mainly in the underground until a twentieth-century generation of German sociologists (Toennies, Weber, Michels, Mannheim) recaptured some of its key insights. Marx's contributions did not fare much better in the revolutionary underground. Instead of being treated as a theory to be developed and refined as new facts and new insights became available, Marxism became a dogma to be polemically defended against all revisions. Near the end of his life, Marx was moved to cry out against his own followers, "I am not a Marxist!" Since the Russian Revolution enshrined Marxism as an official state ideology, Marx's thought has ceased to be a fruitful source of new insight except, ironically, for non-Marxists. The lesson applies not only to Marx; the uncompromising political realism of Weber and Michels has also proved too much for most respectable thought to incorporate, and it remains semihidden in an academic underground.

Marx found one source of illusion about society in the realm of ideology; Freud made an analogous discovery at the turn of the twentieth century when he discovered repression. Freud struck even closer to home. If ideology prevents us from understanding the larger processes that link us to countless others through the economy, politics, and social stratification, repression prevents us from seeing what goes on right before our eyes, including our own actions. Again, the discovery was more in the way of seeing than in the sight itself. Freud was not the first man to notice that men lust for women who are not their wives (and vice versa) or that people can bitterly hate each other even while carrying on polite, even intimate, relationships. Freud's insight was to see how widespread such desires and feelings are and to see that they can exist even in people who would be ashamed and guilty to realize that they felt anything of the sort. Freud unmasked the respectable society of the nineteenth century at its most vulnerable point—the place that was kept most hidden. Repression, like layers of clothing upon bodies, points to what is concealed by the very act of covering it.

Respectable social thought of the nineteenth century, epitomized by Herbert Spencer and the British utilitarians, saw man in modern society as rational and respectable, the upholder of contractual rules that regulated the individual for the common good. Freud looked into those conscious, rationalistic beliefs and those proper, middle-class ideals and found that they could be explained in terms of something else: passions of love and hate turned in upon the self in response to the social restraints that kept them from being outwardly expressed. Where preceding thinkers saw a rational man making decisions to follow the rules, Freud discovered what had long been excluded from such a world view: that man is still a physical animal, a creature of instincts and emotions, and that the civilized, rational part added by socialization does not displace the physical creature, but only reshapes him, sometimes in a mutilated form.

The fate of Freud's insights has been much like the fate of Marx's. His ideas have gained considerable notoriety among people who have heard of him only secondhand through some alleged refutation and who think that they can dismiss him with the observation that "obviously there's more to life than sex." In this way, his insight into repression is itself repressed, along with any recognition that *anything* in the world has to do with sex, hate, or any other emotions impelling our allegedly rational behavior. Freud has also suffered from dogmatic followers who have given the theory a bad name in scientific circles, especially by polemics against equally dogmatic behaviorists in psychology. Between these two extremes, Freud has done much to orient us toward investigating how childhood socialization makes us members of society. The central insights—the view of man as an emotional animal who lives in groups, the existence of repression and identification—are yet largely unexploited; but they are not lost. Freud's discoveries are more appropriately investigated in group interaction than by examining the individual alone. It is in the socially oriented analyses, conducted by such men as the psychiatrist Fritz Perls and the sociologist Erving Goffman, that Freud's insights are beginning to find their explanation and their place in an integrated body of social theory.

We have touched on a number of sources of illusion in our views of social reality: taking our social arrangements for granted because we know of no others, ideological distortions based on the interests and perspectives of our social positions, inability to detach ourselves from an evaluative stance, repression of things that make us feel shameful or guilty. By the time these sources of bias came to light, sociology was on the eve of the twentieth century. We shall touch on only two more kinds of illusions and thereby bring ourselves up to the present: the fallacy of psychological reductionism and the misconceptions that a too-literal identification with physical science can engender. The man who cut through the first of these most strikingly was Emile Durkheim.

A common way of thinking is to explain social events by the actions of individuals: to look for great men in history, agitators in riots, traitors in defeats. By the end of the nineteenth century the dominant evolutionist thinkers—speaking especially in defense of a laissez-faire economic policy—described society as the interplay of individual decisions, in which deliberate social policy could have little effect. Nevertheless, their basic mode of explanation was individualistic: Men struggle for a livelihood and rise and fall according to their individual qualities; modern society itself exists because of contracts among individuals.

Durkheim struck through in a new direction: The distinctive thing about social institutions is that they persist while individuals come and go; they have a force of their own such that individuals who violate social norms not only do not change the norms but are punished as deviants. Furthermore, society can never be logically explained in terms of the motives of individuals. As Durkheim put it, society is a reality *sui generis*. "Social facts," such as the rules that people enforce upon each other, the forms of the institutions within which people act, and even the ideas that they hold, cannot be explained by examining the workings of an individual and multiplying the result a million-fold. These facts must be explained by *social*—that is, supraindividual—causes. Just as living organisms are made up of chemical molecules, yet physiology is to be explained on its own level in terms of the functioning of the parts in relation to each other, society is made up of individuals but is not explicable simply in terms of individual psychology. With his emphasis on social structure as the subject matter of sociology, Durkheim gave the field a distinctive focus of its own. He also showed that such supposedly individual phenomena as suicide, crime, moral outrage, and even our concepts of time, space, God, and the individual personality are socially determined. With Durkheim nineteenth-century individualistic rationalism commits suicide. We know now that we are all social creatures and there is no turning back to the naïve optimism of the nineteenth century that could see in the rational education of the individual the solution to all social ills.

The final major development of sociology took place in the early twentieth century, for the most part in the United States. Instead of relying on historians, newspapers, and their own speculations, sociologists began to go and see for themselves: first with community studies, then with surveys, participant observation of organizations, and small group experiments. This research tradition has done much to counteract the illusions due to ideology and to other biases. We have discovered, for example, that the conservative claims that crime is due to hereditary degeneration or racial traits (theories once popular among biologically oriented sociologists of the evolutionist school) are false, as are liberal outcries that social mobility has been declining in the United States. The great merit of an active research tradition is that it is largely self-correcting; as long as we insist that theories must explain facts, their biases are likely to reveal themselves sooner or later.

But even this research tradition has its dangers and illusions. One of these is the problem of overspecialization and technicism. Sociology has become a large-scale cooperative enterprise; and, as in any large bureaucracy, the individual members tend to lose sight of the overall goals—producing and testing theories to explain all of social behavior and institutions—and are caught up in the immediate details of day-to-day research. One danger, then, has been the trivializing of research and a tendency to substitute purely technical standards, such as statistical refinements, for substantial contributions to our knowledge about society.

The physical sciences provided a model for the modern research enterprise; they have also provided a final, distinctively modern illusion about society. Many American social scientists, especially those who have not fully absorbed the great breakthroughs of Durkheim, Weber, Freud, and Mead, still find their ideas in a version of the nineteenth-century tradition superseded by the above thinkers. Like the British utilitarians and their American followers, they continue to take the natural sciences as an uncriticized model for understanding society. Utilitarian rationalism has been modernized as behaviorism, the doctrine that asserts that human behavior is to be explained in terms of external stimuli—rewards and punishments—without any reference to scientifically inadmissible concepts such as "mind." In sociology, the old positivist doctrine shows up in the notion that the only valid material for a scientific theory are quantitative data, such as those collected in large-scale questionnaire surveys, carefully measured experimental behaviors, and census tabulations. Only "hard data," consisting of observed and preferably quantified behaviors or enumerations, are valid; "soft data," encompassing the experiences of participant observers, in-depth interviews, case studies, historical writings, and introspection, are excluded.

The merit of this distinction turns out to be an illusion. Human social behavior and social institutions are basically symbolic. Society exists and affects the observable behavior of individuals only as systems of invisible names, rules, and positions that individuals can identify with and orient toward. As might be expected, strictly behavioristic theories have not borne much fruit in psychology; rather, it has been in the area of cognitive development and functioning that progress has been made. In sociology the extreme positivists have been found mostly among researchers who have been caught up in short-run technical concerns and hence have contributed little to advancing theories to explain society. It has been by insisting on the principle that we be able to explain *all* the facts that social science corrects itself, even against illusions created by an excessive zeal to emulate the methods of the natural sciences. Symbolic reality is *the* empirical reality for sociologists; it is life as all individuals experience it. Numbers derived by totaling the answers of many individuals to a few short questions about what they believe or have done are quite a long way from the firsthand experience of those individual lives that we are ultimately trying to explain. In this sense Erving Goffman and his students, with their firsthand accounts of how people manipulate the social reality they present for each other to experience, are the latest of the important innovators in sociology.

We are coming to see that there is no necessary battle between "hard" and "soft" in the social sciences. Both quantitative but superficial data and direct phenomenological experience of a few situations have their values and weaknesses. When used to complement each other, they help us both to understand in depth and to check up on the generalizability of the understanding. Like a navigator plotting the position of a point from his own moving ship, we are learning to "triangulate" our accounts of social reality from several vantage points.

THE CONTRIBUTIONS OF SOCIOLOGY

It is often said that the social sciences lag behind the natural sciences and that the latter have created the problems of atomic war, overpopulation, and industrial change that the former must now solve. This view betrays a naïve analogy between the natural sciences and the social sciences, ignoring how unamenable to control by deliberate action the structures of a society are, except—and even here there are serious organizational limitations—by a form of political control that would be likely to create more evils than it solves. If we judge the social sciences, not by the popularistic criterion of practicality, but by their advance toward a comprehensive and powerful explanatory theory of social behavior and institutions, their advance is much greater than has been recognized. Such a theory may not yet be found assembled in the textbooks, but the major pieces have been in existence for some time, and we are slowly learning to put them together. From a time when social thought was little more than myth, ideology, and speculation, we have broken through illusion after illusion, and with each destruction of old belief we have discovered something new and solid.

The great breakthroughs that provide the basis for our modern knowledge took place around the turn of the twentieth century. Durkheim discovered the dynamics of social solidarity, providing us with a way to *explain* how society can operate as a moral order, instead of merely to justify or debunk it. Weber showed how ideas and ideals interact with material and power interests, how we can understand social order in the midst of conflict by seeing society not as a reified abstraction but as a stratified network of groups and organizations. In addition, Weber gave us the most penetrating vision of world history yet produced. Freud revealed man as a social animal in whom civilized mind and physical body guide and torture each other. Mead showed both individual minds and social institutions to be the result of symbolic communication. Since then we have come to see how the unexplained or overlooked facets of one theory could be clarified by the insights of another. Parsons has advanced the synthesis of Durkheim, Freud, and Weber; Goffman that of Durkheim, Simmel, and Mead. Empirical research has fleshed out our general insights, especially on organizations and stratification, where we are beginning to see a core uniting much of sociological theory and research.

This development is not yet widely recognized. Of the great figures in sociology, only Freud and Marx are names widely known to the general public. Durkheim, Weber, and Mead are little known or understood outside the bounds of academic sociology. Even within sociology progress has been obscured, most notably by the conflict between hard and soft approaches and by other controversies over the application of sociology to political issues. Sociologists caught up in these peripheral disputes have thereby blinded themselves, in a way that Marx's analysis of ideology would have predicted, to their opponents' contributions to sociological theory and have even themselves often forgotten that a comprehensive explanatory theory is the major goal of the discipline. But in science as elsewhere nothing succeeds like success. As the demonstrated power of the central sociological tradition is increasingly brought into the light, it advances steadily.

The sociological tradition has shaped our views of the world throughout the last century without our knowing it. It has been the major source of political world views: Radicalism derives mostly from the views of Marx; liberalism in both its laissez-faire and its welfare-state versions from the British utilitarians and evolutionists; corporate statism in Europe from the tradition of Saint-Simon, fascism from, among other sources, the racist varieties of nineteenth-century evolutionism. What is striking about this list is the fact that modern political ideologies all derive from nineteenth-century social thought. The far more profound thought of the great breakthrough—the Durkheim-Weber-Freud-Mead contributions—has as yet had little influence on our thinking about social and political issues. Popular thought lags fifty or seventy years behind the forefront of sociological knowledge. Even the university-oriented liberal proponents of the modern American welfare state have offered little more than a benevolent reformer's belief in the "bad environmental" causes of crime and social unrest and a faith in social work and public education as panaceas. Political ideologists have yet to learn the hard Weberian truths about the dynamics of status stratification and the scarcely controllable momentum of bureaucratic organizations and the Durkheimian and Freudian discoveries of the personal strains in a world of impersonal rules and emotionless organizations.

Modern sociology does not recommend itself to those in search of easy solutions, whether these be of the left, right, or center. Indeed, one of sociology's great contributions is to show that the center is just as subject to illusion as are the extremes. Perhaps we can now see why sociology does not offer easy practical applications in the way that advances in the physics of electricity give rise to color television sets. If we wish our knowledge to advance, we cannot spell out what that knowledge must consist of in advance of the facts. The facts are not what most people would wish them to be, and social science cannot be called in to tell them what they want to hear.

The early social thinkers of the Enlightenment thought they had the key to the world: Man is basically rational; the evils of despotism and war are due to ignorance and superstition. Let man only learn to see things in a rational way, and utopia would be ushered in. This dream has died hard. The generation of Durkheim destroyed its last remnants as far as serious thinkers were concerned, although it has hung on in naïve public ideologies—a further illustration of how little men's social behavior fits the Enlightenment dream. Politicians and social movements pursue their own ideologies and try to impose their ceremonies on reality; the applied sociologist advising them is usually in the position of an anthropologist telling the aborigines what is wrong with their fertility rites.

If sociology has a contribution to make, it is this: If we can be more realistic about our world, more wary of the dilemmas of social organizations, more aware both of the necessities of social coordination and of the dangers of social coercion, and more sophisticated about the illusions with which our institutions populate social reality, we can perhaps make our world more livable. It may be that if enough people realized the connections between political illusion and political coercion and the deadening effect of psychic chimeras on our everyday encounters, the quality of life would improve a great deal. A significant part of the new generation has already shown itself more realistic than those before it—

more capable of cutting through social hypocrisies about sex and politics, through rituals of status deference and illusions about personal relationships. Whether a new culture of honesty and personal emancipation will enable us to control the coercive and alienating institutions of modern society is still in doubt, but greater illumination is one of our few weapons.

THE BOUNDARIES OF SOCIOLOGY

A final note should be made on the subject of disciplinary boundaries. We have attempted to present a brief history of sociology, but we have not insisted on any rigid classification of thinkers, and occasionally we move far beyond what a strictly Durkheimian view of the field would include. One of the reasons for the looseness of boundaries is that sociology did not become a distinct discipline until the twentieth century. Up to that time, it was often not distinguished from economics, and many of the important sociologists—Marx, Weber, Pareto, Parsons —spent some or all of their lives as economists. As economics came to concentrate more and more on the technical analysis of money, prices, wages, and employment, it gradually became a distinct intellectual enterprise as well as a separate university department, although even today institutional and developmental economists, such as Kerr, Galbraith, and Boulding, or Marxist economists such as Ernest Mandel, discuss many of the same concepts and issues as sociologists. Robert Heilbroner's The Worldly Philosophers tells much of the side of the story we have omitted here.

Another discipline whose history is entwined with that of sociology is anthropology. The main difference between the two fields is primarily a historical one: Anthropologists became identified as the investigators of the newly discovered tribal societies of the colonial era, whereas sociologists were concerned with modern societies. The distinction has since broken down. As primitive tribes have been colonized or destroyed, anthropologists have come to study modern Western and non-Western societies, and sociologists to study traditional ones. Today there is little difference between what most anthropologists and sociologists do, although anthropology includes some fields—physical anthropology, archaeology, and linguistics—that are rather remote from the work of most sociologists. It is mainly for reasons of space that this volume does not deal with the great anthropologists, although Spencer, Durkheim, and Freud must be viewed as key figures in both histories. The interested reader is referred to Kardiner and Preble's short book They Studied Man for a sketch of the great discoverers in anthropology.

Political science had origins rather distinct from those of sociology. It originated largely in the study of constitutional law, and its main function has been to train public administrators and high-school government teachers. This background has meant that its orientation has been too philosophical and too ideologically biased to make any very notable contributions to a scientific theory of society. Since World War II the behavioral movement has developed in American political science, and political scientists now do work on political sociology, organizations, and social change that merges with that of sociologists.

Psychology has long been both distinct from and intertwined with sociology. Its distinct branch deals with nonsocial determinants of individual behavior in such areas as physiological psychology, perception, learning, and motivation. The overlapping branch is social psychology, the study of the individual in relation to others. It has been carried on in modern American universities both in sociology and in psychology departments and sometimes in a separate department of its own. We have set the boundaries of sociology rather far over in the field of social psychology out of the feeling that disciplinary boundaries often do more harm by compartmentalizing studies that should be carried on in a broad perspective, than they do good by allowing the concentration of attention. Freud, in particular, might be considered primarily a psychologist, but we give him rather full treatment here for two reasons: First, although Durkheim is surely right that social structures cannot be explained purely in terms of individuals, society is nevertheless created and enacted only by individuals, and our explanations of social order must be founded on knowledge of how individuals function, especially in relation to others. Second, Freud has exerted a great deal of influence on sociology and anthropology—indeed more than on psychology (although perhaps less than on the medical field of psychiatry). American academic psychology has been the bastion of behaviorist orthodoxy, and much of the best thought about cognitive functioning—by Mead and Piaget as well as by Freud—has had to find refuge in sociology. Psychology's loss has been sociology's gain, but one that may eventually be repaid, as the work of the symbolic interactionists, Goffmanians, and sociolinguists promises much progress in understanding the psychological functioning of individual human beings.

Finally, history has considerable overlap with sociology. It would be difficult to place men like Tocqueville, Fustel de Coulanges, Weber, Pirenne, Marc Bloch, Hintze, Rostovtzeff, and many modern historians such as Lawrence Stone or Richard Hofstadter decisively in one intellectual camp or the other. Like sociology, history is an all-encompassing discipline: Everything that has ever happened in the social world is potential material for its narratives, just as it is potential material for sociological theory. The main difference is in orientation: Sociology's is toward a generalizing theory, history's toward the description and explanation of particular sequences of events. The distinction between *generalizing* theory and *particularistic* histories is not an absolute one, however. Historians often apply general principles as a means of ordering the myriad facts available to them, and one of the great tasks of sociology has always been to describe what a particular society (usually our own) is like and to explain the social changes that have led up to our world. In thinkers such as Marx and Weber, the two aims—creating generalizing explanations and capturing a particular historical drama— were carried side by side, to their mutual enrichment. As historians grow increasingly interested in probing beyond political and diplomatic events to social structures, we can expect the two disciplines to draw together even more closely.

Our history of sociology is thus mixed with those of most of the other social disciplines. We draw the boundaries here only to make our subject compact enough to handle. The various disciplines have learned much from each other in the past, and they have much to offer each other now and for the future if only we transcend narrow departmental labels. Having said this, perhaps our various colleagues will forgive us if we indulge a little sociological pride: In the pages of this book, the reader will find the most illuminating tradition in modern social thought.

PART ONE

THE VICISSITUDES OF NINETEENTH-CENTURY RATIONALISM

CHAPTER ONE

THE PROPHETS OF PARIS: SAINT-SIMON AND COMTE

One sign that an era is over is that it begins to be romanticized. Medieval society had become remote enough from the educated Frenchmen of the early nineteenth century for many of them to grow nostalgic about it. It had been a time of faith and order, they thought, when everyone from peasant to king knew his place, and social strife was unknown; when men were poor but happy, and the lords and priests watched paternally over their human flocks. The men of the eighteenth century could hold no such illusions. They were too close to the realities of the Middle Ages and glad to have just escaped.

Men certainly had been poor; but happy? The physical hardships of the Middle Ages were scarcely imaginable—peasants had nothing but bread to eat, and aristocrats were often little better off; dwellings were small, cold, crowded, unsanitary, and ridden with disease. Nor was there much order. Europe had been in continual warfare since the decline of the Roman Empire, and the threat of violence permeated everyday life. It was a world without policemen, in which every man looked out for himself. Towns locked their walls to keep out robbers, and masters could inflict harsh punishment on their servants, and fathers on their children. Torture was the common treatment of public suspects, and execution and mutilation were the punishments for trivial crimes. Men knew their places only because they were kept in them; order existed only as violent oppression.

Nor was that period precisely the age of faith that the romanticists imagined it to be. Religious conflict was almost as chronic as political violence. The Protestant Reformation and the Catholic Counter Reformation were but the biggest and bloodiest battles over the world of the spirit. Heresies and persecutions abound both before and after the time of Luther, Calvin, and Torquemada's Inquisition. The Church owned a third of the land in Europe and provided the financial and spiritual support of kings (and sometimes their soldiers, too), thereby giving virtually all conflicts a religious tone. It was an age of faith only in the sense that the Church was omnipresent, and the belief in heaven and hell was virtually unquestioned.

The universe was seen as highly ordered, as in Dante's description of the world starting with the heavenly spheres, where God dwelt with his angels, proceeding down through the social hierarchies of the earth to the nine underground levels of hell, where the damned were punished according to their sins. Virtually everyone believed dogmatically in this world order, but they disagreed with each other about just where everyone fitted into it—about who was to be Pope, which kings were to be sanctified, which theology should dominate, and whose morals should be absolute. Everyone was sure of his version of the truth and was ready to kill whoever stood in its way. In short, it was an era of waking nightmare, and when peace came and religion waned in the advanced kingdoms of England and France in the 1700s, thinking men heaved a sigh of relief. For them, it was an awakening, an Enlightenment.

The men who entertained the salons of Paris with their conversation were the first intellectuals since antiquity to find employment outside the Church. The *philosophes,* as such men as Voltaire, Diderot, Rousseau, Condorcet, and Turgot came to be known, had found a substitute for theology in science. Isaac Newton was the hero of the age, for his work on the laws of motion, published in 1687, showed how the universe ran of its own accord like a clock. Reason was the spirit of the times, and religion was its enemy. Mankind would at last be happy when the last king was strangled in the entrails of the last priest! declared the freethinker Jean Meslier, to which Voltaire gave assent—although under his breath, since he made a living by ornamenting the courts of "enlightened despots" such as Frederick the Great. The *philosophes* rejected the theology of sin and declared that nature was reasonable and good. It was necessary only to discover the natural laws that governed the world and to put society in accordance with them. History ceased to be seen merely as the record of man's deeds between Adam and the Second Coming of Christ or as a story of continual decline from the golden ages of Greece and Rome. Rather, men began to view history as the progress of scientific enlightenment, in which the eighteenth century stood out as an age of Reason, an age of optimism.

The outbreak of the French Revolution in 1789 brought the opportunity men had been waiting for. Now they could be rid of the old order entirely and build a new one based on principles of reason and justice. The king was overthrown and beheaded, aristocrats dispossessed, and the feudal order abolished. But then the liberal supporters of the Revolution began to fall away. The republicans began to turn against themselves. The Assembly purged more and more of its members, and their heads rolled from the guillotine to the cheers of the Paris crowds. The Revolution became paranoid; enemies of freedom were everywhere at home, war was declared against it abroad. The Reign of Terror was instituted under Robespierre and his Committee of Public Safety. Finally, Robespierre himself went to the guillotine, and France began turning to the right. In 1799 the republican government was overthrown by a general named Napoleon Bonaparte, and the great experiment was almost over.

It took another decade and a half for the drama to play itself out. But behind the grand adventure of Napoleon's conquests and eventual defeat, it was becoming clear that an idea had failed. Reason could be a religion, too, and men could be just as fanatical in defending the Enlightenment as any Grand Inquisitor. Paris in 1815, with a constitutional monarchy back on the throne, was superficially at order again, but intellectually it was in turmoil. Reformers, utopians, and cultists abounded with their explanations of what had gone wrong and what must be done to set it right. At this point entered Saint-Simon, and our story begins.

HENRI DE SAINT-SIMON

Claude-Henri de Rouvroy, le Comte de Saint-Simon (1760–1825), as his name tells us, was an aristocrat, born into one of the most eminent families in France. Like many of his contemporaries, he was brilliant, egotistical, and absolutely unprincipled. His opportunistic career sums up many of the contradictions of his age. He began with a wild and dissolute youth, during which he was even imprisoned by his family as the only means of controlling him—as was his sinister contemporary the Marquis de Sade. Saint-Simon then became an officer in the French army, went to America, and fought in the battle of Yorktown. But we must not think of him as a freedom-loving volunteer like Lafayette; Saint-Simon served purely under the orders of the absolute King Louis XVI, who for reasons of state supported the Americans in order to oppose the British. His political motives did not prevent Saint-Simon from becoming an honorary member of the American patriotic Society of Cincinnatus. If Saint-Simon was cynical, it only reflected the general tone of his age.

Back in Europe, Saint-Simon chafed for some excitement. He cooked up schemes for building canals—one across Central America, another connecting Madrid to the sea—but could not successfully promote them. The French Revolution came along at just the right time. Saint-Simon took on the role of the great republican, making revolutionary speeches, presiding at the local assembly of the area where his estate was located, proposing reforms, and befriending the peasants—while the châteaux of other aristocrats went up in flames. At the height of the republican fervor, Saint-Simon even renounced his title and took the name Bonhomme, equivalent to a Rockefeller today naming himself Jones.

Throughout the political turmoil, Saint-Simon was also busy with private affairs. The Revolution confiscated lands of the Church and of aristocrats who were beheaded or fled the country; Saint-Simon busily bought them up at a fraction of their cost. As the republic's paper currency steadily lost value, Saint-Simon speculated in money and paid for property in worthless *assignats*. To be sure, Robespierre had his eye on such speculators, and Saint-Simon was arrested under suspicion of being a foreign agent. But he had established his republican image well in the provinces, and he mustered enough impeccable supporters to have himself freed. The episode proved only a temporary setback, and while heads were rolling from the guillotine, Saint-Simon amassed a fortune. He entertained lavishly, kept a salon, and conversed grandly with a drawing room full of admirers and wits about his plans for reconstituting society.

But this was not to last. The French Republic was eclipsed in 1799 with Napoleon's coup d'état, and not long after Saint-Simon found that he had spent the last of his fortune. He began to harass his former business partners, his family, and whoever could give him money. He became regarded as a nuisance. He turned again to ideas, wrote them up and sent them in petitions to Napoleon, to members of the *Académie des Sciences*, and to anyone else who might put them into action. His favorite idea was that the world could be saved if the scientists would form an international council and take over the direction of society. Instead of war and strife, men could then turn their attention to building canals and generally improving conditions. Saint-Simon had taken a typical Enlightenment idea, the belief in science, and given it a slightly more practical foundation.

Strangely, Napoleon and the other eminences were too busy for Saint-Simon's schemes. His petitions were usually returned to him unopened. Saint-Simon dropped further into destitution. He came to believe that the scientists were in a conspiracy against him. His paranoia grew acute, and for a while he was confined in the famous madhouse at Charenton (the setting for Peter Weiss' play *Marat/Sade*). He made an unsuccessful attempt at suicide.

Eventually, his fortunes improved a bit. After the monarchy was restored in 1815, Saint-Simon began to make a living as a publicist. The confiscated properties of the aristocrats were now in the hands of a new class of financiers and entrepreneurs; and with the downfall of Napoleon the remaining émigrés returned and tried to reclaim them. The government became the focus for a struggle between these two groups, and Saint-Simon, who had a sharp eye for the winning side, began to put out papers and pamphlets arguing the cause of the "industrialists," as he called them. The word was soon to take on general currency. Saint-Simon's publications were always collapsing, but he made a living by making the rounds of his supporters for contributions to each new venture. Out of this enterprise, Saint-Simon developed his theory of society and began to attract a following.

Saint-Simon's main idea was that industrialism was a new era in history. Progress was not a matter of science alone, but affected all the conditions of life. This new society, growing out of a declining feudalism, would provide the basis for solving all the old problems. Saint-Simon was one of the first to discern the new order emerging, and he took on the role of prophet of how it should operate.

One of Saint-Simon's famous statements sums up his philosophy:

Suppose that France suddenly lost fifty of her best physicists, chemists, physiologists, mathematicians, poets, painters, sculptors, musicians, writers; fifty of her best mechanical engineers, civil and military engineers, artillery experts, architects, doctors, surgeons, apothecaries, seamen, clockmakers; fifty of her best bankers, two hundred of her best businessmen, two hundred of her best farmers, fifty of her best ironmasters, arms manufacturers, tanners, dyers, miners, clothmakers, cotton manufacturers, silk-makers, linen-makers, manufacturers of hardware, of pottery and china, of crystal and glass, ship chandlers, carriers, printers, engravers, goldsmiths, and other metal-workers; her fifty best masons, carpenters, joiners, farriers, locksmiths, cutlers, smelters, and a hundred other persons of various unspecified occupations, eminent in the sciences, fine arts, and professions; making in all three thousand leading scientists, artists, and artisans of France.

These men are the Frenchmen who are the most essential producers, those who make the most important products, those who direct the enterprises most useful to the nation, those who contribute to its achievements in the sciences, fine arts and professions. They are in the most real sense the flower of French society; they are, above all Frenchmen, the most useful to their country, contribute most to its glory, increasing its civilization and prosperity. The nation would become a lifeless corpse as soon as it lost them. It would immediately fall into a position of inferiority compared with the nations which it now rivals, and would continue to be inferior until this loss had been replaced, until it had grown another head. It would require at least a generation for France to repair this misfortune; for men who are distinguished in work of positive ability are exceptions, and nature is not prodigal of exceptions, particularly in this species.

Let us pass on to another assumption. Suppose that France preserves all the men of genius that she possess in the sciences, fine arts and professions, but has the misfortune to lose in the same day Monsieur the King's brother, Monseigneur le duc d'Angoulême, Monseigneur le duc de Berry, Monseigneur le duc d'Orléans, Monseigneur le duc de Bourbon, Madame la duchesse d'Angoulême, Madame la duchesse de Berry, Madame la duchesse d'Orléans,

Madame la duchesse de Bourbon, and Mademoiselle de Condé. Suppose that France loses at the same time all the great officers of the royal household, all the ministers (with or without portfolio), all the councillors of state, all the chief magistrates, marshals, cardinals, archbishops, bishops, vicars-general, and canons, all the prefects and sub-prefects, all the civil servants, and judges, and, in addition, ten thousand of the richest proprietors who live in the style of nobles.

This mischance would certainly distress the French, because they are kind-hearted, and could not see with indifference the sudden disappearance of such a large number of their compatriots. But this loss of thirty-thousand individuals, considered to be the most important in the state, would only grieve them for purely sentimental reasons and would result in no political evil for the State.[1]

By chance, a few days after this was published in 1819, an assassin took the life of the Duke de Berry. Saint-Simon was arrested as an instigator. But Saint-Simon had chosen his sides well, and he was acquitted.

The old era had been devoted to war and religion; aristocrats and priests had lived as parasites on the rest of society. The new era was to be devoted to the production of useful goods and services. Saint-Simon did not distinguish among bankers, manufacturers, engineers, laborers, poets, and scientists—all were producers, in contrast to the parasitic aristocracy. "All men must work" became Saint-Simon's slogan, whatever work one might be suited for. His disciples later put forward the formulation: "Each according to his capacity"—eventually to become famous as part of the motto of communism.

The Saint-Simonians were quite willing to call themselves "socialists," although they meant this in a rather vague sense. Modern ideologies had not yet crystallized, and the Saint-Simonians continued to believe in private property, although they did not assign it very much importance, and were more concerned with coordinating the activities of society through large and centrally directed enterprises. Great undertakings—like canals, railroads, and steamship lines—were the focus of their interest, and these things were "social" rather than individual in nature.

The modern era was to be one of peace. Force would no longer be necessary, since men would turn their powers against nature instead of against other men. The state would virtually cease to exist, at least in its old, coercive form; it would be replaced by a world council of scientists, financiers, and industrialists, who would plan and coordinate for the good of all.

Society would remain a hierarchy but would no longer be looked upon as stratified. Men simply have different innate capacities: Some are more intellectually developed, and these would become scientists; others are more emotional and would become the poets and artists; those who are more motor-oriented would become the workers and organizers. The best of all three types would be given the top positions

[1] Henri de Saint-Simon, *Social Organization, The Science of Man, and Other Writings* (New York: Harper Torchbooks, 1964), pp. 72–73.

of leadership, and the others would array themselves below. Everyone would be happy if he could fill his own true function, be it high or low. In sum, Saint-Simon believed in the rise of a perfect meritocracy.

What Saint-Simon developed has turned out to be the characteristic ideology of industrialism. It is found all over the world today, among the technocrats of the modern French state, in the British civil service, and in the great American bureaucracies from the universities to the RAND Corporation. It is a belief that progress is based on science and that new societies are created out of the old (in the developing nations of the world as well as in the more advanced countries of the East and West), without revolution or conflict, simply by putting the scientists and industrialists in charge. There is no real conflict of classes if everyone works and is able to rise according to his individual merit. The system is elitist, but no one would (or should) mind, since the experts at the top are working only for the common good. This ideology includes what may be called the belief in "the stateless state": that the government exists purely as a technical, neutral instrument for coordinating society, not as a means of oppression or the provider of special interests. As we shall see, even the communists adopt this view of their own state, although they deny that it is true of the state in capitalist countries.

When Saint-Simon died in 1825, his young followers started off on an unexpected turn. Taking up one of Saint-Simon's last ideas, the creation of a "new Christianity" of social harmony, they began to preach love of humanity and formed a utopian community outside of Paris, where all would work for the common good. In a prim and proper fashion, they were the hippies of their day. The experiment collapsed after a year, when their leader Enfantin was brought to trial and sentenced to a year in jail for outraging public morals. After this romantic escapade, the Saint-Simonians settled down to become industrialists and financiers. Among them were the Pereire brothers, the financiers of Louis Napoleon's Second Empire and the organizers of the famous Credit Mobilier speculations. Another of these, Ferdinand de Lesseps, even brought one of Saint-Simon's earliest schemes to fruition: In 1882 he built the Suez Canal.

AUGUSTE COMTE (1798–1857)

In 1817 Saint-Simon engaged as his private secretary a serious young man named Auguste Comte. Comte was well educated, having just graduated from Napoleon's new *Ecole Polytechnique,* where the best of modern science was taught. Saint-Simon saw his new assistant, trained in mathematics and all the sciences, as the disciple who could formulate his loose ideas into a complete system. They worked together for seven years, developing their views on history and on industrial society. From this enterprise was to emerge an entirely new social science.

They split up in 1824 after a series of quarrels. The final dispute came over the question of whose name was to appear on the title page of their most important work. Without a patron, Comte fell into dire straits. He demanded a position at the *Ecole Polytechnique* from which to teach his new science and was refused repeatedly. He eked out a living grading entrance examinations in mathematics, gave public lectures for whoever would listen, and wrote volume after volume of his system. Like his former employer, he barraged kings and officials all over Europe with petitions to support his work. He drew no response, for the garrets of Paris were crowded with starving writers of every variety, and his petitions were part of a deluge of such mail. Comte fulminated against those who rejected his ideas, which he felt could save the world. In classic style, he went through fits of raving mania and was confined for a while at Charenton asylum. He twice attempted suicide. Eventually, he began to gather a cult around him, and his system of Positivism gradually became known.

Comte's system derives from a basic principle, the law of the three stages of knowledge. Comte referred to this concept as "the great discovery of the year 1822" (when he had still been working for Saint-Simon); he had even written down the hour of the day at which he had begun each new page. It was over the publication of this work that the break with Saint-Simon had come.

The law of the three stages states that knowledge of any subject always begins in *theological* form (explanation by animism, spirits, or gods), passes to the *metaphysical* form (explanation by abstract philosophical speculation), and finally becomes *positive* (scientific explanation based on observation, experiment, and comparison). Accordingly, there is a historical sequence of the sciences, as the various areas of knowledge pass through these stages in order of difficulty. The simplest and most remote topics become scientific first, followed by increasingly complex and concrete matters. Thus, the sciences develop in this order:

mathematics
astronomy
physics
chemistry
biology
sociology

Man frees himself from theological and metaphysical notions first in those areas most remote from himself—mathematics and astronomy; it is only after great advance that he comes to apply science to the realms of his own being—biology and sociology. This was, in fact, the first time that society was conceived of as an object for science, and Comte coined the term "sociology" for this new field.

There appears to be a missing link in this list of sciences—psychology. But this was no oversight on Comte's part. As far as he was concerned, the individual psyche or soul was merely a religious and philosophical superstition; a truly scientific psychology would treat man as the activity of body and brain, and hence psychology was part of physiology, a division of biology. Comte's views on psychology at the time consisted of the beliefs of phrenology, a system that explained human temperaments as due to the enlargement of various areas of the brain. This survives today only in the occasional practice of analyzing a person's character by feeling the lumps on his head. Comte's radical rejection of any subjectivistic psychology has its modern counterpart in behaviorism.

Comte's rejection of psychology has another important consequence. In his view, each science constitutes a separately organized level of existence. The social world, although composed of individual men, is not identical with those men, but is structured according to its own principles. Comte thus broke with the prevailing Enlightenment search for an answer to social problems in the elements of human nature. Society is not just the behavior of individuals, but something that accumulates across many generations. Just as language is created by individual men speaking, but nevertheless develops a vocabulary and a grammar that no one man ever does much to modify, society remains and unfolds by laws of its own, while individual men come and go. Comte thus hit on the concept of society as a cumulative *culture,* as we would now put it.

The task of the new science of sociology was to set forth the laws that governed this entity. Accordingly, sociology is divided into two parts: "social statics" and "social dynamics." Comte defined statics as the study of social order, and dynamics as the study of social change or progress.

Comte himself was well trained in the sciences of his day, and he held that sociology would develop by the scientific methods of observation, experimentation, comparison, and historical research. Unfortunately, he himself never did much of this kind of research, although he was fairly well versed in history. He was in too much of a hurry to finish his system, for he believed it contained the answer to the main problem of the day: how to put a society ravaged by revolution and strife back into order. With this in view, Comte invoked some methodological principles that provided shortcuts to his goal.

The first of these was the principle that isolated facts cannot be understood by themselves, but must be seen in their larger context: The whole must be grasped if one is to see the functions of the parts. This principle contains the fairly sophisticated idea, upheld by modern philosophy of science, that one must have an organizing paradigm or set of concepts before one can know what observations to make of the world. But Comte neglected the modern proviso that the concepts one begins with are only provisional, to be modified or rejected as the effort to fit in the facts goes on. Comte was confident that he had grasped the model of the whole at his first try.

According to this model, society is analogous to a biological organism. Society has its various parts (the family, the church, the state) just as a body has its various organs (the liver, the brain, the kidneys, and so on), each serving some function for the whole. Comte did not mean that society is literally an organism; it exists only as consciousness, not as physical individuals, and the various social institutions are parts of this set of ideas that are passed on from generation to generation. The roots of modern functionalism can be found in this analysis.

The various parts of society thus fitted together, and none could exist without the others. The harmonious society, then, was based on *consensus,* a feeling of belonging together as a moral unit. Here we can see how much more conservative Comte was than his mentor Saint-Simon. Saint-Simon was a thoroughgoing atheist and materialist, a believer in science and industry, whereas Comte felt that society could not be held together by reason alone, but demanded faith. Thus, the family, the church, and the community are the core of society, for it is here that men's selfish tempers are controlled by the sentiments of love, duty, loyalty, and respect. Comte thus mixed Saint-Simon's revolutionary heritage with the ideas of the conservative opponents of the Revolution, who contrasted the chaos of the years of Robespierre with a romanticized view of feudal society. The most influential of these conservatives were the émigré aristocrats Joseph de Maistre and Louis de Bonald, whom we shall meet again when we come to Tocqueville. Social thought owes many of its advances to such mixtures.

This constituted Comte's social statics. Two other principles helped him formulate his system of social dynamics: the belief that social change everywhere goes through the same sequence and the belief that all the various elements of a society change together. According to the first of these, we do not need to investigate the history of all societies; we need only locate the most advanced society, and the stages of its history will show us the stages through which all others must pass. The evolution of one society can show the rest of the world the face of its future. Comte was thus able to place all known societies on a continuum of development, from the primitive tribes described by the explorers of America and the Orient, on through the empires of history, and culminating, needless to say, with nineteenth-century France.

The second of these principles tells us that progress occurs simultaneously in all spheres—intellectual, physical, moral, and political. This follows from the idea of society as an integrated whole or system. This provided another shortcut for Comte, for it meant that one kind of change could be taken as an index for all others. Comte chose to emphasize intellectual change, since this was the area he knew best. The result was this capsule summary of the stages of human history:

Intellectual	Material form	Basic social unit	Basic moral sentiment
Theological	Military	Family	Attachment
Metaphysical	Legalistic	State	Veneration
Positive	Industrial	Humanity	Benevolence

Comte's basic ideas have had enormous influence on the development of sociology, both for good and for ill. Society is somewhat like an organism, but it is also unlike an organism in crucial ways. It is inherently full of conflict as well as harmony; and it is held together, when it is in fact held together, by coercion and economic self-interest as well as by moral sentiments. Comte's ideas about social change have been especially pernicious. They have a considerable appeal for the mentally lazy, who do not want to have to understand the intricate paths of history, which are arranged so inconveniently that they do not even progress toward the same goal. The elements of society do not all change together, and the outcomes are neither so inevitable nor so benevolent as Comte believed. For all men's hopes, France did not hold out the vision of the future to the rest of the world, nor does the United States for the Third World today. As we are beginning to understand, the so-called developing nations show few signs of creating our kinds of politics, stratification, or even economy in the foreseeable future, and it has even become questionable whether they are "developing" at all. Today's world planners are guilty of the same haste for favorable conclusions as was Comte: There is no shortcut substitute for the scientific method of collecting, comparing, and analyzing the facts.

On the positive side, Spencer, Durkheim, and others were to make good use of many of Comte's leading insights: the recognition that society would have to be explained on its own level rather than by reduction to psychology, the division of labor among social institutions, and especially the role of moral sentiments in holding society together. Free of Comte's overwhelming ideological concerns, later sociologists have gone beyond merely advocating moral order to analyze it, to search for the conditions that create it at certain times and places, and, thus, to break through to an understanding of the emotions and rituals that harness men to each other below the level of their rational consciousness.

But this was to be in the future. Comte, indeed, ended by turning his new science into a cult. The cult took form after Comte, in 1844, had a melodramatic but strictly platonic love affair with a middle-aged woman. The object of his passion was a lady named Clothilde de Vaux, who had been deserted by her husband, but still remained faithful to her marriage vow. The high point of the affair was an abortive liaison, complete with much hand-wringing and many protestations of duty and honor, which left Comte still physically denied but enraptured with worship of Clothilde's moral superiority. Not long after, she became deathly ill, and Comte forced his way into her bedroom and locked out her parents so that he might spend her dying moments with her alone.

Comte then began a series of ritual devotions, starting with daily obeisance to a lock of Clothilde's hair. He formed his followers into a Religion of Humanity, with Comte as its high priest. He began to refer to society as the "Great Being" and preached universal love and harmony through his system of industrial order. He envisioned mankind advancing to progressively higher levels of spirituality and even imagined a time in the future when love would dispense with gross material forms entirely, and women would be able to give birth without sexual intercourse. He formulated a new calendar, with days of devotion commemorating scientists, saints, poets, and philosophers alike. He planned a council of all such leaders, organized under the High Priest of Humanity, who would rule the world benevolently through the application of Positivism.

The cults of Comte and Saint-Simon, like the other utopias and schemes of the nineteenth century, failed to save the world, of course, or even to have very much effect on it. Saint-Simonianism provided an ideology to justify the activity of some financiers and Industrialists of the nineteenth century. Comte's Positivism attracted scattered adherents around the world, notably in the United States and Russia, and at the behest of some romantic Brazilian aristocrats it was made the official philosophy of Brazil. Indeed, Comte's motto *Ordem e Progresso* (Order and Progress) is still found on the Brazilian flag, an ironic commentary on the actual conditions of that beleaguered country.

The utopian prophets failed to change the world because they insufficiently understood it. They were too optimistic, too sentimental, and too eager for easy change to understand that history grinds out its conclusions through long and hard struggles. In the next chapter we meet the founder of the most successful social movement of modern times, a man willing to see the conflict at the core of things: Karl Marx.

CHAPTER TWO

SOCIOLOGY IN THE UNDERGROUND: KARL MARX

The social thinkers discussed so far have been respectable. They appeal to the established order. They talk in ideals and avoid looking too closely at unpleasant facts about the new industrial order. But the nineteenth century was not simply a glorious era of science, progress, justice, and brotherhood. Saint-Simon's harmonious hierarchy of industrial men or Comte's social organism made sense only by closing one's eyes to what was going on in the mundane world. Black smoke was beginning to hang in the air over the industrial towns of England, France, and Germany, and on the streets behind the houses of the prospering businessmen were growing the tenements where workers crowded with their families in scenes of grime, poverty, and disease. The mines and factories were manned by a tubercular population of men, women, and children, working eleven- , thirteen- , or fourteen-hour days, seven days a week, without respite except layoff or death. For Karl Marx the basis of reality was here, in the harsh facts of material and economic conditions, and the talk of philosophers, politicians, and priests was only a smoke screen designed to divert attention from it.

Marx was the great angry man of the nineteenth century. Indignant at what was happening to men and at the hypocrisy and blindness of those who covered it up, he set out to reveal what was going on, to explain both the inexorable workings of the economic substructure and the deceptions of the political and ideological superstructure. Marx was the first to come to grips with the realities of social conflict instead of wishing it away, and for this he doomed himself to a life in the underground. But this was the fate he wished. Free from the illusions of respectability, he thought he saw the system bringing its own destruction and the outlines of a newer, better world arising in its midst. Karl Marx, the man of conflict, was both a realist and a revolutionist.

It is not surprising that Marx is the most controversial of all modern thinkers, with the possible exception of Sigmund Freud. His ideas have been the handbook of revolutionists and would-be revolutionists. With the success of his followers in Russia, China, and elsewhere, his ideas have been raised to the level of state dogma. In Moscow the Institute of Marxism-Leninism has faithfully recorded the events of every day of Marx's life. Marxism has become a political orthodoxy. On the other side, virtually every opponent of communism has felt he must refute the Marxist system, usually by pointing out that revolution has occurred only in backward countries, where Marx did not expect it, and has not occurred in mature capitalistic nations, where Marx did expect it. The Marxists respond with the notion of imperialism, which internationalizes capitalist exploitation but can only put off the final reckoning, and stoutly maintain the truth of everything Marx said.

In the controversy the intellectual value of Marx's ideas gets lost. Knowledge advances by using and revising ideas to account for the facts we turn up, building on strengths, shoring up weaknesses. Such work is not engaged in by those who want to use ideas as ideologies to stir men to action or to test their loyalty, or as shibboleths to attack. In the long run we are best served by discovering as much as we can of the truth, not by rushing to act on half-truths or outright illusions. Marx's ideas can be best used if we are aware of both their weaknesses and their strengths, and that is what this chapter will try to display.

MARX'S LIFE

Karl Marx (1818–1883) was born in Trier, one of the small, legalistic states of the Rhineland, on the border between a progressive France and the more traditional parts of Germany. His father was a liberal, a Jew from a long line of rabbis, who had nominally converted to Christianity in order to maintain his career as a lawyer—that is, as a member of the local government bureaucracy, since lawyers were not independent professionals in Germany. Young Marx attended the University of Berlin, where he drank in taverns, acquired debts, fought the usual duel and got the usual scar on his face, and studied philosophy. In short he prepared himself for an academic career.

But circumstances conspired to forbid him a respectable career as a brilliant professor. He became caught up in the intellectual movement

known as the Young Hegelians. Hegel (1770–1832) had been the dominant German philosopher of his day. He was a liberal, after the German
fashion, which meant that he believed in the rule of laws rather than the
arbitrary rule of men and hence supported the Prussian state. Hegel's
philosophy culminated the idealist tradition that began with Kant; it held
that the essence of reality is Reason, but that the spirit of Reason manifests itself only gradually, revealing more and more facets of itself
during the course of time. History, he held, is the growth of Reason to
consciousness of itself, and the constitutional, legalistic state is the
culmination of history. Hegel developed his philosophy while Napoleon
seemed to be spreading the achievements of the French Revolution all
over Europe. Later, in the reaction following Napoleon's final defeat in
1815, Hegel found it expedient to declare that history culminated in the
bureaucratic Prussian state, and he became the official philosopher
at Berlin.

Of course, there was no reason why history should come to a halt in
Prussia, especially when that state still lacked a true constitution, and
after Hegel's death the revolutionary implications of his doctrine came
to the fore again. One faction of Hegel's students, the left Hegelians,
unleashed his historical relativism into an attack on the autocratic state
and its ideological bulwark, the state church. Marx's teacher, Bruno
Bauer, investigated the Bible as a historical document and declared the
Gospels to be forgeries and Jesus, a historical myth. For this Bauer was
dismissed from his university post in 1842 as dangerous to the state.
This ended Marx's chances for an academic career, since sponsorship
was even more important in the universities of the time than it is now.
It had been predicted that Marx would be the most eminent professor
of his generation, but this path was now closed. Marx took his first step
toward the underground.

He became the editor of a liberal newspaper in Cologne, a Western-
ized city on the Rhine River. Hard economic realities struck him immediately. He became embroiled in a controversy with the authorities over
their decision to prohibit peasants from cutting firewood in the forest,
although this was a traditional custom. The trees were protected by
laws, Marx wrote acidly, while poor men froze. He began to view
philosophy of all sorts as a distraction from the hard, material realities.
Hegel's idealism stood history on its head, he later wrote; the task was
to set it on its feet. The newspaper lasted five months before being
suppressed by the government. The conservative papers accused him of
being a communist. Marx did not know quite what this meant, but he
resolved to find out.

Now twenty-four years old, he went to Paris, the intellectual home of
all radicals. He read the French historians, imbued with the Saint-
Simonian idea of progress and the image of industrial society breaking
out of the bonds of feudalism, and he encountered the advocates of
utopian socialist communities. To his German Hegelianism and French
radicalism he added the third leg of his system: the ideas of the British

economists Adam Smith, Thomas Malthus, and David Ricardo, who explained how the movements of men and goods in this new era were controlled by the invisible hand of the market.

Among Marx's radical acquaintances was Friedrich Engels, another idealistic young German, who had just returned from his father's textile factory in Manchester, bringing with him a harsh exposé entitled *The Condition of the Working Class in England in 1844.* Their ideas meshed, and they launched an intellectual partnership that was to last the rest of their lives. They were soon expelled from France for their radical writings. They went to Belgium and then to England. In 1847 they attended secret meetings in London of a new revolutionary coalition of labor unions (at that time illegal) called the Communist League. As its platform they wrote a manifesto, which ended with the following words:

The communists disdain to conceal their views and aims. They openly declare that their ends can be attained only by the forcible overthrow of all existing social conditions. Let the ruling classes tremble at a communist revolution. The proletarians have nothing to lose but their chains. They have a world to win. WORKINGMEN OF ALL COUNTRIES, UNITE!

The *Communist Manifesto* was finished in January 1848. In February, during an economic crisis in Paris, a group of demonstrating unemployed workers were fired upon by soldiers, and the city erupted into riot. The French king abdicated, his government collapsed, and a wave of revolt was set off through the cities of Germany, Italy, Austria, and most of the rest of Europe. The nobility everywhere were frightened and on the defensive. In France the wealthy property owners took command of the Second Republic; a popular left-wing revolt in June was crushed by the army in six days of bloody fighting. Around Europe the right wing gradually regained confidence and began to reestablish its power. Marx, who edited the revolutionary newspaper in Cologne during its uprising, was banished by the Prussian government.

Reaction had set in again. Marx went to London, his final place of refuge, and, watched by police spies, began again to write. With him came his wife, his childhood sweetheart and the daughter of a German aristocrat who had been the Marx's neighbor in Trier. Life became a struggle to survive. For a while Marx made a living as a foreign correspondent for the New York *Tribune*, then under a liberal editor. At times the family nearly starved. They lived in the poorest working-class section of London. They pawned their possessions and borrowed money from Engels, who was then working in his father's business in Manchester. Several of Marx's children died of malnutrition and disease. Through it all he managed to work, sitting in the reading room of the British Museum from 10 A.M. to 7 P.M. every day for years. At last, in 1867, his researches were published as *Das Kapital,* a book that would help bring down half the world.

Marx's life work forms a comprehensive system, but for purposes of analysis it may be divided into three parts: his sociology, built around the analysis of class consciousness and class conflict; his economics, which develops the internal contradictions of capitalism; and his social and political philosophy, built around the notion of alienation and its solution in communism. These parts are not equally valid. Marx's sociology has turned out to be basically correct and has been very important for subsequent theories. His economics, on the other hand, is crucially flawed, although it points us to some important questions. His philosophy, in the final analysis, is based on value premises and ways of looking at the world that the individual can accept or reject as a source of inspiration as he sees fit. In short, it is possible to get much from Marx without accepting his whole system.

MARX'S SOCIOLOGY

Classes and class consciousness

"The history of all hitherto existing society is the history of class struggles," Marx declares at the beginning of the *Communist Manifesto,* and classes are the core of his analysis. Marx did not invent the concept of class, of course. In his day one could scarcely avoid noticing them, and the danger was rather to take them for granted. What Marx did was to provide a theory of how classes are produced. He began from materialist premises. Since one could not survive without making a living, he reasoned, the source of one's living must be the most basic determinant of one's behavior. The economy of an era, with its different economic positions, was thus the source of its fundamental class divisions. In the society of ancient Greece and Rome the economy was organized around slavery; hence the basic classes were those whose living came from owning slaves (the patricians or citizens), the slaves themselves, and those who were neither slaves nor slaveholders (the plebeians or freemen). In the feudal society of the Middle Ages the basis of the economy was the manor; the main classes were the nobility, who owned the land and the services of the peasants attached to it, and the serfs or peasants, who provided the agricultural labor. In modern or bourgeois society the economy is organized around industrial production and commercial exchange; and the main classes are the capitalists, who own the factories, the banks, and the goods to trade, and the proletarians, who own nothing but their own labor power.

Within these classes there could be further divisions. For example, in feudal society the nobility was divided into ranks from king down to knight and included the landowning clergy of the powerful Medieval Church. There were also minor classes not based directly on the central economy, such as servants, guild masters, journeymen, apprentices, and free peasants. For Marx the property divisions were crucial because they marked the breaking lines in the social structure. When conflicts became intense, classes would have to group themselves along these divisions. Thus, modern society includes financial capitalists (such as bankers and brokers) as well as industrialists and agricultural landowners; small capitalists as well as big ones; the petty bourgeoisie, consisting of handicraftsmen and shopkeepers who both own their own tools and shops and work in them; the working class or proletariat; and the poorest and most degraded class, full of criminals and people living from hand to mouth, the *lumpenproletariat.* Marx used all of these classes to analyze what happened in modern society, but he expected the conflicts to polarize more and more between the property owners as a whole and the propertyless workers, with the petty bourgeoisie and small capitalists being deprived of their property and dropping into the ranks of the proletariat.

This material organization of society produces what Marx calls "class consciousness." People do not have an objective view of the world; they see it from the restricted point of view of their own positions. Thus, bourgeois writers like John Locke saw private property as an inherent part of the order of nature; feudal lords saw the rights of hereditary nobility as given by God; and the ancient philosophers could not even imagine a world without slavery. This is not to say that people have *no* capacities for being objective nor that they spend all their time thinking about their economic interests. They may occasionally be genuinely interested in the ideas of philosophy, religion, science, literature, history, or art, but where their ideas impinge on the social world, class consciousness goes into action.

Out of the array of available ideas, people select those to believe in that best fit their material interests. Thus, the medieval nobility supported the conservative Christian thinkers who preached the sanctity of worldly authority and diverted the peasants toward the spiritual world and away from the oppressions of the material one. This is the meaning of Marx's phrase "religion is the opiate of the people." Occasionally, it could work the other way, as when the religious upheavals of the Lutheran Reformation provided some alternatives and a peasant revolt broke out under the religious guise of the belief that the Second Coming of Christ was at hand. In modern society bourgeois interests found ideological support in beliefs about personal morality; extolling the virtues of hard work, individual success, self-control, frugality, and respect for law and property were ways of getting people to support the competitive system of free enterprise. In the same way, politicians make speeches about the eternal truths embodied in their laws, even as those laws frame a system of property that benefits the group those politicians belong to.

But there seems to be a contradiction here. If everyone selects ideas to fit his personal interests, how can religion be "the opiate of the people"? How can people have "false consciousness" and be taken in by the ideologies of their opponents? This was a serious question for Marx, since the workers did not always see the capitalists as their enemies, and until they did so, a revolution could not occur. Marx's writings imply two main answers. The first is simply that people's ideas can be controlled by coercion. He himself was familiar with government censorship, treason trials, and the denial of rights of speech to "subversive" thinkers by those who did not want their viewpoint contested. The second, somewhat subtler answer is that consciousness depends on the material resources people have for formulating and communicating ideas. The dominant social classes have most of these resources: They get the most education, are most likely to be literate, and have the time and money to keep up on news and ideas. Furthermore, they can influence what ideas are produced by paying the salaries of teachers or priests, owning newspapers or controlling them by buying their advertisements (or as in the present era, giving research grants). The impoverished Saint-Simon writing publicity for the French industrialists provides an example of how the process works. The lower classes can criticize the upper classes under their breath but not in the center of public attention, and they lack the means to formulate ideas about things happening at a distance from them. The result, in Marx's words, is that "the ideas of the ruling class are in every epoch the ruling ideas."

As history moves, consciousness changes with it. The thinkers of the Enlightenment appeared because material conditions had changed in England and France, and the incipient bourgeois class was beginning to gather the resources to support thinkers of its own. Marx discerned another movement, culminating in the future. As capitalism brought workers into the cities and crowded them together in factories, it created material conditions that allowed the workers to communicate among themselves. Literacy and the press began to give the workers a chance to develop a world view of their own. Beneath the public beliefs of bourgeois ideology an underground consciousness was growing. Here Marx found a role for himself, not unlike that of Hegel: to raise the level of consciousness of the working class until it became fully aware of itself.

Marx's theory of politics

All this culminates in Marx's theory of politics. Politics is the effort to control the state. The state fundamentally consists of the instruments of organized violence in society, and hence it is an enormous power for whoever can control it. The state is a crucial prop for the economy in that it establishes the system of property. Property, after all, is not so much the things that are owned as it is the right of the owner to do what he pleases with them, and the denial of those rights to others. Land, for example, does not "belong to" anyone, even if it is used, until someone claims the exclusive right to use it and backs up the claim with either his own power or the power of the state. In this way, the state creates the rights of property in a system of slavery or serfdom or in a modern money economy. Marx was particularly interested in the fact that since the state creates private property, it can abolish it and substitute socialism. But that was for the future.

Ordinary politics is the struggle to control the state so that its powers can be used for one's personal advantage. The struggle may be between members of the same class (such as nobles fighting among themselves for power in the Middle Ages) or between different class sectors (in modern society, petty bourgeois interests versus industrialists, financiers versus landowners). Beneath the sonorous speeches of the politicians, the real business of politics concerns mundane economic issues—taxes, tariffs, monopolies, franchises, licenses—over which people struggle and bargain for nothing more noble than the opportunity for economic gain.

Occasionally, there are more important clashes. These occur in historical periods when new economic classes attempt to change the existing structure of property. Marx lived in the shadow of the French Revolution, when the entire feudal system of aristocratic privileges and monopolies was swept aside to create the basis for a market economy, transforming the nobleman into a holder of salable land and the peasant into a free laborer, and freeing the entrepreneur from old monopolies and restrictions. These basic, revolutionary conflicts draw together the members of the various classes. Nobles cease to fight among themselves, and the bourgeoisie unite in their common interest. An entire system is at stake.

Who wins in these struggles? There are two main determinants: the distribution of material resources that enable men to struggle successfully for power, and the historical situation that favors a class whose time has come. While these are not entirely distinct, we can see that the first determinant is most important in ordinary politics, and the second is crucial in times of revolution.

During the feudal era, for example, ordinary politics was monopolized by the aristocracy, because they alone had the resources to engage in it. The peasants were tied down to the land; the merchants were a minor group, without military power. Men who owned enough property to afford a horse and armor could be knights; the great landowners could outfit whole armies. Thus the nobility constituted the only "political class," the only group with the time and resources to keep informed of what was going on, to make alliances with other nobles, and to take part in wars and court intrigues.

In the same way, in the industrial era the capitalists control communications, money, and time. They exert an influence over government far out of proportion to their numbers because they command the resources of business and finance. The network of business contacts gives them a class organization; their business and financial affairs keep them constantly aware of what the government is doing that may affect them; their wealth and organizational bases allow them to support politicians who will represent them in office. Not the least of this power is ideological. As we have seen, the class with the strongest resources can control the means of communication and hence hinder other classes' abilities to formulate their own interests. Within the capitalist class, as within the aristocratic class in its era of dominance, the men who hold the largest resources will be able to advance their interests over those of their fellows. But when another class challenges, the class that holds the greatest resources as a whole will usually unite and thus prevail.

This brings us to the second determinant of power: the long-term historical changes in the economy that favor a particular class simply because that class's interests happen to coincide with the interests of the system as a whole. Marx was sure that the bourgeoisie would eventually prevail over the aristocracy in Germany, Russia, and the rest of the world, just as it had in France. Once capitalism developed to the stage where a society depended more on industrial production and trade than on subsistence agriculture for its livelihood, the capitalist economic system had to be supported by favorable state policies. To fail to give it this support would hurt everyone, especially the existing rulers, who would not want to go back to a preindustrial standard of living. But in Marx's time the old feudal laws and government hindered capitalism; kings could only ruin it by their old policies of sales of monopolies, indiscriminate taxation, and special rights for aristocrats. The means of production had outgrown the relations of production; the fetters had to be broken.

"Force is the midwife of every old society pregnant with a new one," declared Marx. The revolution came in France in 1789. The king went to the guillotine, eventually to be replaced by another in 1815—but now the old property system was gone, and a new one, suitable for the bourgeoisie, had taken its place. Instead of the old absolute monarchy, there was a constitution and a representative assembly in which the bourgeoisie could begin to shape laws to its economic needs.

The bourgeoisie won because its time had come. The economy had changed, giving them the resources to contend for power, the ideology to express their interests, and the favored position of being necessary for society's prosperity. A similar revolt in the Middle Ages could only have been a failure. Even if by some chance the capitalists had had the resources to win power, they would have been unable to change the laws upholding feudal society without creating a chaos of marauding warriors and defenseless peasants. They had to wait until history was prepared for them.

Marx's sight focused on another class maturing in the womb of history: the working class. Just as capitalism grew up within feudalism until their conflict kept both systems from operating and the old world had to be smashed to make way for the new, capitalism itself would begin to break up because of its internal contradictions. The periodic financial crises, with attendant bankruptcies and unemployment, were only symptoms of what was to come. As the industrial economy grew, it would come more and more into conflict with the free market and the system of private property that formed its structure. Eventually, a crisis would occur in which the interests of the *workers* alone would coincide with the *necessities* of keeping the system going. Only the abolition of private property and the institution of socialism would restore economic order. The interests of the workers, then, would have at last become the interests of the whole system, and the capitalists would be displaced.

The process was really twofold. Not only would economic change make the workers the necessary dominant class, but it would also shift the balance of weapons with which to conquer power. The factories and industrial cities would bring the workers together in the strength of numbers, and technological change—the press, the telegraph, and so forth—would improve their capacities for communication and organization. Modern advances would thus bring them to full mobilization and full consciousness of their interests. When the moment struck, they would be prepared.

When properly understood, Marx's sociology appears to be basically correct. That is not to say that his predictions about the downfall of capitalism are right, as they obviously are not. But these are specific applications of the theory and not the theory itself. A considerable amount of modern research indicates that one's economic position (that is, occupation) is a major determinant of one's life style, interests, and beliefs; that economic change produces the line-up of classes in a particular historical era; and that the material resources for organization and communication, along with the functional necessities of governing to keep up the economy, tend to determine who will win political power. All of this, however, Marx plugs into a particular theory of *how the economy will develop.* His account of capitalism growing within European feudalism and bringing about the great waves of bourgeois revolutions seems basically accurate. But his theory about the inevitable tendencies of modern capitalism is wrong. It is because Marx's economics fails that the rest of the system does not turn out the way he expected it to. Marx did not, as is sometimes suggested, fail to take account of racial or religious strife that would keep the workers from unifying, or of social mobility that would make workers think of their individual chances of rising instead of their class interests in overthrowing the whole system. He merely expected such conflicts to be dwarfed by an economic crisis so great that men would have to unite along class lines simply to survive. The decline of racial animosity in the United States during the Depression of the 1930s suggests that Marx was right on this point. Similarly, he recognized the possibility of social mobility, but he believed that in a time of economic crisis the only social mobility would be *downward.* No, the problem is with Marx's prediction of an economic crisis that could be resolved *only* by socialism.

We turn, then, to a brief sketch of Marx's economics.

MARX'S ECONOMICS

Labor theory of value

Marx began with a premise common to Adam Smith, David Ricardo, and the other classical economists: that the value of anything is the amount of labor it takes to produce it. For example, if it takes one day's labor to produce a shirt, and two days' labor to produce a pair of shoes, then two shirts are worth one pair of shoes. Given the fluctuations of supply and demand on the market, the market price should eventually come into equilibrium with the real value, and two shirts will sell for the price of a pair of shoes. The labor theory of value, then, describes the basic mechanism of production and exchange in the economy. It also has a special appeal to a socialist like Marx; for if *labor* is what produces value, justice would seem to require that workers receive the proceeds of their labor.

Profit as exploitation

If the labor theory of value is correct, we are left with a paradox: Where does *profit* come from? The market moves toward equilibrium; everything gets exchanged for its true value; one day's labor gets exchanged for one day's labor. How can anyone get more than he puts into it? Marx finds the answer in one commodity that sells for its true value yet can produce more than what it sells for. This commodity is human labor itself—the worker's exertions as he sells them on the labor market. According to Marx's chain of deductive reasoning, labor should tend to sell for its true value, which is equivalent to the amount of labor it takes to produce it—that is, if it takes an average of six hours work by farmers, weavers, carpenters, and others to feed, clothe, and shelter a man for a day, he will be paid the equivalent of six hours work. But if the employer pays him for six hours work, he can nevertheless work him eight hours (or twelve hours or fourteen hours, as was more common in Marx's day). This is possible because the employers own the means of production—the factory and its tools—and hence they can demand this longer working day as a condition of giving a man a job. Profit, then, comes out of the extra hours of work, over and above what the worker is paid for. This extra work is called "surplus value," and profit can be said to be based on the exploitation of labor.

Law of the falling rate of profit

The system can now be set in motion. As capitalists expand production, they compete with each other for labor. Thus, they bid up wages to attract workers. But rising wages cut into the margin of profit. This, in turn, motivates the capitalist to install labor-saving machinery to cut his labor costs.

But here the capitalist starts to cut his own throat. Machines do not produce profit, according to Marx's scheme; profit comes only from exploitation of labor. Any gains a manufacturer may make with his new equipment will disappear just as soon as his competitors catch up with him and install the same equipment. This drives the price of machinery up and the price of the produced goods down; so the upshot is merely that the capitalist has reduced the amount of labor he employs in comparison to machinery and other nonlabor costs. This means that profit has to fall, since exploitation of labor is the only source of profit, and less labor is being exploited. And in fact, the economists of Marx's day agreed that profits did tend to decline. (Modern economics has modified this principle: Profits fall *within* the business cycle, but not *across* cycles, where there can be long-term growth.)

Periodic crises

This brings us to the characteristic drama of the capitalist economy. About every ten years throughout the nineteenth century there was a depression. As new machinery is installed, Marx explained, people are thrown out of work. This means there are fewer people drawing wages and hence fewer people who can afford to buy things. But the machinery has *increased* the rate of production. There are too many goods, too few buyers. Prices fall; profits go down. Manufacturers try to catch up by installing even more labor-saving machinery, but this only makes matters worse. Soon there are great warehouses of goods lying unused, while unemployment grows and people are destitute. Manufacturers go bankrupt, throwing even more men out of work.

Eventually, the crisis reaches a bottom. The stronger capitalists buy up the factories and machines of the bankrupts at a fraction of their value and begin to make a profit. The surplus is used up, workers can be hired for low wages, and employment begins to rise. Soon the cycle begins again: a boom of expansion and profit, then a bust of falling profit, mechanization, and unemployment. The system rises and falls with grim regularity; only each time there are fewer manufacturers, holding bigger and bigger shares of the market.

The final collapse of capitalism

Capitalism, then, moves toward a gigantic industrial monopoly. The smaller capitalists are squeezed out; they lose their property and join the ranks of the proletariat. At the same time the system creates a great reserve army of the unemployed, which keeps the competition for jobs high and wages at a level just above starvation. The proletariat thus becomes larger and more disgruntled. Each successive crisis of the system is worse than the last, because the collapse of big firms throws more workers into destitution than the collapse of small ones. During this period, the economy becomes centralized through these gigantic monopolies, preparing the way for socialism. All that needs to be done is to overthrow the system of private property and let the workers run the system for the common good.

A last crisis occurs, and the workers rise up as a vast majority. The army, the politicians, and the defenders of the state can do nothing to stop them, for all are forced to see the inevitable solution. "The centralization of the means of production and socialization of labour at last reach a point where they become incompatible with their capitalist integument," Marx prophesied. "This integument bursts asunder. The knell of capitalist private property sounds. The expropriators are expropriated."

What went wrong? The capitalist system has not collapsed in the advanced industrial countries, whatever its strains; profits have not fallen in the long run; wages have not stayed near subsistence level. There have been cyclical crises, to be sure, and huge corporations with near monopolies dominate the business scene; but the crucial elements of Marx's picture are missing.

There are two main answers. The Marxist reply has been: imperialism. Lenin, whose theory was based on the ideas of the British economist Hobson, pointed out that modern capitalism has become international. Thus, the more advanced countries, like Britain, France, Germany, and the United States, have been able to avoid domestic economic ills by exploiting the rest of the world. If capitalist countries overproduce, they can dump their excess goods in the markets of India or South America. Extra capital to invest can go to the same places; even labor can be exploited internationally, by using low-cost native labor to produce raw materials cheaply. In short, by exploiting the rest of the world, the wealthy nations can keep their profits up and can even pay enough wages to content their workers.

But the crisis can be only put off, not evaded entirely. Once the entire world is brought into the capitalist orbit, the class conflict will become internationalized. War becomes an adjunct to revolution. Lenin saw World War I as a struggle of the great capitalist powers of Europe over colonial markets; the result could only be to speed up the inevitable chaos of the capitalist system. Thus, Russia underwent a socialist revolution in the economic devastation following its defeat by the Germans. World War II and the Japanese conquest were to have the same results in China. Cuba, Algeria, and Vietnam are only so many more steps along the road toward capitalism's final collapse.

There is another answer to the question of why Marx's predictions have not been realized, one that goes more to the core of the problem. That is: Marx's labor theory of value and the related labor exploitation theory of profit are wrong. Labor, we may reflect, is not the only thing out of which profits may be gotten by obtaining more production from it than it costs. Machinery and improved organization can provide this too, because they can increase the productivity of labor. The United States produces so much more per capita in 1970 than it did in 1870 because our technology is so much more powerful today. This means that it has been possible to produce much more than before; profits can remain high, yet workers can get more, too, by unionization and through government welfare programs. With this extra production the government can even intervene in economic crises, using the techniques of Keynesian economics (such as government employment, spending, and taxation) to keep widespread unemployment and underconsumption from happening.

None of this would be possible if Marx's inexorable economic machine really worked the way he said it did, but that machine is broken at the very center. Marx's thought forms a perfect system: The economy produces social classes, class consciousness, and class power to rule the state; the labor theory of value, the law of the falling rate of profit, and the inevitable progression of economic cycles turn the wheels of the system. But the labor theory of value is wrong; the mainspring falls out. Marx's sociological determinants go on, but free of their inexorable underpinnings. History lapses into indeterminacy.

Still, something may be salvaged from the wreck of Marx's economics. If economic crises are not necessarily inevitable, it is still true that they can occur or at least threaten to occur, and it is worth remembering Marx's prediction of their political effects. The theory of imperialism is of special relevance for today. Maybe there is no inevitable necessity for advanced countries to exploit backward ones to stave off their own economic collapse; nevertheless, there is plenty of self-interested drive for profits that makes European or American businessmen interested in investments under the protection of military dictators in South America, Iran, or Southeast Asia. Indeed, the current conflict between the Communist countries and the Free World cannot be understood if one leaves out economics, for the "Free World" has a primarily *economic* meaning. It does not refer to the world of political democracies, since most of the countries in it, outside of northwestern Europe and North America, are dictatorships; they are "free" only in the sense of markets open for private enterprise. In this era, when we live under the mushroom cloud of potential nuclear annihilation and witness wars slaughtering Asian peasants at the behest of dictators and generals, there is nothing we need more than an understanding of the forces that drive these historical events. The Marxist theory bases the explanation on an economic mechanism that does not quite work. It does not give us the answer, but points us to the crucial questions.

MARX'S SOCIAL AND POLITICAL PHILOSOPHY

Marx's philosophy is woven throughout the rest of his work. It centers around the ideas of alienation, as the distinguishing feature of man's history, and of communism, as the end of history and the solution to alienation.

Alienation has become a common idea as the twentieth century has been infected by a malaise that was scarcely discernible one hundred years ago. We feel there is something about the world we have created that goes against our basic nature—that we are ruled by impersonal forces of the market and the inhuman decisions of bureaucracies. We live in a world diagrammed by Kafka. Marx was one of the first to discern this malaise, although it remained for Weber and Freud to make empirical sense out of it. For Marx alienation was less an observable fact than a basic axiom, derived from Hegel and ultimately going back to a theological notion of sin. To understand what Marx meant, we must take a brief excursion back into Western philosophy.

The idealist tradition in philosophy can best be grasped if we begin with René Descartes (1596–1650). Descartes's famous phrase *"cogito ergo sum"* (I think therefore I am) was the one principle that he found *must* be true, even if one doubted everything else about the world. David Hume (1711–1776) extended the scope of skepticism by pointing out that we can never really *know* that something *causes* something else. If one event always follows another (at least has always done so up until now), we can only *suppose* that it is caused by the first event. We judge the probability that the same sequence will happen again. Causality, then, is something we impute to things out of our own minds, not something that *absolutely* exists "out there." Immanuel Kant (1724–1804), the founder of the German idealist tradition, took this idea one step further. We cannot really know *anything* about the world, he argued, because we never *experience* anything except through our own subjective filters of understanding. Not only causality, but time, space, shapes, numbers, colors, and substance are all part of the framework of our own minds. The "things in themselves" can never be known; all one can know is the contents of one's own mind, imposed on the raw materials of unknowable reality.

This brings us to Hegel, Marx's mentor. Hegel drew the conclusion from Kant that man *creates* his world by the act of perceiving it. But this does not occur all at once; it takes all of history to fulfill. In effect, inert matter has no form until living creatures develop who can perceive it; the higher forms of beauty and truth do not appear until man arrives to see the world through these spectacles. Moreover, man actively fashions the world, making tools, works of art, laws, states, and systems of ideas. Each of these progressively manifests more and more of the world of forms into the world of actuality. Eventually (we are nearing Hegel's own time), man becomes aware that he is the agent of something greater than himself—that the world is a spirit that unfolds more and more facets of itself until it is fully visible. This spirit is Reason, and it reaches its culmination in the constitutional state and in Hegel's philosophy, which is Reason at last conscious of itself.

Alienation enters into Hegel's system because it describes the relationship of man to his creations up until the time he finally recognizes reality for what it is—the unfolding spirit of Reason. That is, man creates things but then fails to understand that he has created them. He mistakes the world for something objective (at least, he did so up until the revelation of Kant). He worships objects as idols and loses sight of his own creativeness and of the spirit flowing through him. Thus, man is cut off, or alienated, from his essential self.

Marx adopted this form of analysis from Hegel but took it off its spiritual foundation. For Marx man creates the world through his labors but then becomes constrained by the very things he has created. He creates religions out of the imagination of his own brain and then falls down and worships his gods as if they really existed. He creates the state and then cannot escape its rule. He creates an economic system by the labors of his own hands and then finds that he is compelled to sell himself on the market he has created.

In a famous chapter in *Capital* entitled "The Fetishism of Commodities" Marx describes how money begins as a means of exchange to buy goods but soon becomes an end in itself. Goods become viewed in money value only, instead of in terms of their use to the consumer. A house is no longer a place to live but becomes a piece of real estate that one can afford to live in only if the market makes it feasible to keep it. The capitalist is a man who cannot enjoy his goods but must turn them into as much profit as possible or else be wiped out by a competitor. In the capitalist system the worker is the most alienated of all, because he becomes a cog in a machine, selling his own labor as a commodity, and is stripped of any meaningful relation with the goods he produces for the capitalist to sell.

Alienation grows progressively worse throughout history. The final revolution that brings down capitalism, then, destroys not only a system of economic exploitation, but a system of dehumanization. History ends with communism, for monopoly capitalism stretches human alienation to the final verge, at which it can at last be abolished. Communism was to be a society without alienation, where man no longer was to be controlled by the system he had created, but instead would control it for his own benefit. The division of labor itself would be destroyed. Man would at last reach absolute fulfillment.

Marx's notion of alienation is not really an empirical entity, but a whole way of looking at the world, of holding up a standard to evaluate it by. Modern sociologists have tried to measure just how alienated people are in various kinds of jobs, and the results are mixed. Certain kinds of labor, such as that on the auto assembly line, are considered by most workers to be rather dehumanizing. Most other kinds of work (and we must remember that most people, even in factories, do *not* work on assembly lines) elicit a fair amount of positive reaction; and some people, although a minority, even like working on the assembly line. Marx's response would no doubt be that men can be so oppressed by the system as to lose even their elementary human wants. In the final analysis Marx believes in untapped human potentialities and holds up a high standard for society to emulate.

The idea of communism is easier to evaluate. Marx himself actively promoted the revolution he wrote about. He helped found the revolutionary trade-union movement, the International Workingman's Association ("the First International"), and Engels carried on the leadership after his death. In some places, notably in Germany, the unionists' Marxism became more and more rhetorical and irrelevant as their organization gained political recognition. But the revolutionary potential of Marxism would not be lost. Marx's most militant and ruthless followers, inspired by his penetrating analysis of capitalism and by his assurances of the inevitability of their victory, created a state in Russia and elsewhere that bears his name.

Marx would probably reject the Russian system of today as a gross perversion of what he had in mind. He wanted a system to dignify the whole man, not to sacrifice everything to material production. But Marx never really devoted himself to the hard question of how his humanist utopia was to be brought about. It is easy to speak abstractly of man's taking control of the system instead of being controlled by it, but it is harder to see just how this may be brought about. Indeed, much of subsequent sociology has carried on a debate with Marx's ghost, as Weber, Sorel, Michels, Mannheim, and others have questioned the possibility of controlling *power* in the same way that the *economy* might be reduced to management for the common good. Events have forced us to go beyond Marx. We have had to look for ways to escape from the Leviathan of the state as well as the Mammon of the marketplace.

Marx, like Hegel, wanted to bring history to a close with himself. Instead, both men are relegated to their places in history.

THE LAST GENTLEMAN: ALEXIS DE TOCQUEVILLE

Thought in the early nineteenth century was no more unitary than it is today. So far we have paid attention to the modernists: prophets of the industrial order like Saint-Simon and Comte, and radicals like Marx who looked further ahead into the future. Not everyone believed in progress, however. The postrevolutionary situation had its conservatives, too, of whom the most famous were the Englishman Edmund Burke (1729–1797) and the French aristocrats Louis de Bonald (1754–1840) and Joseph de Maistre (1753–1821). The last two attacked modern society as the anarchy of mob rule and counterposed an ideology of order, obedience, ritual, religion, and hierarchy—all of which qualities were supposed to be found in the Middle Ages. Restoration France thus created the germs of the major modern ideologies: liberalism, communism, and fascism.

But the heritage of conservatism is more ambiguous than this, and new thought comes from strange mixtures. Comte combined the conservatism of Bonald and Maistre with the industrialism of Saint-Simon and produced sociology as the science of *order* in the new society. Conservatism also produced a man who represents the best of the old order—Alexis de Tocqueville. His conservative stance brought him not to vituperation against the new era, but to the detachment necessary for understanding it.

Modernists are essentially optimists. Tocqueville was a pessimist. He shared the classical Roman and Greek outlook: Life is a tragedy, with its eternal forces always in balance. His classical prose style aims to impose the only order possible upon the dilemmas of existence—the harmony of literature. Thus, equality improves most men's lives; but mediocrity is the price we must pay for it. Freedom is gained in some respects only by the loss of freedom in other respects. Tocqueville holds the classical idea of balance: An excess in any direction leads to a corresponding reaction. In an era of optimism Tocqueville's conservatism enabled him to tear the veil blinding the eyes of his contemporaries. The others shared a belief in the withering away of the coercive powers of the state, whether this was to occur immediately, as Saint-Simon and the liberals believed, or in the revolutionary future, as Marx predicted. The idea of progress made the wars and tyrannies of twentieth-century governments inconceivable for these men; Tocqueville's more timeless viewpoint on the dangers of power has kept him contemporary and relevant.

Tocqueville was virtually the last of the old school of gentleman-intellectuals. This sort of person was not a professor or a commercial writer, but a man of some wealth who owned a well-stocked library, wrote beautiful letters to his friends, and devoted his leisure to composing treatises and essays on philosophy, history, and everything else, to be circulated to his correspondents and sometimes published upon wider request. Some of these men dabbled in science—Darwin was to be perhaps the last of these—before the era of large university and government laboratories. It was a role existing only in aristocratic society and comprised only a very small section of the aristocracy. All in all, it was the best excuse that class had for its existence.

Tocqueville himself was on the margin of the French aristocracy— the *petit noblesse*. His father was a government official, a prefect (governor) in various parts of France. His parents were almost executed in the Revolution; they were saved only by the Thermidorian reaction that sent Robespierre himself to the guillotine. Other relatives of Tocqueville did not escape.

Tocqueville studied law and took up a career as a lawyer, that is, as a salaried official of the royal court system. In 1830 riots in Paris led to the abdication of Charles X. When the dust had settled, the throne was still there but was occupied by Charles' cousin, Louis Philippe, of the rival house of Orléans. The Orléans had been scheming for the throne for hundreds of years and at last achieved their aim by an alliance with the constitutionalists. (The alliance was to survive only eighteen years.) Tocqueville was forced to take an oath of loyalty to the new regime. But as a legitimist, he was opposed to this bastard monarchy, and his views caused much friction with his superiors.

The recurrence of revolution convinced Tocqueville that there was an inevitable trend toward equality and the destruction of aristocratic society, but that France was going about achieving it in the wrong way.

He hit on a plan: a leave of absence and a commission to go to America to study penal reform, currently a topic of interest in France. His real reasons for wanting to go were to escape from an impossible situation for himself personally and to see what lessons could be learned for the future of France. He left in 1831 for nine months of travel in America. Out of this trip came his monumental work *Democracy in America.*

Tocqueville liked America, even though its surface was unappealing to an aristocrat. It was the land of "mob rule," where politics consisted of demagogic bombast and the maneuvers of politicians to stay in office and dispense patronage to their followers; where business dealings were incessant and all-pervasive; where high culture and refined manners hardly existed; where the laws were in the hands of the people, and men shot each other down in the streets of the Western territories. In other words, it was an America like that of today, only cruder, tougher, and above all, more puritanical. "I thought that the English constituted the most serious nation on the face of the earth, but I have since seen the Americans and changed my opinion," said Tocqueville. "An American, instead of going in a leisure hour to dance merrily at some place of public resort, as the fellows of his class continue to do throughout the greater part of Europe, shuts himself up at home to drink. He thus enjoys two pleasures: he can go on thinking of his business and can get drunk decently by his own fireside."[1]

Tocqueville liked this. He himself was rather serious, hard-working, devoutly religious, and prudish, and he admired the Americans for these same qualities. Beneath the surface he saw the Americans as like his beloved Romans—people who believed in laws and used them to rule themselves; who participated actively in public affairs; who showed patriotism, religiousness, and the discipline of moral self-control. Tocqueville romanticizes America a bit, especially in failing to see that the American democracy he describes was run by the middle class and not by the poor. Given these reservations, his analysis of America continues to be sound.

EQUALITY IN AMERICA

The basic premise of Tocqueville's system is the inevitable advance of equality, which Tocqueville took to be so characteristic of modernity as to be a sign of God's will. Equality (which Tocqueville uses interchangeably with the term "democracy") is contrasted with *aristocracy*, as the other great form of society. Equality means the free mobility of individuals; aristocracy means that positions are hereditary from birth. Equality means the extension of the political franchise from the few to the many. It means the end of legal differences in status: of noble ranks and titles with their attendant privileges, and of primogeniture within the family

[1] Alexis de Tocqueville, *Democracy in America,* Vol. 2 (New York: Alfred A. Knopf, 1945), p. 232. Copyright Alfred A. Knopf, Inc.

(by which the eldest son inherits all the wealth). In short, equality means an end of deference based on immutable differences between different ranks of society. Along with this, Tocqueville believed that men were becoming more equal in wealth, education, and culture.

In an effort to be balanced, Tocqueville tried to present both the good and the bad effects of the advance of equality, based on his observations of daily life in America. He pointed out that with the end of dominance by inheritable property and of primogeniture, equality had spread to the relations between fathers and sons and among brothers. The result was a decline in the old authority of the family. But the family did not fall apart, as the conservatives had predicted; the artificial bonds of property were replaced by stronger bonds of personal sentiment. As family members were no longer controlled by each other, they were able to like each other more. The same sort of freedom applied to unmarried women. Since they were no longer bartered by their parents for family connections, they were free to choose their own partners by falling in love. The result, Tocqueville shrewdly remarks, is that such marriages have much less infidelity than the aristocratic marriages of convenience which make no claim on the feelings of the partners.

In the same vein Tocqueville remarks on the effects of equality on manners. The Americans are not great conversationalists, using talk as a display of rank, but talk plainly and openly without signs of deference. The British, he says, are caught in between the clear rankings of the French aristocracy and the equality of America, and the famous British stand-offishness is the result. They still retain the aristocratic belief that people should be given the proper deference, but equality has progressed enough so that it is hard to tell just what deference people are entitled to. The solution is to avoid speaking to people unless they are properly introduced.

Tocqueville found that equality also changed the relationship between employer and employee. Instead of a relationship between a proud master and his submissive servants, it becomes a simple contract between men in which one bargains for a limited portion of the other's labor. The man does not sell his whole self, but only a part. The old loyalties to one's superior disappear, but they are replaced by new ideals, shared by all. In the field of politics, the prevailing sentiment is nationalism. In the field of personal virtues the old military "honor" that had to be defended by fighting duels is replaced by the business virtues of hard work, reliability, and thrift. Modern society is thus not without honor; it is only that the honor appropriate to a time of armed self-defense is changed into the honor necessary in a time of commerce and industry.

Most impressive of all, Tocqueville thought, was the extension of personal sympathy in equalitarian society. He quotes a letter written by an aristocratic Frenchwoman of the seventeenth century, in which she blithely mingles descriptions of the fine weather with news about the tortures that were imposed on the local peasants who were revolting against a new tax. This lady was not an unkind person, Tocqueville explains; her letters show that she was full of kindness to her relatives and friends. It is merely that the range of sympathy extended only to those who were equals, and she could not imagine herself in the place of the peasants. In America, on the contrary, Tocqueville found a surprising display of charities of all kinds, as well as of good samaritanism among perfect strangers. For the same reason tortures disappear as a means of punishment in modern society, and there is a shift toward rehabilitation and general leniency toward criminals. This sympathetic attitude is not inherent in the culture of the Americans, Tocqueville argues, but is rather a product of equalitarianism. To prove it, he points to the inability of the white Americans to sympathize with the plight of the Negro slaves, whom they do not regard as equals: It is the limits of equality, and not the cultural outlook, that set the limits of sympathy. Tocqueville's principle is still illuminating today. It helps explain why Americans often aid each other in accidents on the street, whereas Asians or Latin Americans are more likely to be indifferent to what happens to strangers in public.

On the negative side, Tocqueville noted the pervasive commercialism of American life. Equality, he felt, leads to ceaseless striving for social position. Where all are basically the same, it is debilitating to fall behind. Accordingly, everyone seeks to get rich quick. Tocqueville observantly points out that even though most Americans at that time were farmers, they were not farmers in the European sense. They did not grow food merely to live on, but rather, they developed land for profit. Indeed, much of the land was scarcely cultivated, but was bought and sold for speculation in land prices. Thus, even in 1830 the American farmer was less the virtuous rural citizen he always makes himself out to be and more the speculative businessman.

All this has a negative effect on culture. Business emphasizes practicality, not abstract truth or aesthetic style. As a result, Tocqueville argued, Americans become hazy and bombastic whenever they are forced to speak of any general ideas, for outside of the range of specific practical matters their minds have developed no refinements or distinctions. Culture in America thus is neither very high nor very low; everyone is well-versed enough to get along, but there is no incentive or opportunity to stand out. Lacking the European aristocratic tradition in intellectual endeavor, America remains a land of comfortable mediocrity.

Also on the negative side, Tocqueville finds that the continual business dealings of America add up to a general monotony. The novelty of events stays on the same plane, and nothing rises above it. He found in America the general trait of conformity over a century before David Riesman and others popularized the idea. "I know of no country in which there is so little independence of mind and real freedom of discussion as in America," Tocqueville declared. He saw Americans' individualism as confined to economic competition and as entirely lacking in the world of ideas.

"We must understand what is wanted of society and its government," says Tocqueville.

. . . If a clear understanding be more profitable to man than genius; if your object is not to stimulate the virtues of heroism, but the habits of peace; if you had rather witness vices than crimes, and are content to meet with fewer noble deeds, provided offenses be diminished in the same proportion; if, instead of living in the midst of a brilliant society, you are contented to have prosperity around you; if, in short, you are of the opinion that the principal object of a government is not to confer the greatest possible power and glory upon the body of the nation, but to ensure the greatest enjoyment and to avoid the most misery to each of the individuals who compose it—if such be your desire, then equalize the conditions of men and establish democratic institutions.[2]

But in fact, says Tocqueville, we have no choice. We will have equality whether we want it or not, and if its social consequences are neither very bad nor very good, the *political* possibilities it opens up are momentous. It is with these possibilities that Tocqueville is primarily concerned. Equality is not the same thing as freedom, he is quick to point out. It can result either in an excellent form of self-government or in anarchy and its concomitant danger, tyranny. As examples of the latter Tocqueville had in mind the bread-and-circus mobs of Rome preceding the Caesars' overthrow of the Roman Republic or the crowds at the guillotine in the Reign of Terror that prepared the ground for Napoleon's coup d'état in France. The events of 1830 in France again followed that pattern. The question is, *Why* does equality sometimes lead to one, sometimes to the other of these results?

The United States (along with Britain) is Tocqueville's model of a good government based on equality; France is his example of its bad effects. He did not think of the United States as perfect, however. He objected to the electioneering, the office seeking, the patronage game, the personal attacks in the public press. But these are the inevitable side effects of equalitarian self-government. Despite them, the United States is favored by three kinds of conditions: the structure of its government, geographical and historical accidents, and the culture of its people.

GOVERNMENT STRUCTURE

Tocqueville found the main virtue of American political institutions to be their decentralization. He was impressed with the degree of local autonomy given to towns and counties in administering local matters such as roads, charities, schools, and taxes. By contrast, all such things

[2] *Ibid.*, Vol. 1, p. 262.

in France were handled by a central bureaucracy in Paris. For the same reason, he admired the federal system, which gave the national government the powers necessary to control the currency, wars and foreign affairs, and national commerce, but which left all other matters to the states. He thought the principle exact: The national government should have full powers to take care of things affecting the nation as a whole, but not the power to intervene in what affected only a part of the country.

The effect of this system, Tocqueville believed, was to make Americans public-spirited. Tocqueville felt that the natural effect of equality was to make men individualistic and selfish, since they would be busy competing in business and thus uninterested in the affairs of the larger community. But decentralized institutions counteracted this, for they tied individual self-interest to public-spiritedness. If Americans wanted to get anything done, they could not rely on a government agency to do it for them; they would have to initiate the action themselves. Where cooperation was necessary, they would have to drum up support among their fellows, take part in local government, and contribute their own efforts to getting it done. The man who wanted a road or a canal for his own use, then, would have to come up with a project that would appeal to others' interests as well. Thus, a decentralized government makes its citizens energetic, industrious, and prosperous; by contrast, the tone of a centralized autocracy is one of lifeless quiet.

Tocqueville also admired the way in which the authority that did exist was split up through its own internal balance of power. He liked the presidential and gubernatorial system which separated the executive from the direct influence of the legislature. Tocqueville, thinking of the radical shifts in mood in the French Assembly of the 1790s, considered direct control by the legislature (that is, the parliamentary form of government) unstable. It was liable to those moods in which the majority tries to impose its will by force on the rest of the country—"the tyranny of the majority."

Tocqueville was particularly impressed with the powers of the American courts to pass on the legality of the acts of the legislature, as well as to provide remedies for aggrieved citizens, thus making democracy into a rule of laws rather than merely a rule of politicians. But given the power of the courts in America, Tocqueville thought it important that their power was itself split up and restrained. In France, he declared, such courts would be an instrument of tyranny, for there the government exercised complete control over the courts, just as over any government agency. In America the courts were made independent through the tenure of the judges once they were in office, and the judges' power was itself circumscribed by the separation of prosecution and defense attorneys from the court. (Recall that Tocqueville himself was a professional lawyer, employed by the bureaucratic French courts, and that his visit to America was prompted by his difficulty in working for a regime of which he disapproved.) He also thought the jury system useful in balancing the power of the judges, as well as in educating citizens to participation in the orderly rule of law.

The effect of these balances was that the government could not be too strong or too precipitous in its actions, so that neither an emotional majority nor a would-be tyrant could easily enforce its will. Tocqueville was careful to point out that the United States was *not* a land of unlimited freedom for the individual to do whatever he pleased. Unlimited freedom, in Tocqueville's conservative view, was nothing but license for anarchy. On the contrary, he declared, "more social obligations were imposed on [the individual] there than anywhere else." America was full of agencies for group control over the individual, and Tocqueville cites with approval the New England ordinances that required citizens to go to church, prohibited drunkenness, and severely punished sexual improprieties. This great community power was restrained from creating a political tyranny, however, by being broken up through decentralization and balances of power, thereby making the government both less dangerous to the nation as a whole and more responsive to private interests. Tocqueville's observations on just what "freedom" means in America are pertinent today, as a struggle goes on between the rights of individuals and the public power to control individuals' morals. The "freedom" that is built into American political institutions is the freedom of local groups from unified central control, and there is very little built into the system to protect the individual from the tyranny of these groups.

Tocqueville also devotes some attention to freedoms that he thinks are dangerous in themselves, but that serve to counterbalance other dangers of the system. Tocqueville regarded freedom of the press and freedom of assembly as invitations to spread slander and extremist opinions and to form conspiracies to overthrow the government. This, at any rate, he believed to be the case in France. But in a country like the United States, where power was too decentralized to be easily swayed or overthrown by mass agitation, he believed these freedoms provided a necessary corrective to the other ills of the system. If elected politicians tended to be self-seeking and corrupt, the press could keep them in check by threat of exposure, and political parties created the competition that would publicize their failures in order to try to replace them in office.

Finally, Tocqueville remarked on the beneficial effects of the separation of church and state in America. Again, his contrast is to France, where the state-supported church made religion a bone of material contention. Religion was caught up in defending a particular political regime and hence added another source of political controversy. Political opponents of the regime became irreligious, and contending religions were driven into political opposition. The lack of a state church in America, then, strengthened rather than weakened both state and church.

GEOGRAPHICAL AND HISTORICAL ACCIDENTS

These political structures were the main features of stable self-govern-ment in America, but there were other contributing factors. For example, the United States grew up in the virtually empty continent of North America, with plenty of land for expansion and wide oceans between it and the warring powers of Europe. The result was that America had little fear of wars and no need to maintain a large standing army. This was important, for wars are the great centralizer. In wartime the central government assumes great powers over the nation, not only over local governments, but over the citizens themselves. The entire apparatus of government is directed toward providing the materials for war: Men are conscripted, taxes are high, the economy is regulated. America was spared all this because it was protected by its geography rather than its army. Tocqueville was correspondingly pessimistic about the prospects for American-style decentralization in Europe, where the threat of war-fare from neighboring states necessitated constant preparation by the central government.

Another accidental feature favoring stable democracy in America was the general equality of wealth. Accordingly, there were no overwhelm-ingly great differences among the people and no strong basis for revolutionary conflict. (The one exception, Tocqueville noted, was the existence of slaves, whose unequal condition provided the most ex-plosive feature of American society.) Tocqueville thought it especially important that equality existed in America before the democratic gov-ernment was established. By contrast, in France, where a war had to be fought against the aristocracy in order to create equality, the Revolu-tion aided the process of centralization. The local institutions had been in the hands of the aristocrats, and hence the Revolution took away local autonomy in order to wrest control from the aristocracy; in doing so, it destroyed the decentralized bases of freedom.

AMERICAN CULTURE

Democracy in America was also favored, in Tocqueville's view, by the unique social conditions of its people. They all spoke the same language, were mostly of the same Protestant religion, and had the same educa-tional level of rough literacy. Again, few sharp distinctions, few bases for political conflict. Most important of all, he felt, was the strong hold of the Puritan religion. The church taught men discipline, moral order, and a belief in laws. Moreover, the Protestant churches in America were controlled by their congregations and hence provided a model of democratic self-government. All told, Tocqueville was inclined to view America as uniquely favored by its special characteristics to build equality into a stable form of democratic government, rather than to give in to its inherent dangers.

In the abstract Tocqueville was more pessimistic. Equalitarian society was dangerous to freedom, he felt; his views on the subject have become known as the theory of mass society. The abolition of the aristocracy resulted in there being no one strong enough to resist the tyranny of the central government and its head, whether he be king or dictator. Moreover, the equality of conditions tended to eliminate all independent sources of power which might check unlimited control. Equality among citizens makes them emphasize uniformity; as noted above, no one is willing to stand out against the strength of public opinion. The natural tendency of the public is to demand that laws and rules apply to everyone, without exception; the public feels that it should be allowed to oversee everything, and hence the state takes on the potential for exercising total control over the individual. Since everyone is equal, no one individual has any power, and men must appeal to the only thing above the individual—the state—to do things. The state becomes the only ideal outside of the private person; the overwhelming demand for loyalty is to the nation. Thus, the individualism of a mass society of equals goes together with the total power of the state. As the private individual seeks his personal gain in business or other purely private affairs, his political interests are reduced to a desire for tranquillity—a government that will maintain order so that he can pursue his own affairs. The man of mass society is willing to give great power to the centralized state and in the process loses his freedom to oppose it.

The United States, in Tocqueville's view, had the uniquely favorable political structures, geographical circumstances, and customs to counteract these ill effects of equality. But France and most of the rest of Europe did not. On the Continent the governments were extremely centralized, controlling through their national bureaucracies not only armies, taxes, and public works, but charity and education, finance and workmen's savings, the regulation of manufacturing, and a large section of the public's employment. This centralization advanced irreversibly, through every revolution and restoration; there seemed to be no stopping it. Other conditions were unfavorable as well. France, Germany, and other European nations confronted each other across narrow boundaries and maintained their central governments to support a great war machine. Nor were the cultures of the people favorable to peaceful democracy: Great inequalities in wealth still existed, as did sharp cultural distinctions, religious conflicts, and a widespread absence of any religious faith at all. The prognosis for America was that there would be no more revolutions; only the unequal condition of the blacks, Tocqueville felt, could have that potential. For France and for the rest of Europe he feared more of the cycle of revolution and reaction.

Democracy in America proved very successful after its publication in 1835 (a second part came out in 1840). Of all the many visitors' accounts of America, Tocqueville's was by far the most famous. Its success was due partly to the fact that it says what people wanted to hear. Thus, it was most popular in England and America, whose institutions were praised, and least popular in France, which did not come off so well.

The book contains a very powerful theory of political institutions. Its main weakness is that it makes the United States seem a more perfect democracy than it really was, or is. From his aristocratic viewpoint, Tocqueville mistook middle-class Americans for poor people and hence concluded that the poor people in America were really fairly well off and, in any case, ruled the country. He saw more equality than really existed; in fact, there were poor people in the 1830s, just as now, but they were characteristically invisible, living in the remote parts of town and countryside.

This defect does not vitiate Tocqueville's insights, but it adds a new dimension to them. Indeed, it points us directly at the central dilemma of modern America: Democracy can operate and be very strongly entrenched and yet not serve all the people. As in Tocqueville's day, middle-class businessmen participate in local politics, but the poor are generally unable to do so. There is democratic bargaining for power, and in the process a middle-class majority is well enough served; in a country where the middle class is a majority, a democracy can easily ignore the poor. This is implicit in Tocqueville's analysis, for he saw that democracy could operate among the white majority even while excluding the black slaves. Tocqueville, the man of classical philosophy, would no doubt be willing to recognize his error and let his analysis stand even in that light. He would probably feel (as apparently do many people today) that a democracy of the middle class is better than no democracy at all and would consider the political exclusion of the poor as an unfortunate by-product, but a price one should be willing to pay for what freedom there is. As a conservative he would be unwilling to upset the balance of powers of democracy as it stands in order to extend equality to the poor. That, in his terms, would be paying for equality at the price of freedom.

There is another side of Tocqueville, one that is generally ignored by his admirers and intellectual descendants. He has somber words on the subject of war as creating centralized power and thereby reducing the bases of freedom. For twentieth-century America, modern transportation and communications have ended geographical isolation, and World War II and its aftermath have created just the military megalith that Tocqueville predicted. Moreover, Tocqueville had some wise words on the tendency of military officers, who have a relatively low status in a business-oriented society, to seek wars in order to justify their existence and to give them chances of promotion. Another centralizing factor has also been operating, which Tocqueville missed: the growth of the business system to national and even international scale, which brings about central government regulation, especially in combating large-scale economic crises such as depressions. Such economic crises can have the same effects as wars in concentrating government powers, just as the growth of big business corporations has eliminated much of the individualism that Tocqueville found so much a part of the American scene. By the mid-twentieth century many of the bases of decentralization that Tocqueville thought important in upholding democracy in America had disappeared.

Tocqueville's own career showed how right he was about the structure of politics in Europe. In 1839 he was elected a deputy in the French legislature, representing the district of Vologne, where his ancestral château stood. He was continually reelected until his retirement from politics in 1851. In parliament he led the fight to abolish slavery in the French colonies and interested himself in the French colonization of Algeria. In 1848 he made a speech to the House, which concluded with the words: "I believe we are sleeping on a volcano." The date was January 27, about the same time that Marx and Engels were finishing the *Communist Manifesto.* On February 16 riots broke out in Paris, and another revolution was under way. Tocqueville was elected to the Constituent Assembly, which was called to form the Second Republic; he led the monarchist faction. In 1849 he was named minister of foreign affairs in the government of the new president, Louis Napoleon.

Tocqueville lasted in office only five months. He came into conflict with his president, who was already preparing the coup d'état that in 1851 was to destroy the Second Republic and usher in the ill-fated Second Empire of Napoleon II. France's pattern was becoming set: Third, Fourth, and Fifth republics were in the offing, as well as a short-lived Communist commune in Paris in 1871, a Fascist regime collaborating with the German occupation during World War II, a Communist-based World War II underground, an attempted army coup in 1958, and a student-led near-revolution in 1968. Tocqueville's foresight was already becoming apparent.

After Napoleon's coup Tocqueville retired from government and attempted to search out the origins of France's calamities. The result was *The Old Regime and the French Revolution,* possibly the greatest historical book ever written. Tocqueville broke new ground in several ways. Instead of relying on what other historians had said, Tocqueville went back to the files of provincial town halls for the original documents showing the operations of local government. He compared the development of institutions in France with the development of those in England, Germany, and elsewhere, in order to test his ideas against alternative sequences. The book is a model of good scholarship, scientific thinking, and beautiful style. Its results are still definitive.

It was not the Revolution that destroyed the decentralized institutions of France, Tocqueville found, contrary to what most conservatives held.

Rather, it had been the French kings themselves. Back in the Middle Ages Tocqueville's class, the aristocracy, had jealously guarded their independence from the king. Parliaments and independent courts had been created by coalitions of nobles as a balance of power to resist the control of the king. Such institutions had existed all over Europe, even in Russia and Spain. The kings counterattacked and managed to destroy the powers of the aristocrats by creating a royal bureaucracy, into which the courts were incorporated as subordinate agencies. The aristocrats were made royal officials, and their representative institutions were reduced to virtually nothing.

This process went furthest in Russia and the East and least far in England. In England, in fact, the courts and lawyers remained almost totally independent, and parliament won the final struggle with the king in the seventeenth-century revolution led by Oliver Cromwell. In France the struggle went on the longest. There, the king built a mighty bureaucracy, but the aristocracy still held many powers, and the show-down did not come until the end of the eighteenth century, when a new commercial era had accentuated the trend to equality and created the massed population of Paris which would prove so important in French politics. The inefficiency of the French regime, balanced between an autocratic king and a parasitic aristocracy, led to the government financial crisis of 1789. In the temporary government deadlock the floodgates broke, and the masses attacked. The spirit of equality had been unleashed by the leveling bureaucracy and the growth of commerce, and the aristocrats who lived on with their old privileges but without their old powers and functions were to feel the vent of its fury. In the end the main effect of the Revolution was to strengthen and streamline the central government, something that could not be done as long as the aristocrats stood in the way. The Revolution merely consolidated the structure the kings had labored to create.

This account sharpens the irony of America in world perspective. The United States has the most protection against the instabilities of modern mass society, because it derives its institutions—especially its decentralized courts and local governments—from the early period of British history. The colonists of the seventeenth century who founded American society were from the conservative, minor aristocracy of England, and they brought with them the institutions of decentralized feudal control. America thus escaped even from what centralization the English kings had managed to carry out. The United States, far from epitomizing the new era of politics, has come to have one of the oldest government forms in the world.

The United States, then, is not a hopeful model for the Third World, where, as if to follow Tocqueville's forebodings, revolutions destroy local autonomies in order to modernize and thus set the basis for total government control. For Europe Tocqueville's predictions have been only too true, as shown by the alternations of dictatorships and anarchical democracies in France, Germany, Italy, Greece, and elsewhere.

By 1815, the main outlines of the modern era had already emerged. Napoleon, the little corporal who brought in the army to stop the squabbling of politicians and restore order in France and then set out to conquer Europe for his system, foreshadows another little man with global ambitions, this time on the other side of the Rhine—Adolf Hitler.

Tocqueville's private secretary in the foreign ministry of Louis Napoleon was an aristocrat named Arthur de Gobineau. In the period after Tocqueville's death de Gobineau was to become famous for his scientific theory of history as the conflict between superior and inferior races. History thus provides us with yet another ironic link between the old and the new.

CHAPTER FOUR

DO-GOODERS, EVOLUTIONISTS, AND RACISTS

So far our history has dealt mainly with the thought of France and Germany. We take up now the third of the great intellectual cultures of modern times, that of the English-speaking world. It is not a world of towering individual thinkers like Marx or Tocqueville, with the exception of Charles Darwin, who is not really a social thinker at all. But it does produce some major ideas: the notion of society as organized around a market and the idea of man's continuity with biological evolution. It produces as well the characteristic political philosophy of Britain and America—liberalism, in both its right-wing (laissez-faire) and left-wing (welfare-state) versions. It develops the modern ideology of the application of science to the solution of social problems. For us today, concerned about the potentially dangerous consequences of science, there is a lesson in this. For it was out of the vogue of science, and especially of biology and statistics, that the ideologies of racism emerged. How this happens is still of some interest, for the mode of thought that produced racism has not disappeared along with that particular doctrine.

To begin, we must retrace our steps and return briefly to the eighteenth century. Medieval Christianity had held a monopoly on thought all over Europe, and Latin had been everywhere the language of the educated thinker. It was only in the eighteenth century, when thought broke out of its religious mold, that truly national differences in culture began to appear (although the Reformation paved the way for this by breaking up the Catholic Church into national churches). In France, as we have seen, the movement that we call the Enlightenment was a sharp revolt against religion, in the name of science. The *philosophes* of the Paris salons entertained their listeners with revolutionary principles cloaked over by witticisms. In Britain the break with religion came much more gradually, and the tone was mildly progressive, never revolutionary. Unlike the independent, secular French intellectuals, the British thinkers emerged first of all as university professors in Scotland, where they taught a branch of theology called moral philosophy. Originally this discipline consisted of practical advice on what the good Christian should do in specific situations to avoid sin, but it gradually became secularized into a consideration of how the good society is organized. From moral casuistry, it gradually turned into economics.

THE MORAL PHILOSOPHY OF FERGUSON AND SMITH

The agents of this transformation were two Edinburgh professors, Adam Ferguson (1723–1816) and Adam Smith (1723–1790). Ferguson began with the medieval idea that society is formed like a living body. The king is the head; his soldiers the arms; the church the heart; the artisans the stomach; the royal ministers the eyes and ears; and of course the peasants the feet. (This is a notion from which Shakespeare, a characteristically medieval thinker, drew many of his most elaborate metaphors.) Ferguson applied the model more seriously. If society does in fact consist of specialized parts forming a body, we must conceive of a division of labor among them and a system of exchange by which the services of one part are paid for by the services of the others. And given this natural exchange, one may draw a striking conclusion: that the social division of labor can carry on its exchanges very well on its own, without the interference of the government. The social body does not need the constant supervision of its head.

Adam Smith drew out the consequences of this in 1776 in *The Wealth of Nations*. The market, Smith showed, has laws of its own, the most basic of which is the principle of supply and demand, which regulates exchange for the benefit of the whole. No one could very long persist in producing what was not wanted, for he would get no return; the high returns for those who produce what is so wanted as to be scarce will attract other producers and thus reduce the scarcity. It is neither necessary nor desirable to interfere with this process, for there is an invisible hand that guides the results of men's labors, and in following his own self-interest, each man best contributes to the general good. Smith thus at once founded the new science of economics and a new political philosophy, Liberalism.

LIBERALISM AND SOCIAL REFORM: BENTHAM, MALTHUS, AND MILL

The philosophy of Liberalism has two sides, which were united for a while, but later split into rival viewpoints. These two sides were organized respectively around the idea of rational man and the idea of the natural laws of the market.

On the one side, there is the way of regarding man as *homo economicus,* the rational individual who calculates profits and losses and acts accordingly. This enlightened self-interest was all to the good of the system, as we have seen, and it became thought of as the principle around which all of society could be organized. The leader of this wing of thought was the lawyer Jeremy Bentham, who founded the school of *utilitarianism,* originally as a program of legal reform. The laws of England were a jumble of local and national statutes, full of inequities and grotesque feudal punishments like hanging for stealing bread. Bentham argued that revenge and other sentiments were foolish bases for laws and proposed a set of reforms based on principles of reward and punishment that would induce people to be good. In the utilitarian philosophy the best action could be computed by a "hedonistic calculus," by which one arrived at "the greatest good for the greatest number." It provided a way of combining maximum individual freedom with the good of the whole society.

The other side of Liberalism was organized around the idea of the division of labor and the exchanges of the market, which follow their own natural laws. In the tradition of moral philosophy from which this model emerged, natural laws were regarded as the way in which God (or Nature) had intended things to operate; they were laws about both how things work and how they *ought* to work. Thus, competition, through the principles of supply and demand, results in the production of just the amounts and kinds of goods that are needed and assigns them a fair price. All restraints on trade, whether these be business monopolies, government restrictions, or labor unions, are unnatural and hence must be opposed.

Sometimes the results of these laws seemed to be unfortunate. For example, in 1798 a country parson named Thomas Malthus published *An Essay on the Principle of Population* in which he stated that poverty was the result of a law of nature. As production increases, the population grows, he argued; but whereas the population increases by a geometric ratio (for example, 2:4:8:16:32, or some such *accelerating* curve), the production of food can only increase by an arithmetic ratio (1:2:3:4:5 or other *constant* increments), as new land is brought into cultivation only with effort, and even that approaches a limit of exhaustion. Accordingly, population will always tend to outstrip food supplies, and the less fit individuals will starve. This is not only inevitable, said Malthus, but even good for the system as a whole. Malthus and Smith used a labor theory of value and hence were confronted with the same paradox Marx grappled with: How is profit made, if the market ensures that one quantity of labor-value will be exchanged for an equal value? You will recall that Marx invoked labor exploitation as the answer; Malthus proposes population increase of the poor people as the saving element, for it ensures that there will be too many poor people for the available jobs and hence keeps wages low. Thus, the natural laws of the system are all to the good in the end, and in any case it is fruitless to interfere with them. Trying to save the paupers only enables them to reproduce, which makes the population problem that much worse. Parson Malthus even regarded this principle as evidence of God's moral retribution: Poverty is the punishment that men bring down on themselves for their lack of sexual restraint.

Eventually, a split was to develop between the two wings of Liberalism, but they would retain much in common. They both believed in representative government, the capacity of rational men to rule themselves; in the civil liberties of freedom of speech, press, and assembly, which ensured that truth would arise from the free market of ideas; in religious tolerance and the separation of church and state; and in a minimum of government interference with the freedom of the individual, as long as he does not use his freedom to infringe uopn the freedoms of others. (Just where this infringement begins was to be a subject of bitter debate.) This implied a belief in private property as an individual right. The only way in which all Liberals agreed that one might interfere with others was through education (although not necessarily state-supported or compulsory education), which would enlighten people to see how their rational and moral behavior was best for themselves and for society. Liberals were uniformly opposed to revolution and believed only in gradual change and improvement.

The Liberal position was of course not the only one in England in the early nineteenth century; there were also conservatives supporting the rights of the aristocracy and other vested interests, as well as more radical movements among the workers. But for the educated middle class, Liberalism became a powerful force. At the same time, its two wings were coming more and more into conflict. Not only the harshness of Malthusianism but the evils of the industrial revolution were becoming apparent. Child labor, factory conditions, hordes of beggars and paupers, squalid poorhouses and debtors' prisons, periodic crises of unemployment—the same things that drove Marx to radicalism moved one section of Liberalism into action. The utilitarian wing, with its belief in rational action and its principle of the greatest good for the greatest number, proposed doing something to correct these ills. Soon they were joining in the commissions that investigated conditions in the factories, proposing legislation on child labor, free schools (as a way to take the children off the market), workman's insurance, prison reform, public health, and a myriad of other worthy causes.

The intellectual rationale for reform was provided by the utilitarian leader John Stuart Mill (1806–1873). The "laws" of the market, Mill pointed out in 1848 in his *Principles of Political Economy,* are simply statements of how things will operate *if we let the market operate unchecked;* but there is no *necessity* for us to let it operate that way. Mill, in effect, destroyed the remaining assumption of moral philosophy, which saw "natural laws" as statements both of what *is* and of what *ought* to be. The market is only one system among many, Mill said. It is not God's single law, and if its results do not bring happiness, then we are free to modify it or to try another system.

This created liberalism with a small "l," the modern philosophy of reform, which has led to the modern welfare state. The old, laissez-faire Liberalism (with a large "L") was put on the defensive. In Britain the bolder wing of the liberals went on to support not only legislative reforms but even trade-unionism and eventually the Labour party. A mild reformist version of socialism was advocated by these liberals organized in the Fabian Society, whose membership was to include George Bernard Shaw. The consequences of liberalism were not merely political; they also began the tradition of empirical research in sociology. The investigating commissions in the factories were followed by tours of philanthropic individuals into the slums and poorhouses, resulting in such publications as Charles Booth's *Life and Labour of the People in London.*

SOCIAL EVOLUTIONISM: DARWIN AND SPENCER

Mill had given the reform wing some heavy intellectual ammunition. But just when the battle seemed won, the fading conservatives acquired unexpected help. In 1859 Charles Darwin published *The Origin of Species.*

At a stroke, Darwin set the natural world in order, just as Newton had done two centuries earlier for physics. All the species of plants and animals could now be seen as evolving from common ancestors through the great principle of natural selection. Continual small variations in each generation resulted in gradual change, as those most fit to survive and reproduce in the available environments do so, and those less fit die out. The result is a series of branchings, as creatures evolve until they become adapted to stable habitats.

This was the great intellectual event of the nineteenth century, and its result was to put the capital "L" Liberals back in the saddle. Darwin's model of evolutionary advance through competition and survival of the fittest was strong justification for leaving social processes alone to take their course. Actually, Darwin's system had more than an affinity with laissez faire, for Darwin had hit upon his great organizing principle in biology—natural selection—while reading Malthus on the dynamics of population. Darwin provided Liberals not only with support, but also with the right kind of enemies. The church conservatives naturally regarded evolutionism as contrary to the biblical account of Creation, and their outcry grew even louder in 1871 when Darwin published *The Descent of*

Man, which carried out the evolutionary corollary that man must have a common ancestor with the animals, most probably with the great apes. Liberalism, joining hands with evolutionism, once again drew the most progressive thinkers to its cause.

The most prominent of the social evolutionists was Herbert Spencer (1820–1903). Like Mill and Darwin, he was an eccentric, unsociable Englishman, although unlike Darwin he was poor enough to have to work for a living. Trained in science, Spencer began working as a railway engineer. He was always producing mechanical inventions, including a not-very-successful flying machine. The only invention that he actually made money on was a sort of early paper clip. By the time he was thirty, Spencer realized that more money could be made by inventions in the world of ideas, but he continued to set up weird labor-saving devices around his own home.

Spencer's career was launched as a writer on scientific and political subjects for popular magazines, which were just springing up around midcentury to cater to the growing middle-class audience. To this public Spencer began to sell his combination of evolutionism and laissez faire.[1] Evolutionism, Spencer argued, shows that we are subject to forces beyond what we can see. Our actions, however well-intentioned, will fail to achieve their aims if they attempt something contrary to the laws of nature. Spencer thus backed up the economic principles of laissez faire with an evolutionist view of social stratification as produced by natural causes. Rich men have risen to the top by their talents, and the poor are at the bottom because of their inherent deficiencies. Accordingly, we should not expect reforms to work just because they seem to be reasonable and good.

For example, Spencer said, we need to determine the psychological differences between the sexes before deciding whether to give women the vote. Since all creatures adapt biologically to their environments, it is both useless and cruel to try to civilize the natives in the colonies or to allow criminals and mentally defective persons to produce their inevitably defective children. Spencer even questioned the value of universal education; to educate the intellect, he pointed out, does not change people's emotions or behavior.

Spencer thus claimed that we must know social science before making any changes. And where is that science? Spencer set out to produce it himself. Indeed, he produced not just a sociology, but an entire encyclopedia. Between 1860 and 1896 Spencer turned out a massive series entitled the *Synthetic Philosophy.* Volume I is *First Principles,* followed by Volumes 2 and 3, *Principles of Biology;* Volumes 4 and 5, *Principles of*

---

[1] Spencer was not a literal follower of Darwin, but it must be recalled that evolutionism was generally in the air at the time. From 1830 to 1833 Charles Lyell published his theory of geological evolution, which had already brought down the wrath of the church and popularized the subject. Darwin himself had formulated his ideas in the late 1830s, and they were privately known among leading scientists.

Psychology; Volumes 6 through 8, *Principles of Sociology;* and culminating in Volumes 9 and 10, *Principles of Ethics.* There were volumes planned on *Principles of Astronomy* and *Principles of Geology,* but these were not finished before Spencer's death; these should logically have come first, but they were postponed because Spencer feared he would die before the main part was complete. We should recall that this was the era before radio and television, and the main leisure pastime of the middle class was reading. Spencer lived off this audience for most of his life, selling advance subscriptions to his works and also publishing them in magazine installments. *Principles of Sociology* began coming out in 1872 in *The Contemporary Review* in England and in *Popular Science Monthly* in the United States.

These volumes are full of interesting examples of different customs found around the world—child marriage, savage puberty rites, the forms of tribal kingship, and so on at great length. It is just the thing for a writer who gets paid by the page and whose readers have long hours at home in the evening to fill. For his sociology Spencer hired three professors to gather together all the available data under the headings of "Uncivilized Societies," "Civilized Societies (Extinct or Decayed)," and "Civilized Societies (Recent or Still Flourishing)," and so we get our information, especially from explorers like Captain Cook in the South Seas and Dr. Livingstone in Africa. Spencer supplied the unifying theory.

Basically, his model was like that of Comte, whom Spencer had read and appreciated. Society is like an organism, passing through various stages of development. Spencer updates this theory by showing that change is due not merely to progress in knowledge, but to principles of evolutionary selection. He also emphasizes that society is different from an organism; it is made up of the actions of individuals and lacks a consciousness concentrated in one place. He also rejects Comte's conservative notion that society is a moral unit and, of course, Comte's political scheme for reorganizing the world under a "High Priest of Humanity." Instead, Spencer wanted to show how society develops structures that culminate in the invisible hand of the market, whereby individuals are given a maximum of freedom and yet contribute to the best functioning of the whole.

Spencer gave his system intellectual elegance by explaining all evolution—cosmic and biological as well as social—by a single basic principle: that matter begins as a homogeneous mass of simple particles and gradually becomes organized as the particles come together to form heterogeneous parts of a complex whole. In short, things move from the simple and unorganized to the complex and organized. Spencer took this idea from embryology: An embryo begins as a mass of undifferentiated cells, which gradually become specialized organs interacting with each other. Spencer stated the principle more abstractly and then applied it to the evolution of the solar system, the earth, biological species, and finally to society. Evolution is the process of adaptation to the environment, and its long-term trend, from lower and earlier adaptations to higher and later ones, is from simplicity to complexity.

Spencer thus arranges primitive, ancient, and modern societies in an order reflecting the stages of evolution. Societies build up as small tribes grow, are conquered, or otherwise combine with others. Size brings about a differentiation of structure. From the comparatively structureless tribes, we get first (a) a *regulative system* for dealing with the outside environment, analogous to the nervous system in organisms—that is, the state, which provides offense and defense against other societies; then (b) a *sustaining system* of economic production that provides life support for the regulative system; and finally (c) an *exchange and distribution system,* consisting of communications and transportation networks, commerce and finance, and so on.

As society grows, each of these sectors subdivides in turn. The state becomes more complex; the king must share his power with the royal bureaucracy and eventually finds himself relying entirely on his ministers. The economy becomes increasingly autonomous, as the market system alone is capable of coordinating the diverse productions. Spencer regarded religion as an archaic stage of development. Fear of the gods was based on fear of the spirits of the dead, he argued; society outgrows this sort of control over ·the individual, just as it outgrows the state. Thus, man's mental capacities improve along with society. Man becomes less emotional and more rational; ideas become more definite; lore is replaced by scientific knowledge; customs are replaced by laws.

Viewing the world around him, Spencer saw two main types of societies. One, the militant society, consists of societies in which the regulative system dominates over the sustaining system. Cooperation is compulsory and enforced by the state; the society is autocratic, warlike, and religious. Such societies could be found in Germany and France. The other type, the industrial society, is peaceful and republican; cooperation is voluntary, through the means of the market. Here, the state exists for the benefit of its members and not vice versa. England was Spencer's prime example of such a society. He stuck by his principles, however, and denounced Britain's imperial conquests as a dangerous shift away from the industrial to the militant form of society.

LIBERALISM IN AMERICA

Both of these wings of L(l)iberal thought—the social reform and the evolutionist—spread to America not long after they arose in England. Spencer had a triumphant American tour. Lavish banquets were given in his honor by wealthy businessmen, grateful for the intellectual support he gave them in what was indeed an era of robber barons. The main home-grown exponent of laissez-faire evolutionism was the Yale professor William Graham Sumner (1840–1910). His tone can be gathered from an exchange with his students:

"Professor, don't you believe in any government aid to industries?"
"No! It's root, hog, or die."

"Yes, but hasn't the hog got a right to root?"

"There are no rights. The world owes nobody a living."

"You believe, then, Professor, in only one system, the contract-competitive system?"

"That's the only sound economic system. All others are fallacies."

"Well, suppose some professor of political economy came along and took your job away from you. Wouldn't you be sore?"

"Any other professor is welcome to try. If he gets my job, it is my fault. My business is to teach the subject so well that no one can take the job away from me."[2]

Sumner's system had some advantages over Spencer's in that it concentrated less on the overall form of social evolution and paid more attention to the particular "folkways" or customs that evolved to fit a particular historical situation. Sumner was especially astute in seeing that moral norms, which he called "mores," are simply a kind of custom that takes on considerable emotional force. Sumner took a rather radical stance, considering that he was an ordained minister, as he detailed the varieties of moral beliefs and practices through slavery, torture, infanticide, cannibalism, monogamy, polygamy, public nudity, and sacred prostitution, in order to show that all standards are relative to the customs of the time. "The mores can make anything right," he asserted, thus claiming that there are no timeless verities, except of course the law of natural selection itself. Sumner, who retired from preaching in the pulpit in order to devote himself to preaching in the classroom, elevated natural selection to the status of the fundamental moral law. In fact, Sumner got into some trouble over this. He had a famous academic freedom controversy with the president of Yale, an extremely religious man, who objected to Sumner's assigning evolutionist readings to his students. But the tides were running for evolutionism, and Sumner emerged victorious in the end.

But if evolutionism was strong in America, reformism was even stronger. The reformers simply took what they wanted from evolutionism and ignored the rest. The reform mentality already had roots in America. The 1830s and 1840s witnessed a sprinkling of utopian communities, like the famous Brook Farm in Massachusetts, inspired by Thoreau and the transcendentalists. Some of them were modeled on the ideas of the Parisian prophets, Fourier and Comte. So when the British liberal reformers gathered in 1856 to form the British Social Science Association, the Americans were prepared to follow suit. In 1865 the American Association for the Promotion of Social Science was founded, with guiding advice from John Stuart Mill himself.

The American association was a mélange of reformers of all kinds, held together by a common quest for respectability under the guise of social science. Its diverse ingredients are shown by the groups that successively split off to form their own societies: the American Prison

[2] William Lyon Phelps, "When Yale Was Given to Sumnerology," *Literary Digest International Book Review,* III (1925), 661.

Association in 1870; the National Conference of Charities and Corrections in 1874; followed by the American Public Health Association, the Association for the Protection of the Insane, the American Historical Association in 1884; the American Economic Association in 1885; and from the latter, the American Political Science Association and the American Sociological Society in 1905.

Intellectually, these people were interested primarily in justifying their projects by whatever ideas supported them. But toward the 1880s academic factions began to form, and this stimulated a concern for intellectual coherence. What was happening was the great reform of the American universities, beginning with the foundation of Johns Hopkins University in 1876. The American colleges were adding graduate departments, expanding their student bodies, offering electives and hence a variety of new courses. The universities were breaking out of the old classical curriculum and offering a place for new specialties in everything from modern literature to basketry. "Social problems" courses began to find their way into the curriculum, and gradually, economics, political science, anthropology, psychology, and sociology got footholds in academia. The first sociology department in the world was founded at the new University of Chicago in 1892.

There were no great intellectual figures among the early American sociologists, whose leaders were Lester Ward, Albion W. Small, Franklin H. Giddings, Edward A. Ross, and William Graham Sumner. But they were all morally dedicated men. An extraordinary proportion of them were sons of ministers, and quite a few had careers in the ministry themselves before becoming teachers. (This, however, was not unusual in the religiously oriented American colleges.) Only Ward, who was a paleobotanist with the United States Geological Survey, was not a college professor. Their one overriding interest was social problems, and their main theoretical question (except for Sumner, who preached laissez faire) was how to justify intervening in social problems, given Spencer's evolutionary case for laissez faire.

Their arguments went generally as follows: First of all, they accepted the basic idea of gradual progress through evolution. The problem was to show that it was natural for men to lend a hand in the evolutionary process. The answer, in one form or another, was that evolution in its higher stages acts through human consciousness and volition. Lester Ward called this the "principle of social telesis." The state, then, was not an outdated impediment to evolution, but in fact acted as the conscious agent of the community as it planned its own advances. Sociology played its role in this advance by discovering the laws determining human behavior, so that society might intervene intelligently for human betterment.

What are these laws? A few sociologists advocated research to discover them, but most of them believed the laws were available through theoretical analysis. Comte and Spencer's notion of society as an organism would not do, for the Americans wanted to operate on the individual level, not to reform the entire society all at once. There was much discussion of the ways in which society was or was not like an organism, with the general conclusion being that since society consists only of individuals, sociology must provide an explanation of how the individual acts. Sociological theorists thus began with an effort to describe the basic ingredients of human behavior, whether these were to be called mental faculties, social forces, interests, instincts, or motives. The theories consisted of long lists of them, such as desire for food, pleasure, sex, love, social belonging, and so forth. All social institutions, like the family or the state, were then explained as the results of combinations of these ingredients.

Actually, these were not explanatory theories at all. By the 1920s, a researcher counted 15,789 different "instincts" listed in the sociological literature and concluded that this whole mode of explanation was useless. It did not explain anything merely to give it another name; to try to explain social groups by the "instinct of social belongingness" told us nothing at all about why groups occur at certain times or in certain forms under different conditions. All the theorizing had merely served to give sociology a reputation for intellectual vacuousness.

But the sociologists were not greatly perturbed, for they were not seriously trying to build a real theory in the first place. They were not really interested in what determines social structures; they simply wanted a rationale for their efforts to reform the individual and solve social problems. They already knew the source of social ills before they started, and they wanted to get right at the solution.

What were these social problems? Recall that the sociologists were largely moralistic, white, Anglo-Saxon, Protestants from small-town or rural backgrounds. What they saw as a social problem was the growing industrial city and its immigrant population. Instead of containing clean, law-abiding, church-going, middle-class citizens, the city was dirty and crowded and full of crime, drunkenness, mental illness, illegitimacy, divorce, delinquency, unemployment, pauperism, radicalism, and political corruption. Sociology, then, consisted of describing these urban conditions and proposing what to do about them. Its answers fitted in precisely with the Progressive movement of the turn of the century (and incidentally, with the Prohibitionist movement too, as that rural movement built up for its last assault on the city just around World War I).

The answers consisted of social work and education on the one hand and legislation on the other. Social workers and schoolteachers could train immigrant workers to become good, clean, hard-working American citizens and thus raise themselves out of poverty and its attendant ills. Legislation could eliminate the conditions that bred these effects: reforming the structure of city government to take power from the corrupt immigrant politicians and put it back in the hand of the respectable middle class; encouraging healthy economic competition by breaking up monopolies and checking fraudulent business practices; reforming the penal system to rehabilitate criminals instead of merely punishing them. The most radical of the sociologists, Edward A. Ross, even went so far as to support the right of workers to form trade unions. As a result he got into a famous academic freedom fight at Stanford University with its wealthy benefactress, Mrs. Leland Stanford, widow of one of the great robber-baron railroad builders.

Neither the theorizing nor the research of the early sociologists produced any real advance in knowledge. They were convinced in advance that the "bad environment" of the city produced these ill effects; and they collected facts only to illustrate the conditions and to goad people into doing something about them, not to test their explanations or the efficacy of their cures.

Sumner, like Spencer in England, inveighed against all this. It would not do any good, he said. If you did not understand the historical forces that produced certain customary behaviors, your actions would not bring about the consequences you expected. Sumner himself was not immune to criticism. His own theory of natural selection was extremely general, and he tended to give a great many examples of different institutional forms, without developing a theory that explained just what conditions would produce what kinds of forms.

But in a larger sense, Sumner was right. The reformers did not really understand how society worked, and hence their reforms were unsuccessful and full of unintended consequences. Their solutions were to rehabilitate individuals through education and social work and to legislate so that everyone would have an equal chance to compete in the world. In fact, their politics were naïve, and their rehabilitation sentimental. They were too individually oriented to understand how politics works, how power is bargained for, and how government organizations have a momentum of their own irrespective of the noble ideas that supposedly guide them. They never did solve political corruption (except where the population of cities changed enough so that the middle class could be in control), nor curb monopolies, nor rehabilitate criminals. The modern therapy-oriented prison is no better than the old punitive one in end results; it serves primarily to introduce new inmates into a criminal culture, and it seems likely to do so as long as persons with criminal records are kept out of all but the least respectable careers. Social work has become little more than bookkeeping for handing out welfare payments. The school system, the cornerstone of reformist hope, has expanded to include the vast majority of the youth population, but with paradoxical results: Instead of providing everyone with an opportunity for upward mobility, the mass school system has served mainly to push up educational requirements for employment, so that high-school graduates now search for the same low-level jobs that were once the lot of grade-school dropouts. And as the giant bureaucracies expand to include ever-larger segments of our lives, the rebellion and alienation found at the bottom of a competitive stratification system merely moves into the school system. Instead of a solution to social problems in the outside world, the schools have become the containers and creators of their own problems. Sumner would have shaken his head and barked out something about "You can't change the folkways."

In retrospect the social-problems perspective is most revealing where its problems have disappeared. Divorce, for example, has dropped out of the catalog of concerns—not so much because there are no more divorces (there are just as many as ever)—but because we no longer regard it as much of a problem. Without the old moralistic views of marriage, we have come to see divorce as a better thing for the individuals involved than an unhappy marriage. In the same way we are coming to see mental illness less as a purely individual condition and more as a term by which people label others who do not live up to their demands for social discipline and propriety; thus, the "solution" can just as well be to change the social *demands* on the individual as to try to change the individual to fit those demands. In the long run the profound relativism of Sumner's "the mores can make anything right" is a far more sophisticated perspective than the moral absolutes of the reformers.

The chapter could end here with the admonition that rushing to eliminate social conditions that offend certain people's values, without really understanding the processes involved, leads to both intellectual and practical failure. But there is an even more sobering conclusion.

THE LIMITS OF SCIENCE

The great idea of the late nineteenth century belongs to the evolutionists: the insight of man's continuity with the animal world. This insight gave enormous impetus to scientific efforts to solve social problems, especially in Europe. If man was a kind of animal, the reasoning went, then he could be measured, trained, or selected. A school of scientific criminology sprang up, following the Italian Cesare Lombroso's theory of the criminal type. Criminologists measured the cranial capacities of convicts and of "normal" people in an attempt to show that a hereditary degeneration was the cause of crime. The solution, they claimed, was compulsory sterilization. In England Francis Galton (whose own superior heredity was shown by the fact that his cousin was another gentleman-scientist, Charles Darwin) helped found modern statistics, which he used to demonstrate the family heredity of men of genius and, conversely, of paupers, the mentally ill, and other defectives. On the Continent a large number of statistical studies attempted to show that the superior members of society rose to the top and the inferior ones sank to the bottom—and that superiority or inferiority was shown by differences in the sizes of their heads and in their health, height, weight, vigor, and intellect. Gobineau had already written his scientific history as the conquest of weaker races by the strong; German historians and anthropologists developed military theories of social evolution, in which they argued for the beneficial effects of war in improving society.

This sort of biologism became the dominant (or at least the most popular) mode of social thought in Europe around the turn of the century. In the United States it was reflected in the writings of such figures as Sumner and Veblen. Its main American impact, however, came during and after World War I, when the progressives finally became discouraged about reform and began to conclude that the only way to save American institutions was to cut off immigration from Europe. This was finally done in 1922. Ross, the most radical of the sociologists, typifies the shift. From supporting labor unions, he shifted to writing about the "yellow peril" of cheap labor from the Orient and of the degenerate paupers crowding in from southern and eastern Europe. On the other side of the Atlantic racism focused into a growing wave of anti-Semitism, not only in Germany, but in France, Russia, and elsewhere. The British, always a little aloof from Continental fads, were less concerned about inferior races than about inferior individuals. They turned their attention to such efforts as those of Galton's Eugenics Society, dedicated to the breeding of only the best human stock.

What was the fallacy in all this? Partly, it was a matter of scientific interpretation. Some *individuals* are in fact constitutionally superior to others in intellect and other faculties, and certain societies have in fact conquered others. But society cannot be explained purely on the level of individual traits. Social institutions work according to principles of their own, regardless of the individuals involved, and the military strength of a society is due primarily to its accumulated culture and its form of organization. More careful studies show few discernible differences in intelligence or other abilities among races. On the individual level such differences undoubtedly exist. But the studies of Galton and his colleagues on individual heredity fail to control for social biases in measuring their supposed effects. The fact that poor people have poor parents, and rich people rich parents, is at least *partly* due to cumulative advantages and disadvantages in upbringing, education, and career opportunities, not to mention the inheritance of wealth. And of course differences in health, height, weight, and so on have something to do with the diets of children of different social classes.

But these are purely scientific mistakes, and if the object were merely to develop a correct explanation of the varieties of human behavior, they would eventually be corrected with the further testing of the theory. The damage is done, rather, because the theory is constructed only in order to solve a problem—and a "problem" is not an objective category at all, but a matter of *values*. If paupers are something to be eliminated as a burden on society, then a theory about hereditary degeneration will do very well as a justification. If one defined the problem from a different value standpoint—for example, a humanitarian concern for all people— then even if the hereditary degeneration theory were true, one would not want to eliminate people. Instead of judging poor people by their fitness to compete in society, one might try to fit society to them. In the same sense, arguments pro or con about racial inferiority are beside the point: It is an important question *only* if one is committed to a form of society that reserves all privileges for those on top, not if one cares about universal human rights.

Thus, the scientific approach to social problems is often just a way of cloaking one's moral failings. An objective, scientific viewpoint treats people with detachment, as things to be analyzed to see how they run. This is a necessary stance for the advancement of theoretical understanding, and indeed modern social thought has advanced by transcending a naïve rationalistic model of man and coming to see the nonrational part of his nature. But scientific objectivity does not free us from moral choices. Lombroso, Gobineau, and the rest have been swept into the ashbin of history, mostly in revulsion against the Nazi regime that gave their ideas a bad name, as well as by scientific rejection of their theories. But the underlying attitude has not disappeared. Galton's eugenics survives more modestly in the IQ tests that govern people's passage through our educational bureaucracies. There is a new Machiavellianism that treats people merely as means to ulterior ends; because it understands some of men's weaknesses and susceptibilities, it is willing to treat their lives as humanly worthless. The technical planners of the RAND Corporation and the CIA and their soul brothers in government bureaucracies around the world, with their kill ratios, public relations campaigns, and strategic population movements, are the spiritual heirs to Lombroso and Gobineau. Recognizing this, we enter the bitter world of twentieth-century sophistication.

The great idea of the late nineteenth century belongs to Darwin. And if its consequences were sometimes frightening, they could also be extremely illuminating. Darwin's vision of man in the perspective of animal evolution sets the starting place for a sociology that could finally begin to become a science. It gives us a vantage point, detached from our immediate concerns, from which to see just what it is we should be explaining: the behavior of a smart, hairless monkey, who walks upright and is able to communicate and cooperate in extraordinarily intricate ways. The implications of this vision are carried out by those thinkers referred to in the next section as the makers of the great breakthrough. The symbolic nature of the social world this creature inhabits and the way in which it affects the consciousness of the human animal were to be exposed by Cooley and Mead. Freud was to explore the human animal's instincts and the ways in which they interact and conflict with the pressures of society. Weber was to unravel the complexities of struggle for domination in this human, symbolic world. And Durkheim would grasp the nature of the invisible social structure through the rituals that sustain it. As American social thinkers were complacently refining their technical apparatus for measuring social problems and as Europeans gathered ideological ammunition for a world blood bath, an intellectual revolution was shaking the world of social thought at its core.

PART TWO

THE GREAT BREAKTHROUGH

DREYFUS' EMPIRE: EMILE DURKHEIM AND GEORGES SOREL

1898: Paris in turmoil again. The issue: the Dreyfus affair, a scandal in the French army blown up into a political cause célèbre between the contending factions of France. Dreyfus, a Jewish captain in the French army, had been the victim of an effort to cover up a spy scandal. Secret military documents were recovered from the German embassy. The real culprit seemed to be an aristocratic debauchee named Esterhazy, but the investigation arbitrarily seized on Dreyfus, an outsider to the army tradition, as scapegoat. He was degraded with full ceremonial regalia. Troops lined up on the parade ground, resplendent in gold braid and red-striped trousers; Dreyfus stood at attention while his commander tore the epaulets from his sleeves, his medals from his chest, and broke his sword across the knee. The dishonored Dreyfus was sent off to the inhuman labor colony of Devil's Island, and the army, its honor restored, returned to its arms race with the enemy across the Rhine.

But the case would not stay covered up. Emile Zola, the most famous novelist of France, penned a famous open letter to the president of the republic. *J'accuse!* it began, and it charged the government with deliberate complicity in a miscarriage of justice. Zola was himself arrested and tried for crime against the state. The trial aroused the nation, both left and right; crowds fought outside the courtroom. Zola's ringing speeches had no effect on the court, a sort of Warren Commission of its day; he was found guilty and sentenced to prison. He escaped to England, where he continued to rally the cause. The scandal could not be contained by the ritual of the courtroom. Ministers were forced to resign, fights broke out in the Assembly, students battled in the streets. There were more trials as the army took its revenge on an officer who had dared question the nonexistent evidence against Dreyfus. Unfortunately for the army, the evidence in the new trial was exposed as a forgery. The conservatives had gone too far, and their enemies closed in ruthlessly. The army, the Catholic Church, the wealthy bourgeoisie, and the peasants all fell back under the pressures of a revengeful left—the anticlerical civil servants, teachers, students, and workers.

The victory proved short-lived. The conservatives eventually benefited from a mood of reaction to the changes proposed by the victorious liberals, a series of confrontations with Germany brought chauvinism back to the fore, and France settled down again from the acute to the chronic phase of social conflict. The battles would all be fought again, many times, before the twentieth century was over.

The students of the University of Paris were in the center of the battle as it dragged on through the first decade of the twentieth century, and some of their professors were rallying points for the Dreyfusard cause. Battles between radicals and conservatives often raged in the streets of the Latin Quarter, and the students were organized in an elaborate system of shock troops, spies, and messengers on bicycles to alert their fellows when a conservative gang tried to break up the lectures of popular republican professors. Among the most eminent of these professors, the holder of the first chair of sociology ever established at a French university, was Emile Durkheim (1858–1917), one of the intellectual giants of modern times.

Durkheim's sociology, more than any other, began to make sense of the events that swirled around him: the heavy silence of the parade ground as Dreyfus' epaulets were stripped off, the impact of Zola on the stand at his rigged trial, the waves of public hysteria breaking across France, now in one direction, now in another. Durkheim penetrated these events with a vision of the nature of society that revealed what the rationalist thinkers of the nineteenth century could not see: Society is a ritual order, a collective conscience founded on the emotional rhythms of human interaction. At the peak of scientific and industrial progress, Durkheim broke through into the intellectual world of the twentieth century and its deepest problem: the nonrational foundations of rationality.

DURKHEIM: THE DIVISION OF LABOR IN SOCIETY

Durkheim's basic concern was the instability, violence, and decadence of modern society, at least as it displayed itself in France. The optimistic predictions by Comte and Spencer of continual progress in industrial society had not come true. But Durkheim could not accept the Marxist idea that the modern industrial division of labor is inherently self-contradictory and self-destructive or the conservative idea that we must return to the old order of religion and authority. Durkheim was a bourgeois liberal, a self-conscious member of the rationalistic French educational bureaucracy, neither a radical nor a conservative. He identified with the French Third Republic, which had succeeded Napoleon II's Second Empire after the disastrous war with Germany in 1871. He was a modernist and nationalist, an ardent believer in science and in republican France. He took as his task to defend the modern division of labor without being a naïve optimist. The purpose of sociology was to explain how to make modern society work.

Durkheim was also an ambitious man. He was born the son of a Jewish rabbi in a province of eastern France and made his way to the elite *Ecole Normale Supérieure* in Paris by his high intelligence and hard work in the competitive exams. The *Ecole* was the training ground for teachers and scientists. Most graduates went to the schools of the provinces; the best captured the few prominent positions in Paris. Durkheim's chances lay in the realm of social science, and he played his cards well. In 1885 he paid a visit to the laboratory of Wilhelm Wundt in Germany, who had just created the science of experimental psychology out of an old philosophical field of speculation. But psychology in France was overshadowed by conservative crowd-psychologists like Gabriel Tarde and Gustave Le Bon. Durkheim, instead, adopted the sociology of Comte and Spencer, which emphasized a realm of phenomena above the psychological level. Here one could create a science of social order and could defend the republic and industrial society. The only problem was that sociology remained largely speculative, as well as intellectually naïve. Durkheim set out to do for it what Wundt had done for psychology: to take it out of philosophy and establish it on the research methods of empirical science. The strategy was sound, and Durkheim's brilliance made it work. By 1902 Durkheim was back from the provinces and teaching his new science at the *Ecole Normale*. The modern era in sociology had begun.

Bald, bespectacled, wispy-bearded, intensely serious, Durkheim applied himself to sociology with rabbinical devotion. His fellow students at the Ecole had called him "the metaphysician." His logical mind turned itself to the task of finding a scientific basis for social order. His fundamental hypothesis came from Comte: that the basis of society is a moral order. His first great work, *The Division of Labor in Society* (1893), attacks the problem rigorously from several angles.

First, Durkheim gives a deductive argument. Society cannot exist simply by rational agreement, he states, because agreements are not possible unless each partner trusts the other to live up to them. Think of economic contracts, which Spencer and the utilitarians and economists before him thought of as the basis for modern social cooperation: I'll agree to work for you for a week, if you'll agree to pay me out of the proceeds of this work at the end of the week. But notice: We are agreeing not only to exchange labor for pay; we are also agreeing to uphold the agreement. The second agreement is implicit rather than conscious, but it is absolutely crucial. Without this implicit mutual trust, no specific contracts would be possible; for if this trust does not exist, the truly rational man will not live up to his contracts. If I trust someone but he breaks the contract, then he has a week of work from me for nothing. On the other hand, if he trusts me and I break the contract, I can perhaps collect a week's pay for little or no work. In the absence of mutual trust, then, the rational man will never live up to his contracts and will never trust others to live up to theirs. Modern game theory would put it as shown in the accompanying table. The rational choice for both

		B	
		Follows contract	Cheats
A	Follows contract	Both share gain.	B wins everything. A loses everything.
	Cheats	A wins everything. B loses everything.	No one wins or loses anything.

game players is always to cheat, since they then stand a chance of winning everything (if the other follows the contract), and at least they will not lose anything (if the other cheats too). To follow the contract without being sure that the other player will follow it too is to risk losing everything for a moderate gain.

What this proves, says Durkheim, is that a "precontractual solidarity" must exist before contracts can be depended upon. The facts seem to bear out his analysis. In a factory in which boss and employees do not trust each other, the boss must spend all his time making sure that his employees are working, and his employees do their best to get as much pay as possible for the least amount of work. Sheer economic rationality reduces cooperation to the amount that can be produced by immediate control of one party over the other. On the other hand, tremendously productive cooperation is possible if everyone identifies with a common goal.

This is Durkheim's logical argument that society is based on a common moral order rather than on rational self-interest. The "social contract" of Hobbes, Rousseau, and others is thus revealed to be an impossible fiction; contracts are only possible after society has been established, not before.

An objection that might be advanced is that people live up to their contracts because they are forced to. If a man does not pay me for my work, I can sue him, and the state will force him to pay. This argument is open to the reply that governments have only recently in history come to enforce contracts for private citizens and that exchange before that had to be built up on some other basis. Moreover, Durkheim argues, the state itself exists only because people have banded together and agreed upon certain ways of exercising force; the king did not rule because he personally was stronger than everyone else put together, but because he led a group of followers. The collective use of force, then, depends just as much on a prior solidarity as anything else does.

What creates this fundamental solidarity, then? It is not an intellectual agreement, says Durkheim, but a shared emotional feeling. Men in society have a "collective conscience" (or "collective consciousness," since the word in French means both of these things): a sense of belonging to a community with others and hence feeling a moral obligation to live up to its demands. We share feelings of right and wrong, and these are inseparable from our feeling of belonging to a group, whether it be the human race, one's country, or one's family. The collective conscience does not mean that there is a group mind hanging over our heads, but rather that people have feelings of belonging to a group.

Where do these moral feelings come from? Durkheim proposes that they come from forms of social interaction between individuals, especially in ways that we would now call "rituals." Roughly, he proposed the principle (taken from the crowd psychology of his day) that as people come together and focus their attention on a common object, thoughts and feelings passing back and forth among them become strengthened until they take on a supraindividual force and seem to be detached from the individuals themselves. Thus, the members of a crowd watching a flag being raised and singing a national anthem together focus their attention on these objects and, knowing that others are focusing their attentions, too, come to feel that they are in the presence of a principle or force greater than any of them individually—the nation. Ideas held in common thus become transformed into a world of their own, the world of moral norms.

If moral feelings are the result of social interactions, Durkheim can apply and test his theory in another way. He can go to the historical evidence and see if moral norms change as the result of changes in social conditions. This second argument, an empirical one, makes up the bulk of *The Division of Labor*.

As an indicator of moral norms, Durkheim uses laws. Laws are not a precise indicator of the moral feelings of a society, he says, since they may lag behind or run ahead of public sentiments, but they give at least a general indication of how people conceive of right and wrong. There are two kinds of laws: criminal laws and civil-administrative laws. Criminal laws express a strong state of the collective conscience, for they provide that an individual who disobeys society's law incurs society's anger and must be punished. Looking back through history, Durkheim points out that this collective conscience must have been very strong indeed, for it often prescribes violent punishments for violations of taboos, even when the violations do not involve harm to persons or property. On the other hand, civil and administrative laws express a much milder sense of community conscience, since they carry very different penalties. Whereas criminal laws call for punishment regardless of what damage has been done, civil laws call only for the offender to make amends for what he has done: If he has failed to pay, he must pay up; if he holds someone else's property, he must give it over. On the one hand, the law demands *retribution;* on the other, merely *restitution.*

Durkheim then shows that the proportion of these kinds of laws has changed with the type of society. In smaller, earlier societies, most law was *retributive,* punishing almost all offenses with torture, mutilation, or execution. In the larger modern societies law becomes mostly *restitutive.* Not only do the pages of the law books come to be made up largely of civil-administrative laws, but there is an absolute decline in the number of things that penal laws control and a diminution in the severity of the punishments.

The connection between these societies and their laws, Durkheim finds, is the changing division of labor. Retributive law is found mostly in societies with little division of labor, restitutive law mostly in those with a high division of labor. The former societies are based on what Durkheim calls "mechanical solidarity." By this he means that in a tribal or peasant society like the Hebrew tribes of the Old Testament (which he had studied thoroughly), most people are like each other. Almost everyone is a farmer or a warrior. Accordingly, there is a very strong collective conscience, since people have many ideas in common from their common experiences. Any violations of this collective conscience find crushing punishment from the laws; the individual, being like others, is given no leeway to depart from their collective practices. The individual is integrated mechanically and by force.

Societies with a high division of labor, on the other hand, Durkheim refers to as bound together by "organic solidarity." Men have a great variety of different occupations; they come into contact only because the worker, the farmer, the shopkeeper, the carpenter, the engineer, and so on, exchange services with each other through a complex economic market. Men experience very different life circumstances and thus have much less in common with each other. But they do acquire some knowledge of each other's viewpoints by repeatedly coming in contact with others while making exchanges; hence a newer, milder form of collective conscience appears. This is expressed in the restitutive laws that regulate civic commerce, which provide only enough social control to keep the complex society operating and do not impose the collective outrage of the whole community on violators of a private contract touching only a few individuals. Durkheim calls this organic solidarity because it is the exchanges themselves, like those between the different organs of a body, which provide the basis of collective belonging.

This historical argument bolsters Durkheim's deductive argument about the necessity of precontractual solidarity. Not only must non-rational solidarity come first logically, but it does in fact come first in history. As Durkheim had learned from his teacher Fustel de Coulanges, ancient civilizations like those of Greece and Rome grew up on the basis of religious rituals that regulated virtually every aspect of everyday life; the rational economic contracts came later, after the society already existed. Nor does the collective conscience disappear after the modern division of labor is set up; it merely changes its form. Thus, societies begin in small groups that maintain order through a strong and repressive collective conscience. As societies grow, a larger population presses down on the available resources for living, and individuals begin to specialize. The division of labor begins to grow more and more complex. Thus, men become different from others they come into contact with and are bound together through economic and political ties across longer distances. The collective conscience has fewer things to build upon, for there are fewer things that all members of a society have in common. Its contents gradually become more abstract. Rather than sanctioning specific local customs and taboos, it begins to uphold only the more general and abstract principles of fairness, justice, honesty, and so on. The collective conscience becomes simultaneously less powerful and more principled; its tone is less violent and more humanitarian. Durkheim thus manages to give a theoretical explanation of the phenomenon that both Comte and Tocqueville had noticed without being able to explain: that the scope of human sympathy expands with the progress of civilization.

All in all, Durkheim hoped with this demonstration to prove that modern society is good. A complex division of labor is inherently orderly, for it contains within it its own moral principles. The decline of traditional religion is nothing to worry about; on the contrary, the modern morality that replaces it is more humanitarian and tolerant. The complex division of labor creates individualism, since men must follow specialized life patterns of their own, but there is nothing to fear from individualism, for it does not mean that men no longer have any social ties. On the contrary, individualism is socially produced and expresses only the way men relate to each other through exchanges, rather than via the repressive similarity of mechanical solidarity.

As we shall see, Durkheim was not entirely successful in arguing that all is basically well with the modern division of labor, and he kept returning to the subject again and again as his researches kept turning up evidence that could just as well be interpreted to mean that modern society is self-destructive. But Durkheim was not yet through with his main theoretical task: to show how moral feelings of solidarity underlie social order. To his logical and historical arguments, he added an empirical proof based on observations of the society around him.

The collective conscience is a social fact, says Durkheim. And indeed, you can experience it yourself when you are in a group. It is a feeling of contact with something outside of yourself that does not depend pre- cisely on any one person there, but which everyone participates in together. "An atmosphere so thick you could cut it with a knife." What can produce such a feeling? For Durkheim, examples were all around in the still-smouldering tradition of France: the tense stillness surround- ing Dreyfus on the parade ground, the vengeful excitement of the crowd at the guillotine. What provided the power of these collective situations was the fact that people were gathered, focusing their attention on the same thing, and generating a contagious emotion. From these extreme and powerful instances of a collective conscience existing where men play the role of the Public at its most awesome, we may draw a con- tinuum that shades down through the shared moods of football crowds and theater audiences to parties, committee meetings, and finally to the most casual conversations.

The stronger states of collective feeling are the easiest to notice; the subtler ones we take for granted. But for every case Durkheim pro- vides a method by which a state of collective conscience can be made clearly observable: You know a social norm is there because you encounter resistance to violating it. The sentiments behind minor rules of politeness and deference show themselves most clearly in the uneasi- ness that occurs when someone breaks them; the invisible barrier of social conventions is never so apparent as when someone almost utters an obscenity at a polite gathering. The standards of just what the polite rules are can change between different times and between differ- ent groups, of course. But where the norms are strong, whatever they happen to be, the invisible order of a collective conscience can be clearly seen. This was all the more noticeable in the heavy formalities of nine- teenth-century bourgeois France.

Deviance and social solidarity

Durkheim was especially interested, then, in acts of deviance, because it was here that society's norms could be seen most clearly in operation. Crimes and their punishments, he felt, were among the central features of a society. When one man commits a crime—a murder or a rape, for example—there is a widespread sense of public outrage, shared by people far beyond those who are personally damaged or threatened by the criminal. People show their nonrational, non-self-interested attach- ment to society in general by their reactions to events that have nothing to do with themselves personally. The fact that this is not a feeling of personal interests is shown when the same sort of public outrage occurs over purely symbolic issues, in which no one is damaged at all—for example, cases of public obscenity (the showing of a nude play or movie would be a modern example) or symbolic political acts, like

Zola's letter to the French president. What is violated, in all of these cases, is not someone's personal interests but the collective conscience itself. A ritual order has been defamed, and ritual punishment is necessary to restore its purity. This is why there is so much public concern with ceremonies of punishment such as court trials and executions. It also helps explain why there is so much sentiment favoring capital punishment, in the face of overwhelming evidence that it has no deterrent effect for crimes of violence: The punishment serves a ritual function, not a practical one, and hence it is supported by people who attach themselves to a certain kind of ritual order.

Durkheim even went so far as to argue that crime is functional for holding society together. Without crimes there would be no ceremonies of punishment; and without such periodic ceremonies to bring people together in a ritual reaffirmation of their solidarity, society would gradually fall apart. The argument is overstated to make the point, of course. Durkheim himself later pointed out that there are positive rituals as well as negative ones, which also serve to create a sense of solidarity. The rituals of church services, patriotic holidays, and even family festivities like birthday parties, all serve this function. The entire functionalist school in anthropology follows up on Durkheim's basic insight. Thus, Marcel Mauss (Durkheim's nephew), Arthur Radcliffe-Brown, Bronislaw Malinowski, Claude Lévi-Strauss, and others have shown how marriage ceremonies, funerals, rites of passage, and gift exchanges all function to reaffirm social bonds, especially when the bonds are disturbed by the loss or gain of a member in a group. In sociology W. Lloyd Warner and Erving Goffman have made the most important applications of Durkheim's perspective to the rituals of modern American society.

Durkheim went still further in his study of deviance and solidarity. In addition to his general observations, he produced a study of statistical data which remains a model for scientific research in sociology. This was his great work *Suicide,* published in 1897. Durkheim was not entirely original here. He drew on a tradition that went back to the 1830s, when the Belgian statistician Adolphe Quételet pointed out that the rates of births, deaths, marriages, murders, suicides, and so on remained fairly constant from year to year, even though each of these rates was the result of many independent individual actions. Quételet thus argued for the existence of a realm of social facts independent of the individual and proposed a science, which he labeled "social physics," to explain these facts. But Quételet was only a statistician, and he came up with no explanation beyond a notion of an "average man" who is likely to act in given ways. This line of research was ready-made for Durkheim, for it dealt with acts of deviance—especially suicide—for which he did have a sociological theory. He now had an opportunity to test his theory in a rigorously scientific way.

Suicide was the first really good piece of large-scale data analysis in sociology. Throughout, Durkheim applied the basic methodological principle of all good research: If you want to know the cause of something, look for *the conditions under which it occurs* and compare them with *the conditions under which it does not occur.* This is akin to Durkheim's principle of how to observe social norms by looking for the cases where they are violated. Behind both principles is the strategy of understanding through opposition: Explanations are revealed by contrast and comparison. It is this principle that was behind the insights of Tocqueville as he compared France and America, and it continues to provide the basis for virtually all important advances in modern sociology.

Durkheim, for example, began with the popular theory that suicides are due to individual psychopathology. This was the sort of explanation he wanted to dispose of, since he was engaged in an academic battle for recognition in which psychologists were his major competitors, and he wanted to show that social factors are on a separate and more important level of explanation. In short, Durkheim was opposed to psychological reductionism, which saw events only through the actions of individuals instead of penetrating to the social conditions that moved the individuals. He attacked the psychopathology theory of suicide by comparing the regions of Europe having the highest suicide rates with those having medium and low suicide rates and then showing that there was no correlation between rates of suicide and rates of psychopathology. In a similar fashion he tested other popular theories that attributed suicide to ethnicity, climate, or geography. In each case Durkheim showed that on close examination the variations in ethnic composition, average temperature, and so on, did not correspond to variations in the suicide rate.

Having disposed of these competing explanations, Durkheim proceeded to advance his own. The suicide rate did vary by social condition, he found. For example, Protestants had higher suicide rates than Catholics, who in turn had higher rates than Jews. This could not be explained just by differences in theology, Durkheim argued. If Catholicism made suicide a more serious sin than did Protestantism, Judaism nevertheless made no special prohibition of suicide and yet had the lowest suicide rate. The difference among these religious groups, rather, was in the social environments they provided for their members. Judaism was the most close-knit religious community, Protestantism the least, with Catholicism intermediate in surrounding the individual with a round of ritual activities. In general, Durkheim argued, the more tightly integrated into society the individual is, the more he is prevented from committing suicide.

Durkheim backed up this interpretation by looking at further variations within these categories. In every religious group most suicides are among men, since women have the greatest day-to-day religious participation and are more tightly integrated into the close community of the family. Among the Protestant churches, the Anglicans had the lowest suicide rate, and they were the most ritualistic and Catholic-like of the Protestant denominations. Durkheim went on to point out, rather ingeniously, that the regions of Europe with the highest levels of education have the highest suicide rates, except among Jews. This corroborated the general argument that the lack of social integration caused suicide, since education was an indication of a secularized, individualistic, non-religious society, except among Jews, for whom education of laymen had been a key part of the religious tradition.

From different angles Durkheim corroborated his general theory: Society is what gives meaning to the individual's life; it is when he is cut off from society that he kills himself. Not only did the evidence on religion point to these conclusions, but also the fact that suicide rates declined in times of war, revolution, or other periods of great social crisis that drew everyone together into a common sentiment. The evidence also showed that married persons were less likely to kill themselves than unmarried persons; that widowhood and divorce increased the chances of suicide, but that this was mitigated the more children there were remaining. The more social bonds surrounding an individual, the less the chance of suicide; the fewer the bonds, the more danger of self-destruction. From all of this emerged one of Durkheim's key concepts: the idea of a state of "anomie" or lack of norms that give a clear direction and purpose to the individual's actions. In this concept Durkheim sums up a major cause of the ills of modern society.

Durkheim's *Suicide* is a classic work, and it survives as a model of how to use empirical analysis to corroborate a general theory. It does have various shortcomings. The data are not entirely reliable, and there were mistakes in the analysis. Moreover, Durkheim did not fully explain suicides. After all, not everyone who is a Protestant commits suicide, even if he is unmarried, highly educated, and so on. The full explanation of any individual case of suicide must involve just the kind of psychological factors that Durkheim wanted to exclude. But Durkheim was less interested in providing an exhaustive explanation of suicides than in showing that social integration and social anomie have important effects on the individual's behavior. He was less interested in suicide itself than in what it can tell us about the structure of society.

Suicide remains an important book in the history of social thought, whether it is precisely valid or not. It not only helps to support Durkheim's general analysis of the importance of ritual interaction for social solidarity, but it lays down the model for sociology as a science: to treat general theoretical principles in terms of variables and thus to test them by systematic comparison with the supposed causal conditions. Durkheim thus moved from the methods of nineteenth-century speculation to the sophisticated analysis of the twentieth century.

Religion and reality

These might seem enough major contributions for one man, but Durkheim was not yet through. He organized the first French sociological journal, the *Année sociologique,* and around it a school of researchers to carry on the new tradition. Out of this group came a major school in modern anthropology, which constituted Durkheim's main following in France. Durkheim himself became increasingly interested in ethnographic reports on primitive tribes, some of which material he analyzed in collaboration with his nephew Marcel Mauss, who had done much of the statistical compilations for *Suicide.* In 1912, a few years before his death, Durkheim published his final work, perhaps the greatest single book of the twentieth century. It was entitled *The Elementary Forms of the Religious Life.*

In this work Durkheim carried through to another level the revolution in our view of reality begun by Karl Marx. Every class has its own view of reality, its own consciousness, Marx had argued. Durkheim went even further, to demonstrate the social relativity of even our most general and taken-for-granted ideas. Time, space, causality, God, the self—all of these could now be seen as creations of society. In place of the old absolutist view of reality "out there," Durkheim shows us that the natural world is only a backdrop for the symbolic creations of men and their social rituals. As we have come to see through the applications of this perspective by Goffman and other recent sociologists, there is not one reality but many, and they exist only by virtue of being enacted by human beings.

Durkheim carried out this revolution in our perspectives by analyzing data on the aborigine tribes of Australia, plus some other tribal societies, in an effort to understand the basis of religion. But since religion was all-pervasive in the world views of these peoples, Durkheim had an opportunity to explain the basic modes of thought in a society.

He began by trying to define religion. What is it that all religions have in common? Not the idea of gods or spirits, since religions such as Buddhism and Confucianism lack these. Not the idea of a supernatural realm set apart from the world of nature, since primitive societies have not developed the idea of a realm of nature and hence make no such distinction. In fact, says Durkheim, we cannot find the key to religion in the realm of ideas at all. The only thing that all religions contain is a set of "sacred objects" that are set off from all other objects and toward which men must act with ritual care. Ritual objects in Christianity, for example, include Bibles, altars, rosaries, holy water, consecrated bread and wine, and so on; in the aborigine tribes that Durkheim analyzed the main sacred object was the tribal totem. A totem is an animal, such as a fox, snake, grub-worm, or kangaroo, which men are forbidden to kill or eat; and periodic ceremonies are held in which the tribe comes together to pay respect to this sacred object.

It is impossible to understand this treatment of a totem from a practical point of view, says Durkheim, but if one views it socially, its significance becomes obvious. The totem functions to hold the tribe together. Without it, there would be no tribal unit at all, for it is by sharing a common totem that its members identify with each other. The totem is thus the basis of kinship and of social membership. The whole tribe is assembled only at the periodic totem ceremonies, and it is at these rituals that its members create and re-create the sense of emotional solidarity that Durkheim had argued was so important for social order. The totem thus creates a social and moral order. Since it is forbidden to kill the totem animal, it is also forbidden to kill those who name themselves after the totem, one's fellow tribesmen. The totem, in effect, symbolizes the society and its moral demands on the individual.

In the same way, one can see more modern religions as functioning primarily to maintain a moral community. The church service of a nineteenth-century American village, for example, brought the community together once a week—perhaps the only time the community regularly assembled. The rituals of the service, from the reading of the sacred book to collective hymns and prayers, functioned to create a feeling of moral order. In general, Durkheim argues, the moral commandments of a religion—its Golden Rule, Ten Commandments, restrictions on self-indulgence in the pleasures of the flesh—are fundamentally *social* rules. They regulate men's behavior toward each other and serve to keep up the sense of social unity and restraint on self-interest that makes society possible.

Why do people live up to such moral rules, at least to some degree? Not really because of fear of supernatural sanctions like heaven and hell or of the sacred power of the totem; these rationalizations for religious customs come and go, but the power of the social controls remains. Rather, suggests Durkheim, it is because the supernatural sanctions *symbolize* society and its acceptance or rejection of the individual. The man who lives up to the moral commandments and participates wholeheartedly in the religious rituals gets a great feeling of solidarity with the countless generations who make up his society, and he represents this feeling to himself as being "saved." He who breaks the rules and avoids the rituals cuts himself off from this feeling of belonging and suffers the consequences of his own self-centeredness. As theologists put it, to be cut off from God is the sinner's self-inflicted punishment. Durkheim would agree, but with the added sociological proviso: God is only a symbol for society.

Durkheim thus brings to a close a chapter that began in the Enlightenment with the attack of science on religion. But religion must be more than superstition and error, Durkheim had pointed out, for how could it have survived so long if it were only this? Durkheim at last enables us to understand beliefs about the supernatural, by showing them for what they really are: symbols generated by social behavior that is at the core of every society. God is revealed to be not exactly what his adherents think, but something real nevertheless: the collective conscience of a community. And if this collective conscience changes its symbolizations from the sacred totem animals to more universal gods, until finally even the remote Christian God with his transcendental heaven and hell disappears into the memories of the past, this is only what we would expect from Durkheim's earlier demonstration, in *The Division of Labor,* that a society's moral order changes with its social structure. Sacred objects like totems, altars, and books are only displaced by new sacred objects like flags, which represent the worship of the state. By implication, much that seems bizarre in the behavior of avowedly atheistic and materialistic Russian and Chinese communists becomes clearer when we see that communism has been organized as a political religion, now split between competing orthodoxies. In general, Durkheim's theory proposes that the historical trend is toward a more and more abstract and general collective conscience; concrete symbols of God disappear into a generalized moral belief about the brotherhood of humanity.

Durkheim's sociology of knowledge thus manages to explain men's fundamental religious ideas in terms of their social interactions. In addition, Durkheim shows that society determines even the basic categories of our thought. We live in a world of time and space, but how we conceive that time and space is socially determined. It is Friday; it is 11 o'clock in the morning; it is the year 1971: implicitly this puts me in a world held in common by most other people in our clock-watching, post-Christian civilization. But there is nothing *absolute* about these units. There is no reason why time should necessarily be broken up into seven-day weeks or twenty-four-hour days; we could just as well have ten-day weeks or no weeks or hours at all (as is the case with many primitive tribes). We divide time into units only because we need to coordinate our activities with others in our complex modern civilization, not because hours and weeks really constitute the framework of nature. But as we continually act upon them, these units become part of the framework of our minds, and we make them subjectively into an absolute reality. In just this way, society implicitly furnishes the bases of our world views. The year A.D. 1971 puts us directly in the context of a *Christian* view of history, since the anno Domini orients us in relation to the year 1 of the mythical birth of Christ. The Chinese, whose calendar now stands at the year 4669, inhabit a fundamentally different historical universe.

Time concepts, Durkheim shows, derive first of all from the scheduling of religious ceremonies. Space, causality, number—all of these abstract ideas can also be traced to social origins and continuing social uses. Space is the area the tribe inhabits; this has grown immensely from the wanderings of aborigines in the Australian desert, through the voyages of Columbus and Magellan, but it still has a basic social meaning for us, as the effects of space travel on our thought about the universe continue to illustrate. Our fundamental concepts all grow from a social matrix in a similar way, and our very idea of objective knowledge ultimately refers to things that we can reliably communicate to others. Durkheim tears away another illusion that keeps us from seeing the world as it is: We mistake our socially given images of reality for the reality itself. Only by seeing the social relativity of our ideas are we on the path to understanding ourselves.

It is a powerful intellectual performance that Durkheim puts on, indeed one of the most impressive of modern times. But what about the social issues with which he began, the effort to cure the social strife of modern France? Here Durkheim was less successful. He tried to use sociological functionalism as a basis for a scientific diagnosis of society's ills: not to impose any particular values on how society should operate, but to ascertain the "healthy" state of the social organism and thereby to understand its "diseases." He tried to show that a modern division of labor is basically healthy and well-integrated and that when it is not, it must be because of special conditions. Thus, Durkheim believed that strikes, political conflict, and labor violence were forms of the "abnormal" division of labor. But he was never able to propose a clear solution. His theory told him that the problem must lie in a lack of sufficient integration of the individual into the moral order of a social community, and in his famous Preface to the second edition of *The Division of Labor,* Durkheim proposed that the lack of solidarity could be cured by organizing men into occupational guilds.

The solution was not convincing, for there is no reason to believe that such occupational communities would not continue to conflict with each other. Durkheim's main shortcoming was that he never came to grips with the existence of stratification and the realities of political conflict; he concentrated on the bases of social solidarity to the extent that his image of society excluded all nonsolidarity features. Durkheim would have been more successful in his search for political solutions if he had followed Tocqueville's lead on how political organizations can intensify conflict or limit it.

In general, Durkheim's optimistic argument that modern industrial society is *normally* well-integrated is not convincing. His own theories tend to refute it. If man is an emotional animal who derives his sense of purpose from the rituals he performs with others, then the gradual suppression of emotions and the elimination of ritual in our highly bureaucratic society should produce considerable malaise. Such, in fact, were the more pessimistic conclusions of Weber and Freud. Although Durkheim did not want to draw this conclusion, his evidence on anomic suicide resulting from the loosening of ritual social bonds supports a pessimistic interpretation.

THE REVOLUTIONARY PHILOSOPHY OF GEORGES SOREL

One of Durkheim's compatriots drew the implications better than he did. This was Georges Sorel (1847–1922), a retired engineer, whose values and politics were as far removed from Durkheim's as possible, although both men held each other in considerable respect. Sorel was an acquaintance, among others, of Lenin, Mussolini, and Fritz Ebert (the Socialist who was to become the first president of Germany after World War I). His politics seemed an equally bizarre flux, from monarchism on the far right to anarcho-syndicalism on the far left. But there was a basic principle underlying Sorel's shifting political sympathies. He regarded modern society as completely decadent, lacking in any real virtue, dedication, or brilliance. He despised the petty squabbling of the academics, saw the business world as entirely self-seeking and corrupt, and politicians as equally contemptible. The failure of the Socialists to take a stand on the burning moral issue of the Dreyfus affair at the time when Zola was putting his life on the docket convinced Sorel that the organized left was equally decadent. By 1907, when he wrote *Reflections on Violence,* Sorel had come to identify with ultrarevolutionary anarcho-syndicalism.

Reflections on Violence takes up the anarcho-syndicalist idea that a general strike of all workers will someday bring down bourgeois society and usher in the new era of the revolution. This revolution, says Sorel, is a myth. It will never be, for society after the revolution would not be greatly changed, and in any case the chances of victory are nil. But— and here is where Sorel parts company with most other "practical" thinkers—the myth of the general strike nevertheless serves a purpose. It unifies the group of workers and gives them a feeling of participating in a moral cause. In the same way, violence has an important value, for it unifies men in a struggle for their common ideals and against their common enemies. In modern society, says Sorel, only social movements in battle have this high moral tone, a sense of joyous spontaneity as the individual feels himself dedicated to something greater and higher than himself. For this reason, such revolutionary movements are the only source of value today, even if they are doomed to fail. It is not the actual goal that counts, but the feelings that go along with struggling to attain it in the company of others.

Sorel throws light on the appeal of violence in modern society, although his analysis applies just as well to nonviolent movements. The civil-rights movement and its succeeding peace and student movements of the mid-1960s often had much of the sense of euphoria among their participants that Sorel describes as the main value of such movements. And if these movements have generally failed to bring about their goals, that does not make them any the less worthwhile. Sorel's lesson foreshadows later existentialist insights: that in a world of dilemmas and well-entrenched injustices, the value of an action is to be judged less by its consequences than by its intrinsic rightness.

Sorel has always been a puzzling figure, since his point of view lends itself to many interpretations. Sorel himself defended the Communist revolution in Russia, while Mussolini praised him as a source of Italian fascism. But Sorel was not really a fascist. He did not want a society that tries to impose an imitation of old-fashioned order by brutal suppression; his values, rather, were for the spirit of perpetual movement. More than anything else, Sorel was a true anarchist. And whatever the political implications that could be drawn from his work, Sorel clearly pointed out two characteristic phenomena of modern society: its emotional starvation and the irrelevance of its ideals to workaday reality. This was more than Durkheim allowed himself to see, although he spent most of his life probing the conditions of the same feelings of solidarity.

Durkheim wanted very strongly to believe in something, and in the end it cost him his life. World War I turned his ardent French nationalism into a paroxysm of anti-German sentiment. When his son André was killed at the front, defending the flag that Durkheim considered the modern version of the most sacred object, Durkheim went into a depression that culminated in 1917 in his death. It was not the first time that a man's insights, so valuable to others, had gone unused by himself.

CHAPTER SIX

MAX WEBER: THE DISENCHANTMENT OF THE WORLD

Max Weber (1864–1920) has exerted more influence than any other social scientist except Marx and Freud. His ideas have had wide currency, first in Germany and then throughout the scholarly world. His term "charismatic leadership" has passed into general usage, and all of social science knows something of the concepts of legitimacy, bureaucracy, rationalization, *verstehen,* ideal types, value-free science, the three-dimensional approach to stratification, and the Protestant ethic with its links to the origins of capitalism. Yet Weber's general sociology and his vision of world history are as yet barely known; they remain hidden behind isolated selections and popularizations, and we are continually surprised as more and more powerful portions of Weber's world view are brought into the light. Weber himself is partly to blame. His works are voluminous but unfinished and scarcely succinct, and even a superficial acquaintance with them turns up notions of such utility that one is tempted to inquire no further. Now, with Marx and Freud passing from view (if not mined out), Weber increases his hold on our attention. The most commanding figure of the great period of German social scholarship, Weber still towers over the world scene fifty years after his death.

Like many great sociologists, Weber (pronounced "Vay-ber") was a man at the center of things, pulled loose from illusions by constant exposure to contradictory points of view. Born in 1864 into a prosperous family of German industrialists, he grew up in Berlin where his father was a judge and a successful politician. Backstage acquaintance with the *realpolitik* of Bismarck's empire made Weber a political realist from his childhood. His father sat in the Reichstag with the National Liberals, representing the interests of the big manufacturers and standing between the Junker aristocracy on the right and the Social Democrats (socialist labor unionists) on the left. It was not a propitious time for liberals in Germany (indeed, it rarely ever was, except during the short-lived revolution of 1848). The landowning aristocracy and the army took a rigid stand against democracy, and the Socialists preached revolution according to Karl Marx. The liberals had no one to turn to except the state bureaucracy, and their ideals went down the drain as their nationalism increasingly became their only political resource. From an early age Weber scorned the unrealistic claims of left and right, but found himself increasingly uncomfortable with the center. Throughout his life an ardent nationalist, he nevertheless saw Germany blundering steadily into a war that would destroy it. His sociology confirmed his fears of imminent disaster, and Weber came to see himself as a twentieth-century Jeremiah, prophesying doom.

He began a career like his father's, studying law at Heidelberg and Berlin. But his pessimism about politics and his own overpowering urge to exercise his independent intellect steered him into an academic career. Germany in the nineteenth century led the world in the eminence of its universities. It was especially prominent in the historical fields. It had been here that Leopold von Ranke and Friedrich von Savigny transformed history from the status of antiquarian chronicles into a science, with its canon: to tell things "as they really were." With German thoroughness, the Herr Professor Doktors had produced detailed accounts, not only in conventional military and political history, but also in economic, legal, and cultural history and in archaeology, ethnography and linguistics. German philosophy, too, since the days of Hegel had a strong historical flavor. Weber trained himself in virtually all of these fields, with the result that his knowledge of world history probably exceeded that of any man who has ever lived.

In an age of growing specialization Weber's feat was the mark of an extraordinary individualist. But Weber was nothing if not extraordinary. Tall, stout, black-bearded, and moody, he impressed all who met him. His colleagues viewed him as a towering intellect. At the end of Weber's doctoral exam Theodor Mommsen, the most eminent historian of his day, rose and said that he knew of no man better qualified to succeed him "than the highly esteemed Max Weber." But Weber stood in an intellectual circle even wider than the world of German historians and philosophers. At his father's house he had met the eminent politicians and academicians of Berlin. In his own house at Heidelberg met the leading intellects of all fields, as well as artists and musicians. Among his circle would be found such men as Karl Jaspers, the future existentialist psychiatrist, Ferdinand Toennies, Georg Simmel, and a young radical who could not get a university position despite Weber's intercessions on his behalf, Robert Michels. He was fully acquainted with Marxist underground thought. He read many languages, traveled broadly, and knew the English evolutionists and the French positivists as well as the German historians. Weber was a one-man crucible for the intellectual currents of the nineteenth century, and from his central position he forged a viewpoint for sociology as both a science and a study of meaningful human creations. His twin methods of *verstehen* and ideal types emerged from his position at the center of intellectual cross-currents: Social reality is not merely to be explained by mechanical analogies to the natural world, but must be understood (in German, *verstehen*) by imagining oneself into the experiences of men and women as they act out their own worlds. Ideal types, as we shall see below, are the tools for making scientific generalizations out of our understanding of this infinitely complex and shifting world.

A sociologist must sympathetically understand the people around him —indeed, also those who have been dead for centuries—and he is bound to feel acutely what is closest to home. Here, too, Weber was at the center of powerful antagonisms. Beneath the surface of a proper German bourgeois family, Weber's father and mother carried on psychic war. His father—harsh, self-righteous, and authoritarian—clashed incessantly with his altruistic, self-denying, and religious mother. Between the two poles Weber may have discerned the remnants of a rigid Protestant ethic whose discovery is his most famous contribution. Certainly Max Weber himself was a prime example of the ethic: Immensely hard-working, impeccably honest, dedicated, serious, methodical, he drove himself with an inner vehemence that left him insomniac for years and dead at the age of fifty-six.

The family conflict finally took its toll. In 1897 when Weber was thirty-three and just beginning his career as a professor of economics at Heidelberg, he became involved in a quarrel while visiting his parents. Years of suppressed bitterness broke through the respectable patrician formalities, and Weber angrily threatened to break off all contact with his father if he did not change his treatment of his mother. Not long after, he heard the news: His father had fallen dead of a stroke.

Depression set in. A powerful, even charismatic lecturer, Weber found he could no longer teach. When he tried, his arms and back became temporarily paralyzed. He found it difficult to speak; serious thinking was impossible. He took a leave of absence from his job, finally resigned it entirely. He traveled incessantly, yet spent hours in hotel rooms staring at his fingernails. He spent several weeks in a mental institution. The experience opened a new side in him. "Such a disease has its compensations. It has reopened to me the human side of life," he wrote his wife. "An icy hand has let me loose. In years past my diseased disposition expressed itself in a frantic grip upon scientific work, which appeared to me as a talisman. . . ."

Slowly, he began to recover, and in 1904 he was back at work. He took a trip to America on an invitation to speak at the St. Louis World's Fair. The loftiness of American ideals and the corruption of American capitalism fired his imagination, and he returned to Germany to finish his first famous work *The Protestant Ethic and the Spirit of Capitalism.* From then on his production never flagged, although he was unable to bring himself to teach until the end of his life, after the close of World War I. He had lost seven years. The work of the next sixteen has never been surpassed.

Weber's sociology is often obscured behind the maze of crosscutting definitions that make up the opening chapters of *Economy and Society,* his major work. Clear and distinct concepts are essential to make sense out of a subject as complex as the workings of society. But concepts are easiest to grasp if we can see them as they are actually put to use. Weber set himself the task of explaining the greatest development of world history: the rise of modern industrial civilization. In order to do this, he had to push his sights progressively back from economics to law, politics, and religion; to chart the interconnections between kinship and stratification, bureaucracy and warfare, until every institution was connected with every other, and the web of explanation stretched from the present to the beginnings of human life on earth. In exploring the question of economic development, Weber created nothing less than a sociology of world history. His contributions to general sociological theory consist of the models he developed in an effort to grasp the key processes of society without doing violence to the complexities of history as it actually occurred. Weber had nothing but contempt for evolutionist or cyclical theories that blindly simplified the facts to fit a few preconceived principles of growth. In his tightrope walk between vague or inaccurate generalizations and the myriad particular forms of world civilization, Weber moved toward a comprehensive theory of men's social behavior and of the institutions men create. We shall take up first Weber's general sociology, then his vision of world history.

WEBER'S SOCIOLOGY: STRATIFICATION, ORGANIZATIONS, AND POLITICS

Stratification: class, power, and status

Weber's sociology centers around three interrelated subjects: stratification, organizations, and politics. Of these, stratification provides the core theory of society, to which all else is related and within which may be found the forces that move society. Weber was a thoroughgoing nominalist; for him, real people in real physical places are the subjects and movers of all that exists and happens in society. To be sure, cultural ethos (such as the Protestant ethic), legal systems, and large-scale organizations all have their own logical structures and laws of development. But they never develop by themselves; they develop through the thought and action of real people.

Weber might well have adopted Marx's slogan as his methodology: "Men make their own history, but they do not make it just as they please." Weber could not accept a reified abstraction like "Society" as it appeared in organic analogies, nor the *Weltgeist* (world spirit) of Germanic cultural theorists. We never see society, but only groups of men and women. Furthermore, these groups are very different, even within one society. It is an error to suppose that the ethical philosophies of the upper classes express the beliefs of middle-class shopkeepers or peasant laborers. India cannot be summed up in Brahmin philosophy, nor Germany in Hegel. If we are to understand society and culture, we must begin with the actual diversity of separate groups, not with some easy generalization based on a single perspective. Stratification, for Weber, provided the link between the diverse groups we can actually observe and the invisible order through which thousands and millions of individual actions add up to results that individuals neither intend nor control.

What kind of order is it that ties people to others whom they may never see? Weber found three such orders: economics, politics, and culture. A man sells his labor in a factory that exists only because of a nationwide division of labor, and affects the price of goods by the ways he spends his wages; he pays taxes and is killed on a distant battlefield because far-off government ministers struggle for power; his family walks in a funeral ceremony elaborated long ago by a hierarchy of priests and changed slowly from one repetition to another. Each order affects man's behavior, lays down the conditions within which he must make his life, determines both his view of the world and which people he will associate with. But not all men are affected alike. The life chances of the financier's son are not those of the farm laborer's; the ordinary citizen's world view is not that of the party leader; the pious housewife does not inhabit the social milieu of the intellectual. We can see the social order comprehensively if we think of it as a stratification of individuals into groups based on similar economic, political, or cultural positions. Groups of people who associate together are the basic units of society. Much research since Weber's day has shown that it is in such face-to-face groups that people acquire their identities, their values, and their world views. Thus the diversity of society is produced by its major institutions—businesses, states, armies, churches, schools. At the same time, the members of the various groups are tied together through their positions in these institutional networks.

Weber did not find it necessary to ask the general question of what holds society together. He saw that societies over the sweep of history were always coming together and falling apart, shifting and changing from one set of institutions to another. History shows nothing permanent, but continual war, conflict, and change: states conquering and disintegrating, trade and finance spreading and shrinking, religions and arts slowly shifting from one theme to its opposite. What does remain beneath the change, the concrete basis of human society, are groups of people bound by ties of common feeling and belief: families, households, kinsmen, church and cult members, friends, communities. The core of Weber's view of stratification is thus a theory of group formation, a set of hypotheses about the conditions that bring men together into solidary groups. These conditions are found in the way men relate to the institutional orders that link groups together into a society.

Weber accepted certain motives as a basis for an explanation of human behavior: need for food and material comfort; fear of death and avoidance of physical pain; desires for sexual gratification, for membership and status in a social and moral community, and for a meaningful view of the world. Weber did not attempt to explore the psychological dynamics of these motives nor to account for individual differences in motivation; in these respects his theories may be complemented by the insights of Freud and Mead and by the social theories of group solidarity of Durkheim and his followers. Weber took these motives as given because he found them manifested throughout human history. They enter his theories as the three main sanctions by which men influence each other's behavior: offers of economic gain, threats of physical coercion, and appeals to emotion and belief. Economics, politics, and culture are corresponding institutional realms; class, party ("power group" might be a preferable term), and status group are the groups formed on their bases.

Weber's central hypothesis is that men who share common positions and interests in the economic arena, in the political struggle, or in the realm of culture are likely to act and associate together and to exclude all others from their company of equals. In the economic market classes are formed as men come together with others who experience similar work conditions. Here Weber follows Marx's discovery: The peasant laborer, the factory worker, the skilled craftsman, the rural landlord, the industrialist, the merchant, the stock-market speculator all inhabit distinct social worlds. Material conditions have a powerful effect on men's lives, throwing factory laborers together in urban tenements and drawing country gentlemen together in their round of visits between estates. Economics shapes not only how men live and in whose company, but also how they see the world and how they will act. Economic position gives men distinctive interests: The worker sees an advantage in demanding higher pay, forming a union, or supporting a socialist party; the peasant tries to keep down his duties to his lord and his taxes to the king; the industrialist opposes unionization and socialism; the financier is concerned about the price of gold and the prevailing rate of interest on loans. Men are thus moved to act on their economic interests, and the resulting conflict draws men of similar economic position closer together and isolates them from those of opposing positions. How many such opposing groups there will be and how extensive the conflict among them depends on the nature of the economic system in that particular society and on the relationships between economic stratification and political and cultural stratification. Weber incorporates Marx's basic model into his theory of stratification, but he sees economic determinism as only one of three factors.

Weber viewed politics, like economics, as a realm in which struggle is widespread. History, after all, reads most obviously as a record of military conquests and feudal rivalries, palace intrigues and coups d'état, peasant revolts and urban insurrections; the activities of peaceful eras consist of the ups and downs of politicians' careers, the shifting authorities of officials, and the power play of interest groups in voting and lobbying. Thus, men may be stratified by their political interests as well as by their economic interests. Minor government officials are drawn together in a distinct group, as are military officers, independent feudal knights, modern party politicians, or municipal judges. Coercive power is a scarce good; many men are concerned with getting as much of it for themselves as possible, and virtually all men wish to make it bear on themselves as little as possible. As we shall see below, politics may be analyzed as a continual struggle to gain authority for oneself and to evade subjection to the authority of others. Political interest groups may overlap with economic interest groups—feudal knights may represent the landowning class; politicians, the classes of industrialists or workers. But power is a separate pie to be carved up, capable of inducing alignments of its own. The kinds of political stratification and political group formation in a particular society depend on the nature of its political institutions.

It should be apparent by now that Weber saw society as a complex and ever-shifting interplay of forces. Political stratification is influenced by economic alignments and vice versa; both of these interact with cultural stratification. Weber was forced to devise a strategy for talking coherently about this world in which nothing ever stays put long enough for us to pin a label on it and in which our labels always oversimplify what is going on. For this purpose he conceived the notion of the *ideal type*, by means of which he could abstract from reality a form of social action that is rarely or never found by itself. We can discover the dynamics of stratification, for example, if we mentally decompose it into its constituent elements—the ideal types of class, power group, and status group. We can thereby discover the dynamics of economic class formation without having to bear in mind the processes of power politics. Having done this, we can successively take up political struggles and the status-producing effects of culture. Finally, we can apply these insights to the overall stratification of any society resulting from the interaction of these three processes. The technique is similar to that of the chemist, who explains the properties of a compound first by identifying its constituent elements and then by noting their interactions. The modern sociological research method called the "multivariate analysis" of survey data reflects the same general strategy.

The interaction of culture with economics and politics is especially subtle. As already noted, economic and political positions have considerable influence on the values and beliefs of their occupants. Marx was the first to notice this for economics, and Weber carried out a parallel analysis of politics. We can speak, then, of economic and political determinants of culture. But there is a third way in which culture enters stratification, a discovery of Weber's own. If culture were merely the result of economic and political position, one could not say that culture was important for stratification. People would be stratified by their income or their power; and whatever deference they received or had to give, whatever boundaries were drawn between them and people who would not deign to associate with them (those ranking above them) and people whom they did not care to associate with (those ranking below) would be based on money or power, not on anything to do with their culture. Weber saw that this was not so: that in addition to the stratification produced by class and power, there were numerous possible hierarchies in the realm of culture. Historically, the most important of these cultural hierarchies have been based on religion. There is a definite stratification within every religion: At minimum there is a difference in status between believers and nonbelievers. The former consider themselves more virtuous and enlightened than the latter, regardless of their respective wealth and power, and such cultural strata are just as likely to associate together and exclude outsiders as are economic classes and power groups. Most religions have much more than this minimum stratification. There are hierarchies from popes, gurus, and high priests on down through minor ceremonial assistants, devoted worshipers, merely formal members, and intermittent sinners. Admittedly, this is not necessarily an exclusive basis of stratification; churches often have property interests and political connections, and clergy may associate socially with correspondingly wealthy or powerful laymen.

Cultural stratification is important especially because it is closest to the way most people actually view their worlds. We feel that we associate with certain people and not with others, not usually because we see ourselves as economic or political allies, but because we like and respect certain people and not others. If we analyze that liking, we find that it usually involves cultural stratification. Respectable churchgoing people prefer others like themselves, not hard-drinking denizens of bars and pool halls; hostesses who practice gracious etiquette and converse about the arts do not invite the backyard barbecue set.

Cultural stratification is thus the most complex and subtle of all the forms of stratification. There are relatively few distinct political and economic groups in any society, but the varieties and ramifications of cultural hierarchies can be enormously refined, especially in a modern industrial society. Indeed, cultural stratification can subdivide the lines of status distinction to such a degree that virtually every group or individual may have a status of its own. In addition to religion, cultural hierarchies can be based on secularized religious ideals like honesty, hard work, ambition, and self-control (Weber's Protestant ethic); on achievement or understanding in science, literature, music, and art; on good manners, tastes in decoration and clothes, or even on one's prominence as a player or spectator of sports. Cultural stratification may be formally recognized in a society, as in the Hindu caste system based on ritual acts that keep members of the "higher" religions from coming into close contact with those who once belonged to "lower" religions. The ranks of European aristocracy, with their elaborate etiquette and code of honor, illustrate a similar development on a non-religious basis.

Cultural hierarchies are the substance of the world as most people experience it, but their great significance comes from the ways in which they are connected with the rest of the social order— with economics and politics and their corresponding forms of stratification. This connection can operate in two ways. First, cultural stratification can be the basis for economic and political stratification. The New England colonies are one of the best examples of this: The church leaders were also the political authorities, and only members in good standing of the church congregation—a minority of the people—could participate in governing the community. Moreover, the religious upper class took the lead in organizing commerce, farming, and fishing and thus became an economic upper class. The religious, political, and economic hierarchies began to separate in the eighteenth century, but even today Americans (especially middle-class, white, Anglo-Saxon Protestants) tend to judge people's status according to their "respectability" in religious terms— essentially, according to how well they live up to the vestigial norms of the Protestant ethic.

Second, economic and political stratification tend to turn into cultural stratification. The cold realities of wealth and power are too blatant for most people, for both those on the bottom and those on the top. There is a widespread need to feel that those on the top merit their good fortune. Thus, people who rise in wealth or power attempt to cloak themselves in cultural respectability. The conquering tribesmen of antiquity called on priests to sanction their conquests, just as Charlemagne had himself crowned by the Pope after building a kingdom by war. Later, the way to the top is forgotten; the aristocracy claims that it rules, not by force, but by hereditary right and by the merits expressed in its code of honor and its patronage of the arts. A similar mutation occurs between the robber barons of nineteenth-century finance and the high society of today.

Economic, political, and cultural goods can be traded off for each other, and Weber postulates a tendency for the three hierarchies to come together in times of social tranquillity. The wealthy try to become powerful and cultured; the powerful use their influence to become rich and surrounded with high culture; cultural elites try to use their prestige to acquire wealth and power. But changes and competition within the realms of economics, politics, and culture periodically upset the composition of classes, power groups, and status groups, and we find the three hierarchies consolidating, breaking down, and rearranging again and again. History is a continuous battle, not only of knights against officials, bureaucrats against politicians, landowners against financiers, industrialists against unionists, and priests against scientists and intellectuals, but of each of these orders against the others. The processes of stratification not only make up the fabric of our everyday lives, but as we shall see below, they turn the engines of history as Weber saw it.

Organizations: patrimonialism and bureaucracy

Surveying world social forms, Weber noted that there are two general ways in which people can stabilize their relationships: either by establishing strong personal ties or by setting up general rules. These were ideal types, of course. Reality is always a mixture of them, although the organizations of traditional societies have usually fallen near the personalistic pole, and modern organizations near the abstract rules pole. Weber often speaks of the former type of organization as patriarchal or patrimonial and of the latter as bureaucratic. The distinction follows broadly from that which Weber's older colleague Ferdinand Toennies made between *Gemeinschaft* (community) and *Gesellschaft* (society).

Personalistic organizations usually begin with the family household. We find the lord in ancient China or Assyria, or the citizen in Athens or Rome, or the baron in medieval Europe running his estate and his politics like a great family enterprise. Sons and brothers are his most trusted assistants, whether in supervising farming or trading expeditions, fighting a war, or collecting taxes for a higher authority. Servants and slaves are like part of the family, subject to the same loyalties and jealousies and to the same patriarchal whims. No distinction is made between public and private, between the official finances and the domestic purse. The king collects taxes equally for his troops and for his wine cellar, and his subaltern lord pays his own expenses and profits out of what he can collect before passing it on up. This form of organization can be extended across large numbers of people by linking together chains of masters and followers. In a patrimonial regime the king has trusted lieutenants who administer distant sections of his realm; they in turn assign their trusted followers to various areas and tasks; and so on down to the lowest official, whose job it is to coerce the peasants to give up their produce. Premodern trading companies and factories were organized in the same way, but on a much smaller scale.

The main disadvantages of the personalistic form of organization are that it is neither very efficient nor very easy to control. Lines of communication from top to bottom are virtually nonexistent, and orders from above are likely to emerge as rumors below, if indeed they are passed on at all. How tasks are carried out depends almost entirely on the energy and initiative of the individuals involved. Under the circumstances such organizations tend to fall back on tradition—to do a job as it was done last time and as far back as anyone can remember, since there are no other guidelines, and it may not be safe to do anything that a vengeful superior could criticize. At the same time, such organizations continually slip from the control of their founders. Again and again in history a lord conquers a large territory and appoints his most trusted followers to collect the spoils, and they in turn appoint their assistants. By the time the conqueror dies, and sometimes before, the central authority begins to dissipate. Only a small portion of the taxes or booty collected comes through to the king. Eventually the more powerful lords may make themselves totally independent. Sometimes the process continues until the jurisdictions are fragmented down to the lowest level (as happened in medieval Germany); sometimes it is arrested halfway in a feudal compromise splitting authority among the levels; sometimes it is reversed by another conquest.

These political disadvantages provided the impetus for developing the other main type of organization: bureaucracy. Kings and lords long ago found that they could arrest the dissipation of authority, not merely by setting servants to spy on each other (which tended to make an organization secretive and clique-ridden), but by laying down general rules. Instead of leaving procedures to the discretion of subordinates, the ruler himself could control matters from afar by selecting, training, and checking up on men whose only job was to follow the rules. Instead of having general authority over a territory, an official could be confined to one specialized kind of job; power was thus split up and controlled from above. If abuses came from the lack of distinction between personal property and the king's property, a rigid line between public and private could be drawn. Instead of tasks being performed intermittently by local barons, they could be handled by officials recruited for full-time careers and paid specified salaries.

Weber found elements of this type of organization as far back as ancient Egypt and China, but its main development occurred only in Europe as the absolutist monarchies were built on a bureaucratic basis, ending the period of medieval feudalism. The first great bureaucracies (after the Catholic Church of the Middle Ages) were developed in France, Prussia, and Russia in the seventeenth and eighteenth centuries. By the nineteenth century the form was widely imitated, not only by governments, but by industrial enterprises that needed an efficient form of control over a large and complex division of labor. Since then bureaucratization has spread to all forms of social life—so much so that Weber regarded it as one of the main themes of modern history.

Considering its advantages, why did full-blown bureaucracy develop so late? Weber pointed out certain social and material prerequisites. The development of writing and then a large group of literate officials were necessary for an organization carrying out specialized rules and keeping records of its activities. A money economy was needed if officials were to be paid in salaries instead of in land or booty. Improved transportation and communication (roads, navigable rivers and canals, a courier system) were necessary if a king was to keep track of what his officials were doing in distant realms. Changing material conditions aided the development of centralized administration. Firearms made the self-equipped knight obsolete and aided the rise of the large, bureaucratic army of foot soldiers. Similarly, the invention of industrial machinery helped replace scattered handicraft production with the bureaucratic factory. But the bureaucratic form itself is historically primary; without its development through the struggles of politics, modern industrial innovations could never have been used and hence would never have been invented.

Moreover, bureaucracy is hardly utopian. The kings who created it in order to control their errant knights soon found that their new machinery was slipping from their hands. Once established, the bureaucracy could do its work of administering regulations without a ruler and could even make up new rules as the occasion provided. Indeed, rulers soon began to get in the way of its smooth functioning, and hereditary monarchs grew progressively weaker until they fell in revolutions or degenerated into figureheads. Nor is bureaucracy the epitome of efficiency. Cabinet ministers and industrialists often have little more control over it than do kings. Weber saw in the world around him all the phenomena that have become famous under the labels "red tape" and "Parkinson's Law": the tendency for officials to see rules as ends in themselves rather than as means to ends, the difficulty of finding responsible decision-makers amid a maze of rules and regulations, the tendency for organizations to drift, to expand mindlessly, to make their own survival the highest value. Many of these themes have been explored in subsequent research by such sociologists as Philip Selznick, Peter Blau and Michel Crozier.

Always a political man, Weber discovered organizational politics even in the supposedly neutral instrument of bureaucracy. As was noted with regard to his theory of stratification, Weber saw how men's views and interests develop from the positions they hold, and he saw how rules and regulations could be used in the continual jockeying for authority and autonomy that human beings carry on. What American sociologists have since come to think of as "informal organization" within "formal organization," Weber saw as part of the implicit dialectic of the struggle for control. Personalistic and bureaucratic forms of organization, after all, are ideal types, and reality is always a mixture. As the Weberian scholar Guenther Roth has recently pointed out, the clever administrator uses *both* strategies of control—a mixture of personal loyalties and bureaucratic impartiality and the use of special emissaries with diffuse authority to carry out tasks that the rules and regulations impede. Franklin D. Roosevelt and John F. Kennedy were masters of the technique of mixed strategies. Both methods have their drawbacks, but only by tireless juggling between them can an organizational leader actually lead.

Politics: traditional, charismatic, and rational-legal legitimacy

Politics is conflict over who shall control the state, the apparatus of coercion in a society. To call the state an apparatus of coercion means only that its ultimate appeal to force is the one thing that all states have in common; it does not mean that all states necessarily coerce most of their members most of the time. A democracy is a type of state in which power is split up among contending parties and separate jurisdictions, so that in fact the state does relatively little coercing. That perhaps is an ideal, and Weber would agree with Hegel's verdict that "history is the chopping-block at which the happiness of peoples, the wisdom of states, and the virtue of individuals have been victimized."

Politics is made up of three components: the groups contending for power, the organizations through which power is sought and exercised, and the ideas and ideals that legitimate authority. We have already considered the first two: the contending groups are found in the stratification of a society and may consist of economic classes, existing power groups, or status groups—each interested in manipulating the state to further its ends. We can have various kinds of political movements: those Interested in economic policies and the state protection or control of property; those interested in power for its own sake or in extending the power of an organization (whether it be a party, welfare bureaucracy, army, police force, or court system); and those interested in having the state sanction some particular culture with official status (those interested in or opposed to a state religion, the prohibition of alcohol, sexuality in movies, psychedelics, and so forth). We have also seen the various kinds of political organizations that have existed and noted some of their preconditions and dynamics.

There remains the dynamics of legitimacy. Weber saw that men have material and power interests, but that they also see the world in terms of ideas and ideals. Men will fight and die for world views as well as for money and power. The difference between Weber's view and the naïve conservative view that sees the state as a spiritual unity is that Weber realized that men's ideals *differ* within the same society. As Weber put it, men have both material and ideal interests, and their interests often conflict. As Weber noted, a society cannot be held together by force alone. Obviously, an army can control an unarmed populace. But within the army the general is not necessarily the strongest man, and he may not even carry a gun. Why then are men afraid to disobey him? Because if one man disobeys and the others obey, the single dissenter will be shot. Why don't all the men disobey together? Because if they want to act together, they must have some sort of organization, and that again raises the question of who shall lead and how his authority will be enforced. To the old philosophical question "Who shall guard the guardians?" Weber replied that organizations can be based on force provided widespread beliefs about legitimacy exist. The general's orders are obeyed because each man expects others to obey him, and this expectation is based on the widespread *belief* that the general has legitimate authority.

Weber was well enough acquainted with history and with the daily newspapers to know that orders are not always obeyed, that the legitimacy of a leader or regime can rise and fall. Accordingly, he was interested in the dynamics of legitimacy. Out of his historical perspective, Weber produced three ideal types of legitimacy. First, authority could be based on *tradition:* A king rules because his family has always ruled (so he says), because he is chosen by the gods, or because the tribal council selected him through traditional ceremonial methods. Second, authority could be based on personal *charisma:* "It is written . . . , but I say unto you . . . ," proclaims the prophet, the hero, the dominant personality, discarding tradition in favor of his own revelation. Third, authority can be *rational-legal:* The laws provide the procedure for selecting legitimate presidents and chancellors; bureaucratic regulations delegate authority to the policeman and the passport clerk. Each of these forms of legitimacy has a corresponding form of organization. Traditional rulers are found primarily in patrimonial and patriarchal organizations; charismatic leaders usually have a personal retinue of disciples and a large unorganized following; rational-legal officials are found in bureaucracies.

Each form of legitimacy has its advantages and drawbacks. The traditional leader seems to have little to worry about. Tradition says he is king or chief, and there is nothing anyone can do about it (except of course his enemies in other kingdoms and tribes). Still, Weber points out that political struggle is never entirely absent, although it may be underground. The traditional ruler is often limited by the very tradition. His advisers, noblemen, and priests are seldom idle about interpreting tradition to their advantage and against the powers of the king. If he wants to do things his way, he must continually struggle to interpret traditions to *his* advantage. But there are dangers in success, too; if he extends his power too far beyond tradition, he may lose his traditional legitimacy. Ancient history (and modern, too) is full of kings turned tyrants who were overthrown and replaced by one of the noblemen waiting in the wings.

One possibility for the ambitious traditional monarch is to mix his traditional authority with personal charisma. But this has its difficulties and dangers too. First, in order to be charismatic, one must have some extraordinary personal qualities. To be sure, these can often be evoked by stagecraft and public relations, but the charismatic leader has entered an arena in which the pressure is on, and he must live up to his billing or disappear into that special obscurity reserved for has-been charismatics. Every emergency—famine, riot, invasion, or special omen—calls for a corresponding miracle. If the charismatic leader does not live up to his own reputation, he soon loses legitimacy to a rival charismatic or to an "I-told-you-so" traditionalist. The tides of legitimacy can ebb and flow with startling rapidity, as the history of modern coups d'état demonstrates.

Finally, authority can be rational-legal. But rationalization is another dangerous beast to ride. Once this force is unleashed, there is no individual who cannot be found dispensable. The European monarchs who tried to consolidate their traditional authority by building a purely legal state found in the end that there is no justification for kings in a rational-legal code. The descendants of Louis XIV and Frederick the Great paid for the power they built. Rationalization attempts to remove the arbitrary, to provide a clear and sufficient reason for every social act. Not only kings, but party leaders, prime ministers, dictators, and individual bureaucrats themselves can be found wanting by the standards of the rational-legal regimes they control. Every regime that proclaims its principles—whether in the ideals of socialism, the United States Constitution, or the Declaration of the Rights of Man—is subject to the judgment of its people. Of course, regimes can get away with consideral deviations from their avowed ideals, since they control powerful organizational and material resources, including the communication facilities, which can define much of the reality its people observe. Still, ideals create a rallying point for potential opponents (like the dissident writers in the Soviet Union or the antiracist and antimilitarist movements in the United States) and constitute the weak link in the authority structure of a regime weakened by defeat, economic crisis, or internal conflict among its power holders. The traditional ruler, at any rate, did not have to spend much effort in justifying his actions. Thus, even where they are not lived up to (that is, almost everywhere), rational-legal principles of legitimacy set the basic context in which political dispute goes on.

WEBER'S THEORY OF HISTORY: THE RATIONALIZATION OF THE WORLD

The great transformation in history was that unmistakable phenomenon called "modernization," which turned a world of peasants, lords, and priests into a buzzing hive of organization, machinery, and movement. Weber found the core of that change in the new industrial economy. An explanation of the emergence of modern capitalism would thus be an explanation of modernity, and Weber's search for its roots led him to describe the social outlines of world history.

Weber began by analyzing the modern economic system. The key attribute is predictability. There is no point in manufacturing large amounts of goods unless you can be sure of a regular market for them, and you cannot get the benefits of modern machinery and specialized division of labor unless you can continuously produce large amounts. Moreover, you cannot run a factory unless you can depend on having a regular supply of workers to hire and unless you can borrow money for capital expenses when you need it and under fair and reasonable conditions. In short, modern industry depends on large and stable markets, a dependable and economically motivated labor force, and a trustworthy financial system. Weber saw that these preconditions were missing throughout most of history and that a long chain of prerequisites had somehow to emerge before the modern economy could take off.

Markets, for example, had been mostly local—peasants producing their own necessities and bartering or selling the rest in nearby towns. Of the many factors that limited larger markets, three important ones were: (1) the riskiness of transporting valuable goods in a world of continuous warfare and conquest, where robbers and barons were equally dangerous and civil order existed only within the walls of one's town or sometimes only in one's house; (2) the general lack of a widespread system of money and credit to facilitate large-scale trading; and (3) distrust of strangers—from other lands, other religions, other villages—which made trading a matter of crafty haggling and merchants often indistinguishable from pirates.

Labor, in the modern sense, was also a historical rarity. Industries cannot run efficiently and competitively if workers are not available who will move from job to job as demand for products changes and who can be attracted to the areas of greatest profit by offers of commensurate wages. (As we see, Weber's economics is in the classical English tradition.) But workers in traditional societies are for the most part not free economic agents. Peasants are often bound to the land as serfs; industrial laborers are usually family members, household servants, or slaves, bound to the enterprise, and a continuing expense whether they are overworked or underworked. Guild monopolies control most of the remaining labor supply. All these various obstacles had to be broken down before the industrial labor force could be brought together in the factory system.

Finally, modern finance is also a recent development. Only in the large kingdoms and empires did a widespread system of money exist at all. Even then, there were many obstacles to a dependable system of loans. Widespread literacy was necessary before the more complex forms of credit—such as the stock market—could arise. Money was lent only at exorbitant rates of interest as long as the risks of nonpayment and failure were great—as they were in an era when courts and police did not exist to back up contracts and when every business enterprise was risky. Not the least of the danger came from the state itself. Taxes were capricious and often little more than robbery; if a banker lent money to a king, there was no guarantee that he would ever get it back. Thus several great German banking houses—including the famous Fuggers of Augsburg—were wiped out in bankruptcies of the King of Spain in the fifteenth and sixteenth centuries. In such a world the life of a businessman was a precarious one. If by chance he was successful and amassed a fortune, he did not reinvest it in expanding his business, but made every effort to buy himself some land and a title of nobility and thus get out of the business world entirely.

Weber's task was to trace back through history to find out where and how each of these obstacles fell—to determine the one time and place where all the circumstances were right and where the industrial takeoff could begin. The story begins in remote antiquity in a world of tribal societies—some agricultural, some made up of nomadic herdsmen and hunters. Religion played a key role in their social structure and in their world views. Men lived and worked almost entirely with their kinsmen, and the kinship network and the community were united by a common set of ceremonies surrounding all aspects of life. God and spirits were everywhere—in the sky and the trees, guarding the hearth and the door of the house, and legitimating the authority of the patriarch-priest-chief. Like Durkheim, Weber recognized the integrating force of religion in primitive society.

Change came about especially by political struggle. Hunting tribes conquered agricultural tribes, creating two-class societies of peasants and warrior-aristocrats. Conquests went wider and wider; empires rose and fell; kings emerged; complex stratification grew within the ranks of the aristocracy; and royal administration (primitive bureaucracies) came into being. The familiar pendulum swings of world political history began: Overextended patrimonial regimes disintegrated into feudalism and then reconsolidated under a new conqueror. In these larger, more complex societies, wealth became concentrated. A division of labor developed around the royal courts, as artisans, servants, scribes, and merchants specialized to satisfy royal tastes. Priests developed separate hierarchies of their own, amalgamating war gods and nature gods into new syncretisms and pantheons.

In a number of these large societies—notably China and India—and in independent cities and small states on their peripheries—notably in Greece and Israel—a great change took place in the realm of religion between the sixth and fourth centuries B.C. Talcott Parsons, a leading interpreter of this phase of Weber's work, calls it the "philosophical breakthrough"—the rise of the great world religions. In each of these—Confucianism, Brahminism, Buddhism, Greek ethical philosophy, monotheistic Judaism and its later offshoots, Christianity and Islam—the nature of man's relationship to the physical and social worlds changes. The change consists of *separating* the idea of the natural world from the idea of the spiritual world. Instead of gods and spirits routinely intervening in the world around us (as in Greek mythology), there exists another, very different realm: heaven and hell, another sphere of reality, a world of ideal principles.

The consequences of this change were far-reaching. As long as the world is in the play of gods and spirits, it cannot be taken as a very predictable place. One can only try to placate its invisible rulers by ceremonies and sacrifices or to control them by magic. But once the spiritual realm becomes separate, both nature and society can be treated in a more stable way.

First, by removing animistic entities the world becomes open to rational explanation. The door is opened to scientific investigation and explanation. This new-found rationalism can spill over into the social realm as well. Men can think of laws based on consistent general principles, instead of bowing before the eccentricities of sanctified tradition. Political and social arrangements, too, become subject to a rational critique—although this latter implication was not really seized upon until the French Enlightenment of the eighteenth century.

Second, religion itself can develop in new directions. Primitive religions merely describe an accepted if invisible side of the ordinary world. A man placates the gods in order to kill his enemies and make his crops grow; he does not worry about being good or going to heaven. (Think of the heroes of the *Odyssey* or the early part of the Old Testament.) The philosophical breakthrough opens up two new possibilities: (1) The spiritual realm can now be a place to which man escapes from the trials and tribulations of the world. If the righteous man—the one who follows all the rituals and does all his duties—nevertheless has bad fortune in the world, it does not fundamentally concern him. In fact, the material world can now be seen as a dangerous temptation, for the truly holy man concentrates only on his salvation. (2) The ideas of good and evil can develop separately from the ideas of worldly success and failure. For the primitive man sin simply means misfortune; as long as he is prosperous, healthy, and powerful, he has a clear conscience. The philosophical breakthrough puts a new ethical obligation on men. They are now to be concerned with justice and injustice toward their fellow men; conscience becomes its own reward and punishment.

These new possibilities, especially the second, are potential forces for great changes in society. The new ideas of good and evil and the concept of a world of perfection can provide tremendous leverage for changing the world to make it live up to these ideals. Here in antiquity we find the basis of Weber's Protestant ethic, which was to play a powerful role in the takeoff of industrialization 2,000 years later.

There is one more crucial attribute of the religions of the philosophical breakthrough: They are all *universalistic*. Earlier religions are limited to the members of one family, one tribe, or one ethnic group. The world religions, emerging in or near empires with unlimited ambitions of conquest, exclude no one. Indeed, earlier religions are tolerant; they conceive of a pluralistic world of many peoples, each with their patron gods. But for Confucianism, Buddhism, Christianity, and so on there is only *one* god or spiritual reality; all else is false, illusory, or subordinate. This shift is crucial because religions mark the limits of solidarity in society. In primitive and traditional societies, men are bound together with those who share a religious community. One can and must trust men who worship the same household or tribal gods. But strangers—men with different gods—are alien beings who cannot be trusted. One result of this setup was a widespread prohibition on usury—lending money at interest to other members of one's own religious group. Outside the group one could bargain in as cutthroat a fashion as possible, since there were no ethical obligations toward outsiders. Thus, to universalize a religion was abruptly to broaden the community within which peaceful social transactions could regularly be carried out.

The philosophical breakthrough opened many of the doors to industrialization: laying the basis for a moral community of trust underlying peaceful commerce, rationalizing the legal system, motivating men to remake political, social, and economic institutions in keeping with an imperative to transform the world more closely to the ideal. But these implications took a long time to work themselves out, and not all of the world religions opened up just the right path to the transformation of society. Weber made a sweeping set of comparative studies of the various religions, of which *The Protestant Ethic and the Spirit of Capitalism* is only a preliminary version of the case of Christianity. The others were *The Religion of China, The Religion of India,* and *Ancient Judaism;* he died before he could begin his studies of Islam and early Christianity. His broad conclusion was that only a certain kind of breakthrough—the mixture of the ethical and scientific rationalism of Greek philosophy with the legalism and world-changing activism of Judaism that made up Christianity—gave the impetus for rationalizing social institutions and changing the world in the economic and political upheavals of modernity. Confucianism, Brahminism, Buddhism, and Islam he found entwined with the patrimonial order of stratification in such ways that they strengthened the unpredictable, irrational aspects of their societies rather than weakened them.

In Europe the key story concerns the growth of the Christian Church—the first large-scale, truly rationalized bureaucratic organization in history—and its growing consolidation with the remnants of the Roman Empire, itself legally rationalized under the influence of Greek culture. The age-old pendulum of political consolidation and disintegration swung on, but was nearing the end of its monotonous cycle through time. By the sixteenth century kings began to build the bureaucracies—using priests as their first bureaucrats—that would eventually destroy the fragmented and conflict-ridden feudal system, establish a predictable set of laws and a trustworthy monetary system, bring peace and order to large expanses of territory, and carry out regular tax policies. Commerce spread; mechanical inventions were sought and made; and handicraft industries developed. Western Europe perched on the brink of industrialization, held back only by government mercantilist policies of establishing monopolies and by the feudal bondage of labor to the soil.

The final obstacles fell in England—ironically, the Western European country in which the feudal gentry had fought the most successful battle against the king and in which royal absolutism was least far advanced. After the civil war of the seventeenth century the small gentry class gained control of the state bureaucracy and used it to further their economic interests—moving the peasants off the land, thereby creating a labor force for the textile mills, and establishing an economic policy that would remove restraints on competition. The battle was fought and won by radical Protestants: men who felt that work, honesty, and rule following were the commandments of God and were further impelled by a powerful vision of the ideal world of heaven and hell. Their emergence at this propitious time in history is not yet understood, but the tradition from which they emerged is clear: They revived the early spirit of Christianity and brought to fruition the world-transforming potential of the religious breakthroughs of antiquity.

Once the industrial revolution was in full swing, its progress was unimpedable. New social classes appeared, transforming politics from the exclusive province of military aristocrats and court cabals to an object of mass movements and bureaucratic manipulations. Science, education, and mass communications were unleashed, to transform again and again the nature of stratification and of industry. England rose to wealth and world power. The rulers of other nations, however fearful of modernization's destructive effect on the old order that supported them, were forced to emulate England in order to keep pace militarily; otherwise, they faced the risk of becoming colonies of the modernized states.

From his towering intellectual vantage point, Weber watched the panorama of events flow through the centuries. *Die Entzauberung der Welt,* he called it—the master trend of history, the disenchantment of the world. Rationalization steadily pushes back the uncertain, the mythical, the poetic. Once all the world was seen through a veil of ritual and ceremony, goddesses and fire-breathing dragons, and the thousand fearful chances of everyday life; now daily railroad trains bring tourists to the castles of Transylvania. Even the God-fearing Protestant entrepreneur has disappeared, replaced by the bureaucratic employee. Once the modern system is established, it runs of its own accord. But the Protestant ethic is not dead, it is merely secularized. Its spirit hangs on in the very institutions of modern society and in the tightly controlled personalities of the men who work in a world of rules and regulations, merit ratings, and bureaucratic security. In an America split in cultural war between a white middle-class generation still deep in the Protestant ethic, and their own sons and daughters rejecting the "uptight" world in alliance with the members of a black culture that escaped only by being kept at the bottom, Weber's sociology strikes the central theme. No one saw more clearly than Weber the ways in which our lives are "haunted by the ghosts of dead religious beliefs."

For all his voluminous writings, Weber was first and foremost a political man. From his early career he was active in the law courts and government agencies of Berlin. His interest in economics was first stimulated when reform groups commissioned him to study the problems of labor immigration in East Prussia and stock-market manipulations. He began with his father's upper-class imperialist loyalties, but increasing exposure to the hardships of the lower classes shifted his sympathies gradually to the left. But he had no illusions about the costs of reform. He regarded the socialist utopia as an ideology with which the leaders of the Social Democratic party kept their followers in line, and he was in accord with his young friend Robert Michels' analysis of the "Iron Law of Oligarchy" in party politics.

The Marxists' flaw was that they failed to see the bureaucratic nature of the modern economy, whether it be capitalist or socialist. Weber became interested In Russia during the abortive revolution of 1905 and learned Russian in order to follow the events firsthand. His analysis was a remarkable foresight of the Soviet period. Should Russia lose a major European war and the revolutionary left come to power, he predicted, Russia would experience a bureaucratization of the entire social structure such as the world has never seen. Considering Weber's views on the quality of life in a bureaucracy, his expectations were anything but optimistic. "The dictatorship of the official and not of the proletariat is on the march," he wrote.

The situation in Germany was scarcely more hopeful. Weber's growing disillusionment with conservative nationalism came as he watched Germany's inept foreign policy, losing allies and progressively isolating herself while at the same time carrying on an arms race and an increasingly strident campaign of nationalist self-glorification. He placed the blame on Germany's political structure: an impotent parliament incapable of controlling an irresponsible state bureaucracy; an army staffed by the defensively arrogant aristocrats of a bygone era; and a foolish hereditary monarch initiating policies that trapped the rest of the nation in their wake. In the 1890s Weber took part in efforts to create a responsible democratic party, but he dropped out when its hopelessness became apparent.

When World War I finally broke out, the release from years of tension came as a relief. Weber was at first enthusiastic. "In spite of all," he declared it "a great and wonderful war." As a fifty-year-old reserve officer in the German army, he was called to duty as the director of military hospitals in the Heidelberg area. A year later he retired and went to Berlin to wield what political influence he could to end the war.

After his first enthusiasm had worn off, Weber quickly realized that Germany's military and political leadership was incapable of carrying out a victorious policy and that a prolongation of the war could only result in the destruction of German—indeed, of European—power and the turning over of world domination to America. By 1918 his last loyalties to the Kaiser were gone, and he published a series of newspaper articles calling for a democratic constitution for postwar Germany.

The fall of the old regime seemed to take a personal weight from Weber's shoulders. From the Versailles peace conference, where he served on the German delegation, he wrote that he slept soundly at night for the first time in many years. Even his inability to teach was overcome. He accepted a professorship at Munich, where he lectured to enormous crowds of students, intellectuals, and public dignitaries. Politics suddenly showed opportunities. Weber became the leader of a new liberal democratic party. An arch realist, he nevertheless saw a ray of hope. Political parties might be corrupt oligarchies, but only within free parliamentary competition might leaders arise capable of controlling the recalcitrant state bureaucracy and giving the nation intelligent policies.

But time had run out. In 1919 Weber fell ill of pneumonia, and he died the next year at the age of fifty-six. His party collapsed; the first of the German republic's many economic and political crises was upon it. Responsible leadership would not be forthcoming; the irresponsible ones were already gathering in the beer gardens of Munich. Politics is a dangerous and morally taxing vocation, Weber had told his students in one of his famous last lectures. The idealist as well as the cynic is caught in webs of consequences far beyond those intended in his acts. Ideals alone are not enough; they must be accompanied by hard realism, sympathetic imagination, and an unyielding sense of responsibility. The following might have been his own epitaph for his accomplishments in the realm of knowledge as well as his failures in the realm of politics:

Politics is a strong and slow boring of hard boards. It takes both passion and perspective. Certainly all historical experience confirms the truth—that man would not have attained the possible unless time and again he had reached out for the impossible. But to do that a man must be a leader, and not only a leader but a hero as well, in a very sober sense of the word. And even those who are neither leaders nor heroes must arm themselves with that steadfastness of heart which can brave even the crumbling of all hopes. This is necessary right now, or else men will not be able to attain even that which is possible today. Only he has the calling for politics who is sure that he shall not crumble when the world from his point of view is too stupid or too base for what he wants to offer. Only he who in the face of all this can say "In spite of all!" has the calling for politics.[1]

[1] Max Weber, "Politics as a Vocation," in H. H. Gerth and C. Wright Mills (eds.), *From Max Weber: Essays in Sociology* (New York: Oxford University Press, 1946), p. 128.

CHAPTER SEVEN

SIGMUND FREUD: CONQUISTADOR OF THE IRRATIONAL

The cataclysmic twentieth-century wars had yet to burst upon the face of mankind; Darwin's *Origin of Species* was three years away from publication, and Einstein's birth lay twenty-three years in the future, when Sigmund Freud (1856–1939) was born in Freiburg, Moravia. Western civilization was intact. Europe enjoyed an uneasy peace, while America was on the verge of civil war.

In modern times Freud has become a legendary figure in the history of science. He is remembered as the founder of psychoanalysis, a method for understanding human motivation and a technique for healing the psyche. He presented himself in his autobiography as a scientist; yet he opened a crack in the scientific edifice of Reason which had dominated the intellectual scene since the Enlightenment. The social philosophers of that period, including Montesquieu, Diderot, d'Alembert, Rousseau, Condorcet, and Turgot, subscribed wholeheartedly to the Aristotelean dictum that man is a rational animal. Their vision, which the founding fathers of sociology attempted to put into practice, was of free rational man emerging from centuries of ignorance, fear, and superstition into a bright new dawn of Reason, science, and unlimited progress. Man, the moving force of society, was to be guided by rational knowledge in a conscious attempt to remake the world in his own image and thereby shape his planetary destiny.

Freud's greatest discovery was the systematic unearthing of the vast and hidden continent of the human unconscious. Via the method of psychoanalysis he probed the depths of the psyche and uncovered the irrational side of human nature. It is one of the paradoxes of Freud's biography that the work of this eminent scientist and man of reason should have heralded the end of the Age of Reason. The Enlightenment dream of the eighteenth-century philosophes died in Freud, a child of that Enlightenment. No longer could Western man trust solely and naïvely in Reason to solve the problems of collective living. Freud showed that the individual is basically a nonrational being, driven by such emotional forces as "sexual instincts" and "repressed wishes."

Although Freud did not discover the unconscious, he was the first to give content to what had previously been an unfilled form. The idea of the unconscious had been brewing in the German intellectual climate since the publication of Eduard von Hartmann's *The Philosophy of the Unconscious* in 1859. But the metaphysician von Hartmann did not claim to have explored the region of the unconscious; rather, he arrived there by a process of abstract reasoning and found "will" and "intellect" (parallel to Freud's formulations of "id" and "ego") in a state of conflict. Nor was the nineteenth century the first age in the history of Western thought to have conceived this idea; it may be traced back to antiquity. As the idea of the "atom" was present in the writings of the Greek philosopher Democritus some 2,300 years prior to Einstein's discovery of the energy latent in that minuscule entity, so the idea of an unconscious in man lurked in Plato's parable of the cave more than two millennia prior to Freud's advent.

EARLY LIFE AND WORK

As a child, Freud was the center of attention of his family's Viennese household. He was so much his mother's favorite that she discontinued his younger sister, Anna's, piano lessons because the ten-year-old Sigmund complained that the "noise" disturbed his studies. Sigmund was a child prodigy who began reading Shakespeare at age eight and was later fascinated by Thiers' *Consulate and Empire.* During adolescence Freud was a hero-worshiper and dreamed of becoming a great general. He was so taken with the romance of Napoleon that he pasted onto the backs of his toy wooden soldiers little labels bearing the names of the French emperor's marshals.

Freud graduated summa cum laude from high school. For the last six of his eight years at Sperl Gymnasium he ranked number one and occupied such a privileged position that he was hardly ever questioned in class. His choice of profession was determined to a great extent by his social position as a Viennese Jew. The alternatives open to him were those of industry, business, law, and medicine. His intellectual bent eliminated the first two, and he considered taking up the study of jurisprudence. Although he felt no direct attraction to medicine, he was motivated by the sort of curiosity that is directed more toward human concerns than toward natural objects. It was a period of indecision. On the one hand, he was influenced to study law by a school friend who was later to become a famous politician; on the other hand, he was attracted by the then topical evolutionary theories of Darwin, which offered hopes for an extraordinary advance in understanding the world.

Freud reached his decision to enter the field of medicine upon hearing a dramatic reading of Goethe's essay on Nature. His youthful idealism was given direction by the old master's romantic picture of Nature as a bountiful mother, who allowed her favorites the privilege of exploring her secrets. Freud had come to believe that the secret of power lay in understanding rather than in force. Swayed by the late-nineteenth-century *Zeitgeist,* he questioned man's relation to himself as well as his place in Nature.

With his father's blessings and financial support, Freud embarked on his career as a medical student at the University of Vienna in the autumn of 1873. His work load averaged over twenty-five hours per week, including lectures and laboratories, in such broadly diversified fields as anatomy, chemistry, botany, microscopy, mineralogy, physics, spectrum analysis, biology, histology, Aristotelean logic, physiology, and zoology. The budding genius thereby acquired a solid scientific background in addition to the habits of hard work and self-discipline. During this academically successful period Freud began to recognize the limitations as well as the capabilities of his intellectual gifts. He learned also the truth of the Mephistophelean dictum: "It is in vain that you range round from science to science; each man learns only what he can."

After having received his first grant in 1876 to study the gonadic structure of eels, Freud found a temporary home in Ernst Brücke's physiology laboratory. Brücke was for Freud a role model as well as an intellectual mentor. He was an exemplar of the man of science—uncompromising, ascetic, disciplined. An austere Protestant German professor with a Prussian accent, Brücke represented the antithesis of the Viennese *schlamperai* (or "sloppy thinkers") with whom Freud was already familiar.

Brücke's Institute of Physiology was part of a far-reaching scientific movement known as the Helmholtz school of medicine, whose teachings made a lasting impression on Freud. Its founders, all to become famous scientists, had sworn a youthful oath to uphold the principles:

No other forces than the common physical-chemical ones are active within the organism. In those cases which cannot at the time be explained by these forces one has either to find the specific way or form of their action by means of the physical-mathematical method or to assume new forces equal in dignity to the chemical-physical forces inherent in matter, reducible to the forces of attraction and repulsion.[1]

By 1870 this current of thought had achieved complete dominion over the minds of the German physiologists and medical teachers; it stimulated research everywhere.

Helmholtz's mid-nineteenth-century mechanical view of the universe, which reduced all natural phenomena to the forces of attraction and repulsion, was incorporated by Brücke into his *Lectures on Physiology* (1874). The student Freud was captivated by his teacher's account of physical physiology. Brücke defined physiology as the science of organisms as such. He distinguished between organisms and machines; the latter were mere dead material entities in action, while the former possessed the faculty of assimilation. However, both were considered to be phenomena of the physical world. According to the principle of the conservation of energy, organisms and machines were similarly composed of systems of atoms and driven by forces. In science the real causes were symbolized by the word "forces." The less scientists knew about these causes, claimed Brücke, the more kinds of forces they had to distinguish: mechanical, electrical, magnetic, light, heat, and so forth. Progress in knowledge had reduced these forces to two—attraction and repulsion. Brücke extended this line of reasoning to the human organism. He incorporated this nineteenth-century image of man into two volumes of what was then known about the interplay of physical forces inside the living organism. That Freud was influenced strongly by the content and spirit of these ideas is revealed in his 1926 characterization of the dynamic aspect of psychoanalysis as forces that assist or inhibit one another and combine with and enter into compromises with one another. His image of the human being, as we shall see, was tinged heavily with the mechanistic view, which he absorbed as a student at Brücke's institute.

With the aid of a photographic memory Freud passed his final medical examination in 1881 with flying colors. During that year he found Theodor Meynert's lectures on psychiatry of particular interest because of their nonlaboratory approach to medical science. Although he wanted to pursue a theoretical career, his financial situation upon receipt of his M.D. was so shaky that he accepted Brücke's advice to abandon this ambition. He served as doctor in residence at the Vienna General Hospital, where he gained three years of experience in surgery, internal medicine, dermatology, and psychiatry.

One year before his marriage to Martha Bernays in 1886, the twenty-nine-year-old Freud was seeking the professional recognition that would enable him to establish a private practice and to start a family. He hoped that his discovery of the clinical use of cocaine as a local anesthetic would earn him early fame. Using himself as a guinea pig, Freud

[1] Ernest Jones, *The Life and Work of Sigmund Freud,* edited and abridged by Lionel Trilling and Steven Marcus (New York: Doubleday Anchor Books, 1963), p. 29. Reprinted by permission of Basic Books, Inc., Publishers, New York, 1961.

observed that cocaine produced exhilaration and lasting euphoria; it increased his capacities for self-control and intensive mental work. Although it aided him in controlling the contents and flow of his consciousness, preoccupation with the magical rather than the medicinal properties of the drug cost him credit for the find. A younger colleague, Carl Koller, won the distinction of inaugurating the use of cocaine on the sensitive eye surface. Freud had yet to prove his worth.

The interpretation of dreams

Prior to Freud the field of psychiatry was relatively virgin territory. The great French observers Jean Charcot and his student Pierre Janet had established a lone outpost with their work on hypnosis and hysteria.[2] The relationship between Charcot, with whom Freud studied during the years 1885–1886, and Janet was akin to that between Saint-Simon and Comte. Saint-Simon and Charcot were the inspirational thinkers, while Comte and Janet, their disciples, were the systematizers. It was Janet who delved deeply into the psychic process of hysteria and found, according to the theories of heredity that dominated *fin de siècle* French psychology, that the disease was a form of degeneration of the nervous system that manifested itself in congenital "weakness." Since Freud's pioneering psychiatric work, forms of mental illness (including hysteria) have come to be viewed largely as socially conditioned, although organic causes can combine with social ones. The background role of heredity in mental illness remains obscure, after almost a century of research.

Upon publication of *The Interpretation of Dreams* in 1900 Freud began to emerge from obscurity. He had been practicing neurology and psychiatry for a decade in Vienna. In 1897 he began an arduous self-analysis, which gave him greater insight into the resistances of his patients and laid the foundations for his system of psychoanalysis. His revolutionary scientific work showed for the first time in a comprehensive and systematic manner the previously unsuspected notion that the fulfillment of a wish was the essential motive of a dream. The conquistador of the irrational had struck ore in an unexplored land.

His first great discovery on this hidden continent was the "dirty little secret" that people lust and hate. Although this came as no surprise to the lower classes, the established middle and upper classes, including their learned scientists and scholars, were shocked by such a picture of themselves. The mere mention of Freud's name was considered impolite and risqué in the genteel drawing rooms of Viennese society. Respectable society followed the leaders of nineteenth-century European intellectual life in considering *their* civilization the summit of human progress. The social evolutionary trend of nineteenth-century sociological and anthropological thought, including the work of Comte, Frazer, Morgan, Tyler, and Spencer, had convinced the modern European of his

[2] Hysteria may be briefly defined as the experiencing of mental anxiety and/or bodily pain without an apparent physical cause.

cultural superiority to the so-called barbaric or primitive peoples. The modern European, secure in his conversation parlor, stereotyped native tribesmen as painted packs of savage, drum-beating cannibals and promiscuous sexual libertarians. Since the nineteenth century had a way of turning Victorian moral absolutes into hereditary categories, European man came to believe the myth that he was racially superior to black Africans. The latter were considered to be subhuman, abnormal, and sexually unrestrained. Freud disturbed Europe's sleep by showing in his case studies and dream analyses of respectable society matrons that the moral barrier between "normal" and "pathological" scarcely existed and that the sexual underground was much bigger than anyone was willing to admit.

Repression

Freud's greatest discovery on this new continent was the phenomenon of repression. The entire structure of psychoanalysis is based upon the foundation of repression as it operates in the human being. According to Freud, random thoughts, dreams, slips of the tongue, neurotic symptoms, and daily mistakes all have meanings (that is, express intentions or purposes) that are unknown to the person. They are what he calls "unconscious ideas." The individual who is undergoing psychoanalysis resists becoming aware of unconscious ideas that may threaten his established sense of self. The individual's rejection of an idea or a desire that he nevertheless possesses is repression. It functions to keep things out of consciousness; its consequence is that the individual refuses to recognize the realities of his or her human nature.

In his first major work Freud divides the mental apparatus into three components. He compares the unconscious system to an anteroom, which houses the various excitations, desires, ideas, drives, and instincts. These elements push forward to gain admission into a second and much smaller room which houses consciousness. A doorman or "censor" stands between these two rooms in the parlor of the preconscious, so to speak. The doorkeeper scrutinizes ideas and excitations that seek admittance, and those that are turned back at the threshold are repressed. Freud found in numerous clinical cases that repression occurred where there was a conflict between opposing wishes and desires. In addition, he found that experiences that were the occasions for such conflict almost invariably had a sexual content.

Freud relates the case of a girl who felt great relief upon her older sister's death. Since she could not recognize consciously the envy of her deceased sister, whose husband was now available to marry *her,* the girl became hysterical. She had repressed the thought, "Now he is free and can marry me." During the course of psychoanalysis she was able to remember the thought and to reproduce the intense excitement that she had experienced upon the occasion of her sister's death. In a burst of emotion, her conscious mind had suddenly recognized the unconsciously repressed material. By reliving that trauma from her past, she effected her own cure.

Next came one of Freud's keenest insights: that people with the highest ideals tend to have the greatest repression of strong aggressive and sexual desires. This empirical generalization, based on his observations of patients, suggested that ideals were *founded* on repression and that they took their vitality from the suppressed feelings themselves. In short, the uptight, honest, hard-working, righteous, authoritarian believer in the Protestant ethic derives his energetic tension from love and hate turned in upon himself. Freud later cited Woodrow Wilson's intense moral idealism as an example of this character type.

A third discovery, one that stemmed directly from the theory of repression, was that children have sex lives. The seemingly obvious notion that children are sexual creatures so roused the ire of his contemporaries that they ostracized him. However, Freud stuck to his empirical guns. In analyzing dreams and neurotic symptoms, he found that they contained a core that represented a return or regression to early childhood experiences. Assuming the validity of the hypothesis of the unconscious, children learn to repress their emotions. At one point they are innocent and unrepressed. The unconscious and conscious are not yet separated. Wishes to play with their orifices, genitals, and feces are freely indulged. It is only in the process of socialization, when the child begins to internalize the parents' values of cleanliness, propriety, and order, that the child learns to behave in a "proper" manner and to tailor himself to his society's norms.

FREUD'S EXPLANATORY SYSTEMS

Freud evolved several major explanatory systems during the course of his career: (1) the theory of primary and secondary process; (2) the theory of stages of sexual development; (3) the libido theory; (4) the trinitarian theory of the psychic apparatus; and (5) the theory of Eros versus the death instinct. Although none of these systems is self-contained and discrete from the others, we may isolate each for the purposes of analysis. The fabric of Freud's thought is sewn with many threads, and in order to unravel the whole, it helps to proceed from earlier to later systems.

Primary and secondary process

His earliest system began with the act of repression itself, which he explained in terms of the "primary process," as expressed in wishes, symbols, and fantasies, and the "secondary process" of our socialized awareness, which censors and controls the former. Each concept may be used to refer to either ways of thinking or ways of managing energy. Freud contends that man transcends his animality by undergoing a basic change from primary process, ruled by the unconscious system and the vicissitudes of the id instincts, to secondary process, dominated by the conscious system and the demands of the ego. Although primary process persists into adulthood, the mature ego is able to control the childlike id by delaying gratification, restraining pleasure, working to achieve rational goals, and remaining secure from irrational passions. Freud describes this dynamic shift within the human psyche as the transformation of the pleasure principle into the reality principle. Beyond seeking mere instinctual satisfaction, the human being develops the faculty of reason and learns to test reality; he discovers that making distinctions, such as good from bad, true from false, and useful from useless, is the beginning of wisdom.

The human being has metamorphosed from a pleasure-loving baby into a conscious, thinking subject located within a social system that demands that he function properly in his economic role. Of course, he is free to have a fantasy life; however, he must ultimately subordinate his mentality to the reality principle (that is, he must obey society's norms and live according to its values). He may have strange dreams, weird thoughts, irrational wishes, powerful desires, or immoral fantasies, but he must not let the imagination run away with itself to the point of excluding external reality. For example, James Thurber's beloved character Walter Mitty imagines himself to be a famous brain surgeon in the midst of performing a crucial operation on a millionaire banker who is a close personal friend of Roosevelt, only to have a parking lot attendant shout at him to stop his car before he slams into a Buick.

The stages of sexual development

One of Freud's major hypotheses is that the first five years are crucial in the further psychological development of the person. It is during this phase of life that the link between the individual and society is forged. Talcott Parsons later interpreted this to mean that the child acquires a superego (or conscience) during this period by identifying with parental values. Since the parents are society's cultural agents, the child will learn the dominant values from them. If cultural values are success oriented, as they are in America, the child will be encouraged to gear its organism toward the achievement of such desirable goals as position, power, and prestige. The will toward acquisition of goods, from soap to status, is thereby built into the individual by society from an early age.

From his observations of patients and their neuroses Freud developed a model of five overlapping stages of psychosexual development: oral, anal, phallic, latent, and genital. During the earliest state infants derive gratification from sucking the mother's breast. The erogenous zones of the mouth and lips are the first to come into play in deriving sexual pleasure. During this oral, or cannibalistic, phase the amoral baby makes no distinction between taking food and sexual activity. The suckling aims to incorporate the object (mother's breast) into his own body; it still lives according to the primary process of striving for instant gratification and has not yet developed the secondary process by which it distinguishes itself from the world and separates subject from object. The baby *is* the universe; it is at one with the environment. During the latter part of this stage the child begins biting; he becomes oral-sadistic. He begins to objectify and to differentiate himself from his surroundings. Although he does not yet know their names, he begins to locate such objects as the breast, the nipple, the blanket, the rattle. He encounters his first significant "other"—mother. He is cutting his first teeth and he explores the world by grasping things, shoving them into his mouth, and chewing on them. He is not sure whether to bite or suck. He is ambivalent. This primeval uncertainty, Freud argues, is the prototype for the polar emotions of love and hate.

During the anal phase of the organization of the libido the child concentrates his energy on the anus as a source of gratification. The child becomes fascinated with his feces and enjoys playing with them. Excrement is viewed as an extension of himself without any connotations of good or bad; it is neutral waste. Through the mother the child learns that excrement is bad via the diaper change. This routine is a rather unpleasant task, however loving the mother. The helpless nursling, who is emotionally sensitive to even the subtlest nuance of facial expression and tactile sensation, sees and feels the parent's distaste at this daily ritual. The role of this early memory trace or psychic imprinting upon the baby can hardly be overestimated in the course of individual development. Excrement becomes negative, associated in the child's mind with the smelly, dirty "bad-me." The clean "good-me" of the child is rewarded with parental smiles and verbal acclaim for not soiling his clothes. Toilet training is the beginning of civilization in the individual. The seeds of society and repression are sewn by teaching the child self- (that is, bowel) control.

During the phallic stage of psychosexual development the individual discovers the genital erogenous zone as a source of pleasure. The penis for the male and the clitoris for the female become the primary organs of sexual excitement. Freud understood the initial sexual instincts of childhood to be largely objectless, or "autoerotic." The key stage of development is the phallic, at which the Oedipus complex emerges, for this is the point at which sexual drives become firmly attached to an external object. Harking back to the Greek myth of Oedipus Rex to find an archetype for his clinical diagnoses, Freud theorized that the young male desires his mother and hates and fears his father. (For the female child, he expected the process to be the reverse.) The male child resolves this conflict by repressing the wish to kill his father; he identifies with him instead and makes him his personal ego-ideal. Thereafter, the internalized father (or superego) punishes the child by making him feel guilty whenever he wishes for something forbidden. The external punisher has taken up residence inside the child's own mind.

According to Freud, sexual interests are submerged during the latency period between the ages of five and twelve, to reappear again at puberty in the genital or adult stage of sexual organization. During these years between the phallic stage and puberty, the child learns from his initial social environment, his family and school, how to channel his sexual feelings into socially acceptable behavior.

Although Freud postulated the Oedipus complex as sociologically universal, ethnographic work by Malinowski and other cultural observers has disconfirmed this hypothesis. The concept does, however, provide the student of man with a heuristic device for understanding the individual's advance from bondage to freedom. As long as the individual remains attached in an emotionally dependent way to the parents, personal independence has yet to become a reality. Freud based his encompassing theory of neurosis upon fixation at the oedipal or one of the preoedipal stages, due to some conflict over gratification. In addition, some personal trauma in adult life may bring about temporary neurotic regression to an earlier mode of gratification.

The theory of libido

Freud's image of man reflected the mechanistic bias of his contemporaries. For Freud, as for middle-class thinkers of his time, man was perceived as primarily isolated and self-sufficient. He was alone in a universe not of his making and found himself, somewhat akin to Hobbes' imaginary atomic individual, surrounded by others in the same predicament. Uprooted from the medieval context of soil, hearth, and community, the nineteenth-century urban man's need for commodities drove him to the marketplace, where he encountered other individuals who needed what he had to sell and who had to sell what he needed. Society's cement consisted in this mutually profitable exchange. The wheeling and dealing for the material advantages took place on the vast stock-exchange floor of life under the guidance of Adam Smith's "invisible hand" of the self-adjusting market. Freud's libido theory, as we shall see, expressed the same idea in psychological rather than economic terms.

The French aristocrat and *homme de belles-lettres* La Mettrie argued cogently in 1748 that man is a complicated machine. Although Freud probably never read La Mettrie, he did pick up this theme. Freud's mechanical man was driven by libido (basic sexual energy) and regulated by the need to reduce tension to a certain minimal threshold. Pleasure consisted in an unwinding or reducing of tissue tensions and in the avoidance of pain. The barometer of well-being was a kind of tepid mean between ecstasy and depression. Men and their mechanical brides sought each other out in order to arrive at mutual satisfaction of their libidinous needs. Nevertheless, they remained as fundamentally alienated from one another as seller and customer on the market. Despite their mutual attraction, they remained at opposite magnetary poles and could never transcend their separateness. According to Freud, man's nature is fundamentally aggressive and asocial, and he is a social animal only by virtue of the necessity to satisfy the ravenous libido.

The concept of libido is essentially a nineteenth-century economic idea in psychological dress, in the sense that it is conceived of as a fixed quantity subject to the laws of matter. One may spend it as one pleases, but once it is spent it cannot be recovered. In the same way, Freud treats love as property or capital. Love was considered as a valuable commodity to be invested wisely and not merely to be frittered away on every passing stranger. Hence, Freud despaired of the possibility of brotherly love, except among the psychoanalytic elite; he ridiculed the commandment to "love thy neighbor as thyself" as an absurdity.

The trinitarian theory of the psychic apparatus

Freud's mature system emerged as a three-element conception of the psychic topography. The ego (cognition of the external world), the id (the emotional or instinctual being), and the superego (identifications and social ideals) were portrayed as dynamically interrelated regions or "psychic localities" within the mind of man. These concepts are ideal types in the Weberian sense. They function as diagnostic categories, which are neither separately observable entities nor physical portions of the brain; rather they are interactive mental principles that are always found in mixed form. For example, the primitive id drives become fixed on (or "cathected to") certain objects, such as mother, father, or self. These object cathexes are incorporated by the unconscious system of the mental apparatus and act as the building blocks of the emerging character structure of the individual.

The ego is a structure or organization of the mental process by which the human being stays in contact with social reality. It represents the viewpoint of Reason, which constrains the limitless passions and impulsive desires of the irrational id. The ego simultaneously draws energy from and acts as the agent of the id. The current outpouring of "how to" books for single men and women—on how to find a mate or how to seduce a member of the opposite sex most effectively and deliciously— illustrates this point.

The superego emerges as a function of the ego. It arbitrates the relationship between the ego and the external world and even punishes the ego. The superego is the interior judge, which represents the moral demands of society and reinforces the authority principle as it operates in the affairs of men.

One of the major fruits of this tripartite system was Freud's essay "Group Psychology and the Analysis of the Ego," in which he set forth an explanation of the foundation of social unity and its dissolution. Taking Gustave Le Bon's treatise on *The Crowd* as a springboard for analysis, Freud sought to fathom the willingness with which the ordinarily civilized individual subordinates his ego to the mindlessness and destructive tendencies of the group (that is, individuals en masse). Since Freud's basic premise was that social cohesion is based on sexual organization, it followed that the libidinal bond, rather than a community of interest, was the power that cemented the group.

Beyond sex, what held society together was the dynamic psychic mechanism of identification, whereby a number of separate individuals join together by substituting a common object for their ego ideal. Freud interpreted the ruler as a father image, an answer to people's wish to be led. Thus, the persecuting primal father becomes the "cultural super-ego," or what Comte called the "Great Being of Humanity," who is incarnated as the totalitarian dictator and invested by the people with supreme temporal power. The charismatic leader, as Weber reminds us, derives his dominion from neither legal nor traditional sources; rather, his authority and power to command are founded in the collectivity's perception of his possession of extraordinary, unique, and magical qualities. Alexander the Great, Caesar, Charlemagne, Genghis Khan, Ivan the Terrible, Napoleon, Lenin, and Hitler are examples of such politically charismatic personality types. The divine-right monarch Louis XIV of seventeenth-century France epitomized the secular sanctity of this administrative function in the famous historical aside, *"L'état, c'est moi."* (I am the state.) The absolutist political leader thereby places himself in the stead of the subjects' parents, and the subjects tend to obey readily and even to worship him.

Eros versus the death instinct

Freud's culminating explanatory system seeks speculatively to understand the individual and history in life-and-death terms. In the history of culture Eros may be distinguished from Agape; the former recalls the Greek ideal of passionate love between human beings by means of which each overcomes the sense of separateness, and the latter refers to the concept of brotherly love, according to which we are all one. Freud treats the two of these together in contrast to Thanatos, which represents the personification or mask of death in Greek mythology; it is the harbinger of suicide, war, pestilence, and famine. Like elliptic cycles, each of these heavenly powers, as Freud called them, recurs periodically in the rise and fall of civilizations and individuals.

PARADIGM OF FREUD'S METAPSYCHOLOGY

	Eros	Thanatos
Individual	Love	Death
History	Regeneration	Degeneration

In the life of individuals Eros stands for the sexual instincts. More specifically, it points toward those modes of human sexuality that have been categorized as heterosexual, homosexual, and bisexual. Whereas heterosexuality may be understood as the attainment of genitality, and homosexuality as oedipal identification with the wrong sex, bisexuality gained little or no stature in Freud's psychomorphology, except for the indication that polymorphous perversity might be a characteristic of early childhood. However, one of the most revolutionary implications of Freud's psychology of sex is the postulate of the universal bisexuality of human beings. In seeking to explain neuroses and perversions, Freud borrowed his colleague Wilhelm Fleiss' concept of constitutional bisexuality. Fleiss contended that this condition is biologically based in male and female characteristics, which are present in both men and women. Although Freud rejected the organismic in favor of the psychological viewpoint, he accepted the validity of the theory of bisexuality as explaining many traits of human behavior. Freud's brilliant and wayward disciple Carl Jung picked up this theme of male-in-female and female-in-male, translating it in terms of archetypes of human consciousness rather than biological fixtures or psychological entities. Whatever the individual's mode of conduct, the theory of bisexuality sheds light on Agape as well as Eros, for it shows the human being as capable of expressing tender as well as aggressive emotions.

On the historical level Eros expresses itself in the form of regeneration of the life force amid a decaying civilization. On this plane Eros transcends the various modes of sexuality among individuals and encompasses the spirit of the times or *Weltanschauung* of an epoch. Such an age of spiritual rebirth occurred, according to the social-existentialist philosopher Karl Jaspers, during the "axial period" of human history between 800 and 200 B.C. with the independent emergence in China, India, Persia, Palestine, and Greece of spiritual leaders such as Confucious, Lao-tzu, Buddha, Zarathustra, the postexilic prophets (including Elijah, Isaiah, and Jeremiah), Homer, and Socrates. In concord with these appearances, man began to gain an awareness of his place in nature. This self-consciousness was accompanied by an unprecedented efflorescence of religion, philosophy, and art. World-historical religions were founded; schools of philosophy from skepticism to materialism flourished; and tragedy was born.

According to this interpretation, the second great thrust of Eros on the historical plane took place during what numerous scholars have dubbed "the Renaissance of Western civilization." After twelve centuries of darkness, during which Western man paid obeisance to the rigid authority of the Church, he was born anew to the joys of classical art and learning. The "new birth" of Europe found its most heightened and particular expression in Italy, where painting, for example, combined the genius of original masters (such as Leonardo, Michelangelo, Raphael, and Titian), the overarching medieval theme of Christianity's Holy Trinity, the Greek love of form, and the Latin sensibility. Beyond the revival of classical antiquity, a major motif, which saturates Renaissance art, is the Christ story. As the coming of Christ had crowned the axial age with the jewel of universal absolution from sin, so the Renaissance reincarnated the Crucifixion saga in its art and mores by elevating the individual to the altar of selfhood and moral responsibility. To this day, Western man's ego is at once his mark of Cain and his shining star.

Looming in the Freudian unconscious are death as well as sexual instincts. Drawing upon August Weismann's heuristic division of the living substance into mortal (or "somatic") and immortal (or "germ plasmic") parts in multicellular organisms, Freud deals with two forces operating in the substance. While the sexual instincts perpetually strive to renew life, the death instincts seek to lead the living toward death. In *Beyond the Pleasure Principle* Freud postulates the "nirvana principle," according to which "the dominating tendency of mental life, and perhaps of nervous life in general, is the effort to reduce, to keep constant, or to remove internal tension due to stimuli." This proclivity in the life of human beings finds partial expression in the pleasure principle, which strives to reduce the tension of desires by satisfying them. In addition, Freud uses the nirvana principle as a basis for believing in the existence of death instincts. He assumes that life is striving to return to an initial state of things from which it originally departed. Thus, "the aim of all life is death."

On the supraindividual or historical level the death instinct manifests itself in periods of cultural degeneration, civil war, and international antagonisms. Indeed, the present age has been characterized by Raymond Aron as "the century of total war." Of course, history is replete with wars, plagues, famines, revolutions, crumbling civilizations, and the like. It was Hegel who once remarked that "what we learn from history is that we learn nothing from history." The radical difference between today and yesterday is that with the recent technological development of hydrogen bombs and sophisticated methods of chemical-biological warfare, our species has within its power the means to extinguish itself entirely. Freud was a pessimist with regard to human affairs. He recognized a death wish in the collectivity as well as in the individual. But he had not completely given up hope. In the concluding paragraphs of *Civilization and Its Discontents* Freud invokes the life force, Eros, as the other heavenly power to rise up and defeat its equally immortal adversary, Thanatos.

LATER CAREER

In his later years, Freud turned to the elder-philosopher role and began to comment on the issues of war and peace, the drift of modern secular history, and the place of man in the biological cosmos. To the end of his days in 1939 Freud wore the mantle of scientist-explorer. In a lengthy letter to Einstein in 1932 Freud expressed the hope that a combination of the "cultural attitude" against war and the fear of the consequences of a future war might result in its elimination as an outmoded institution.

In *Civilization and Its Discontents* he posed the key question of the modern era: Is not civilization founded upon repression, and, if so, is not the universal neurosis of mankind its price? Unlike Marx, who sees the historical deck as stacked against the collectivity, Freud sees it as stacked against the individual. In lieu of *homo economicus* Freud presents us with an image of man as *homo sexualis,* whose irrational drives must be channeled into productive labor in order for civilization to carry on. Society sublimates sex into the striving for success.

As a champion of the Enlightenment, Freud was highly suspicious of any notions that would contradict his famous dictum, "Where id is, there shall ego be." Although he was not blind to suffering and to the sources and means for overcoming it, he maintained his rational posture and dismissed religion as a consolation for the person who possesses neither art nor science. In *The Future of an Illusion* he psychoanalyzes religion as a projected superego of the helpless individual who identifies with an omnipotent and omniscient God, the father-king. Like the skeptical Voltaire, Freud wanted to live without illusions and preferred to cultivate Reason's garden.

The epidemic of psychoanalysis

Within the span of a half-century, the psychoanalytic movement gathered disciples, both wayward and orthodox, and established professional associations in countries around the globe. Psychoanalytic thinking has penetrated the social sciences as well as the humanities. Whole societies have been explained by a cultural "unconscious," and studies on the sexual customs and habits of populations have been published. No longer is a classic appreciated on the sole basis of art for art's sake; nowadays, we inquire à la Freud into the artist's early childhood secrets or sexual hangups to see what really makes him tick.

By 1909 Freud had achieved international recognition. In that year he journeyed to America to deliver a series of lectures at Clark University in Worcester, Massachusetts. He gave five talks in German to large audiences on the fundamental techniques of psychoanalysis and was generally well received by such American psychological luminaries as Adolf Meyer, Edward Titchener, and William James. The lectures were published as *The History of the Psychoanalytic Movement.* In this polemic he explained his revolutionary ideas, sketched the movement's history, and castigated Alfred Adler and Carl Jung as heretics.

Whereas Freud's ambition was the modest one of minimizing the harm men might do to one another, Adler and Jung leaped beyond their teacher in a quasi-religious attempt to find a *cure* for man's suffering. Jung was a kind of spiritual medicine man, who guided his patients on the path to "individuation" by helping them to realize underlying and universal archetypes of human nature. His search for salvation focused on man and his symbols in an effort to reveal the mythical infrastructure in the history of consciousness. Jung is becoming increasingly popular among today's young, with their increasing interest in spiritual rather than psychological knowledge. His scholarly concern with Tibetan and Chinese religious classics has helped to awaken this interest.

Adler was more concerned with the phenomenon of power in society, and he based his psychotherapy upon the patient's neurotic sense of powerlessness or inferiority. The thrust of his teaching was the attempt to understand and to cure this condition by the psychotherapeutic reawakening of social interest. Adler comprehended sexual conflicts more as products of the individual's maladjustments in his later social milieu than as reflections of early childhood difficulties. Adler, Karl Menninger, Harry Stack Sullivan, and Carl Rogers emphasized social more than sexual factors in the etiology of mental illness. Notwithstanding Freud's early indignation, their work has made the greatest impact upon the practice of psychotherapy in America.

Freud's last testament

Freud continued to live in his beloved Vienna until the situation there became intolerable. With the rise of Hitler to power in Germany the predicament of the Jews worsened. Psychoanalysis was "liquidated" in Germany. Freud's and other psychoanalytic books were burned in Berlin in 1933, and Jews were forbidden to serve on any scientific council. The Nazis seized control of the German Society for Psychotherapy, renamed it the International General Medical Society for Psychotherapy, and required all members to make Hitler's *Mein Kampf* the basis for their work. Several official Nazi psychotherapists met with representatives of the Society and informed them that psychoanalysis could continue only if Jews were excluded from membership. Threats accompanied pressure, and the leveling process continued as the various branches of science were "nationalized," brought under a central control, and geared to serve National-Socialist aims. In lieu of Freud's psychoanalysis and Einstein's theory of relativity, Nazi science adopted the doctrine of Aryan racial superiority.

With the Nazi invasion of Austria in March 1938, the streets of Vienna were lined with roaring tanks and train loads of patriotic "extras" shouting, "Heil Hitler!" Freud was surprisingly reluctant to leave his native land; but his biographer and friend Ernest Jones managed to convince him and arranged the complicated diplomatic details of Freud's emigration from Austria to England. However, the Nazis extracted their pound of flesh. They confiscated Freud's bank account and demanded a fugitive tax, without which they threatened to confiscate his library and art collection. During these trying times Freud worked an hour a day on his *Moses and Monotheism,* which tormented him like a "ghost not laid."

During his short stay in London Freud continued to practice psychoanalysis, kept up his correspondence, worked consistently on *Moses and Monotheism,* and received visiting dignitaries. His callers included the writer H. G. Wells, the anthropologist Bronislaw Malinowski, the painter Salvador Dali, and the Zionist leader Chaim Weizmann. Three secretaries of the Royal Society asked him to sign its Charter Book, which contained the signatures of Newton and Darwin. Although Freud was in agony from a jaw cancer that eventually claimed his life, he received these accolades with the grace of a nobleman and maintained his sense of humor to the end. Upon hearing a radio announcement to the effect that this war was to be the last war, a friend asked Freud if he believed that. Freud replied, "Anyhow it is my last war."

Freud's last will and testament was *Moses and Monotheism.* In this quasi-mystical, novelistic essay of self-discovery, Freud develops his general theory of monotheism, which focuses on Moses as the father figure and lawgiver of the Judeo-Christian tradition. Saul of Tarsus, the renegade rabbi who is commonly known as St. Paul, was to organize Christianity in early-second-century Rome on the foundations of original sin and salvation through sacrificial death. Saul's revelation was that human suffering is the effect of having murdered God the father, and his mission as the Apostle Paul was to preach that the sacrificial victim was indeed the long-awaited Messiah in the person of Jesus Christ, the Son of God. Freud argued that Christianity, which emerged from ancient Judaism, became a "Son religion" as a result of having displaced the slain primal father. In *Moses and Monotheism* Freud not only amplified and extended the insights of *Totem and Taboo* and *The Future of an Illusion;* he was also reacting covertly to the oncoming pogrom. He concludes his book about Moses with the wry observation: "Only a part of the Jewish people accepted the new doctrine. Those who refused to do so are still called Jews."

Beyond the personal meaning that this rather speculative work had for Freud, *Moses and Monotheism* is highly suggestive theoretically. Its methodology rests on the projection of the psychoanalytic procedure onto the world-historical plane. The history of a people may be read as if it were the history of an individual, with the intention of unearthing the cultural secrets or "repressed content" of the collectivity, whether the latter be a cult, a nation, a religion, or a civilization. Research along this line might illuminate the phenomenon of leadership in accordance with Freud's emphasis on leaders as embodiments of the collective superego. Such an approach would allow freer reign for what Mills called "the sociological imagination" to come to grips with what is going on in today's world at the fine point where biography intersects with society and history.

CRITICISM AND ADVANCES

Freud's theories gave rise to a flurry of psychological experiments in the 1930s and 1940s. Most of these were dubious tests of his hypotheses; for example, attempts were made to test repression by seeing if people find it harder to remember unpleasant things than pleasant ones, even though the mechanism of repression was postulated only for strong instinctual drives and their derivatives. A combination of behaviorist orthodoxy and middle-class America's reluctance to deal with any of the strong emotional drives that Freud was discussing has meant that academic psychology has done little to follow up his leads. Clinical practice, on the other hand, has heeded Freud's recommendations to pay attention to emotions and behaviors of which we are not ordinarily conscious (for example, childhood experiences, sex, and aggression). That clinical psychologists and psychiatrists are ambivalent about the veracity of Freudian theories and the effectiveness of his therapeutic methods should not obscure the fact that Freud's most basic discoveries have been vindicated, so much so that they have almost passed into the realm of common knowledge.

Another criticism that may be leveled against Freud is that he reified his concepts. Notwithstanding his analytic disclaimers, he treated such mental ephemera as ego, id, superego, consciousness, and unconsciousness as if they were real objects. Although definitions are arbitrary and concepts only heuristic devices, Freudian terminology has come to be used by many professionals and laymen as if these ideas were real in themselves. There is a measure of truth in the assertion that concepts, once entrenched in the literature, develop a life of their own; however, this linguistic phylogenesis must not blur the distinction between the real and the nominal. It should be underlined that Freud's conceptualizations are analytic tools rather than actual entities.

In addition to having observational bias and tending to reify concepts, Freud was culturally bound in his thought. His Eros/Thanatos duality is subject to this critique, in the sense that Freud's attitude toward death reflects a pessimistic period of Western thought. In conjunction with his contemporaries, Freud regarded aging and death as the irresistible antitheses of life. This viewpoint contrasts with such recent Western European psychological paradigms of inner growth as Erikson's "ages of man" and Maslow's "hierarchy of needs" and contradicts Eastern doctrines of spiritual rebirth, through which aspirants attain enlightenment and come to see the world through the eyes of one newly born. Neither age nor sex is a barrier to this experience, as long as life is understood as a process of interior growth and personal development rather than as a slow decline into the grave.

The most valid criticism of Freud is that he observed repressed, middle-class, Victorian men and women and generalized from them to all mankind. Twentieth-century anthropological research by Bronislaw Malinowski, Margaret Mead, and others has shown that neither the latency period nor the Oedipus complex is universal. The type of adult sexual repression that Freud found in the social milieu of his day is by no means characteristic of all cultures. In addition to traditional societies on the Asian, African, and South American continents, contemporary lower- and middle-class subcultures in Europe and North America have mores different from Freud's formulations.

However, these conditions do not warrant abandoning Freud. One should rather make the appropriate theoretical modifications. A primary reason for the general unwillingness to update Freud has been the dogmatism of neo-orthodox Freudians, who resist seeing their master's work as just one phase of discovery rather than as the essence of knowledge. This is the school of "right-wing" conservatism, which heavily emphasizes biological sequences and the determining effect of early childhood. But there is also a group of "left-wing" Freudians, including Erik Erikson, Karen Horney, Erich Fromm, Geza Roheim, Herbert Marcuse, and Fritz Perls, who have opened up a broad path for social and historical factors to enter this ongoing colloquy on human nature.

If Freud's work is understood as describing a particular historical period, it is a valuable complement to that of Weber. The Protestant-ethic personality—hard-working, uptight, repressed, puritanical—is exactly what Freud was depicting. Thus, the dictum "Neurosis is the price we pay for civilization" is the clinical insight corresponding to Weber's pessimism about the effects of rationalization and bureaucratization on the quality of modern life.

Freud also complements Durkheim and Sorel. Durkheim was of two minds about modern society. At first he argued that "organic solidarity" was a sufficient condition for social order, even though the contractual network first had to emerge from the emotionally binding "mechanical solidarity" of traditional societies. Later, after the Dreyfus affair and the tremendous conflict of turn-of-the-century France, Durkheim reconsidered and concluded that a purely formal, rules-and-regulations type of society created widespread anomie. As a social remedy for the normless state of affairs he advocated a return to workers' guilds, in which emotional solidarity could be found. Freud bolsters the later phase of his French contemporary's theory by suggesting that if peoples' feelings are overly repressed, any strains in the social order are likely to cause a channeling of pent-up emotion into social movements that allow them an outlet.

Sorel, writing in Durkheim's day, says the same thing from another point of view when he describes how group solidarity can express itself through violence against an alien group. The civil-rights, peace, and now Maoist revolutionary movements draw their psychological strength from the same "us-them" principle. Its hidden side manifests itself as solidarity in group martyrdom as well as in committing what Sorel called "purifying violence." Recent rebellions on university and college campuses throughout the world owe at least part of their motivation to a striving for solidarity in the streets that cannot be found in official bureaucracies. Here, as in the emerging synthesis of sociological theory, Freud maintains his contemporary relevance.

CHAPTER EIGHT

THE DISCOVERY OF THE INVISIBLE WORLD: SIMMEL, COOLEY, MEAD

SIMMEL

At about the same time when Emile Durkheim was giving sociology a distinctive scientific identity in France, a similar attempt was being made in Germany. The German Durkheim was Georg Simmel (1858–1918), whose career is strikingly similar to Durkheim's—and also strikingly different. For Durkheim was successful, and Simmel was not. Like Durkheim, Simmel formulated a view of society as a level of analysis independent of observable individuals, with laws of its own that required a separate science to investigate them. Simmel pointed out more clearly than anyone that since only individual men are physically real, the subject matter of sociology must be an invisible world of symbols and forms of interaction. He thus avoided some of the possible mystification inherent in Durkheim's "collective conscience." But Durkheim went on to become one of the most prominent thinkers in France, while Simmel spent twenty-nine long years waiting to be called to a professorship in Germany. All his life Simmel was an outsider, and his work shows both the strengths and weaknesses peculiar to that position.

Simmel came from a wealthy and cultured Jewish family, and indeed his work is full of the echoes of music, art, and drawing-room conversation. After studying philosophy, he became a *privatdozent* (private lecturer) at the University of Berlin in 1885. Not until 1914—just four years before his death— was he to gain the long-sought promotion to full professor. Forces conspired to keep him out. He was a Jew in a time of growing anti-Semitism, a liberal in Imperial Germany, the proponent of a discipline, sociology, that was associated with the un-German politics of Comte and Spencer. Simmel retreated more and more into the world of art and sociability, his sociology becoming a collection of insights—a theory of society, as it were, as if seen by a passer-by, catching a few features as they strike the eye but never penetrating to the heart of the edifice. Like the subject of one of his most famous essays, Simmel was the stranger who sees things that other men, wrapped in their familiar routines, cannot see, the man privy to secrets given him because he has no one to tell them to.

The formal background of Simmel's sociology was the tradition of German philosophy—Kant, Hegel, Dilthey, Wundt—which showed how man sees the world through a veil of his own perceptual forms and how these forms were passed on through human history in language, artistic ideals, myths, and legal systems. Accordingly, Simmel argues that society is an *invisible world* with laws of its own. These laws are found in the flow of culture—language, technology, social institutions, art— which molds each new generation along the lines of the past, and in the forms or patterns of interaction among men that have effects on what they may individually do. But man is also a living individual. The culture that molds him and the interactions that constrain him are what make him human, but they are also something external and alien. The drama of man is, then, a struggle between the individual and the social—a drama that is fundamentally a tragedy, for the two forces must always exist together in every living man.

Simmel's sensitivity to these two simultaneous levels of existence resulted in a striking insight, one that has been followed up only recently: The social institutions that make up the relatively permanent heritage of a society—the state, the family, the economy, the class structure—are only an extended version of the everyday interactions of men and women meeting on the street, in stores and offices, or at a party. Thus, by studying the formal structure of the more fleeting encounters, we reach the essence of our invisible society.

"The interactions we have in mind when we talk about 'society' are crystallized as definable, consistent structures such as the state and the family, the guild and the church, social classes and organizations based on common interests," wrote Simmel.

But in addition to these, there exists an immeasurable number of less conspicuous forms of relationship and kinds of interaction. Taken singly, they may appear negligible. But since in actuality they are inserted into the comprehensive and, as it were, official social formations, they alone produce society as we know it. . . . Without the interspersed effects of countless minor syntheses, society would break up into a multitude of discontinuous systems. Sociation continuously emerges and ceases and emerges again. Even where its eternal flux and pulsation are not sufficiently strong to form organizations proper, they link individuals together. That people look at one another and are jealous of one another; that they exchange letters or dine together; that irrespective of all tangible interests they strike one another as pleasant or unpleasant; that gratitude for altruistic acts makes for inseparable union; that one asks another man after a certain street, and that people dress and adorn themselves for one another—the whole gamut of relations that play from one person to another and that may be momentary or permanent, conscious or unconscious, ephemeral or of grave consequence (and from which these illustrations are quite casually chosen), all these incessantly tie men together. Here are the interactions among the atoms of society. They account for all the toughness and elasticity, all the color and consistency of social life, that is so striking and yet so mysterious.[1]

In one of his essays Simmel speaks of men whose profession is to sit at home in full dinner dress, ready for a call from superstitious hostesses who find that they have a dinner party of thirteen about to sit down at table. Simmel was himself something of a "fourteenth man at dinner." Always the outsider, even in his chosen sphere of fleeting encounters, Simmel could not divest himself of his sociologist's detachment. Even more so than his later incarnation Erving Goffman (whom we shall meet in Chapter 12), Simmel was simultaneously within and without; neither completely participant nor completely observer; and his writings are a texture of insights that never quite make a solid system.

Simmel was the first to remove sociability from the realm of the taken-for-granted and to analyze it as part of social structure. Sociability, he pointed out, is a little world within the world, with laws all of its own. Here one did not allow practical and serious matters to intrude. The doings of the outer world might provide the starting place as subject matter for conversation, but the conversation was to rule the subjects and not vice versa. In the hands of skilled conversationalists, politics, business, art, gossip, the weather all become the vehicle for talk that is carried on for the sake of talking, as raw material to be shaped by the formal requirements of these artists of fleeting symbols. Sociability is thus a world of make-believe, making the world of "outer" reality into a fantasy-land that exists solely for the pleasure of the players.

In the same vein, Simmel offers a perceptive analysis of the game of flirtation (which suggests that he must have been experienced at it— as do his knowledgeable remarks on love affairs and secrets). In its most refined form flirtation takes the raw material of sex and weaves from it a fabric of delight and fantasy, a symbolic world which turns the simplicity of physical passion into the subtle universe of love. By such

[1] Georg Simmel, *The Sociology of Georg Simmel,* Kurt H. Wolf, ed. Published in 1950 by The Free Press Division of The Macmillan Company. Reprinted by permission.

sketches Simmel takes us into the heart of the salon society of Europe in one of its most dazzling eras.

But Simmel never really pushes through to a sociological theory of the causes and effects of sociability or pursues the ramifications of his view of man's symbolic performances into a general model of society. He does not draw the implication, just recently being developed, that men create their world views out of just such encounters—not only in polite upper-bourgeois drawing rooms, but in all classes of society—and that it is just such shared fantasy-worlds that bind some men together and set them off against others. Simmel's payoff is aesthetic rather than sociological. He concludes his discussion of sociability with the observation that polite conversation has the same sort of function as a majestic view of the ocean: Both give pleasure because they transmute the turmoil of life into a pleasing spectacle, viewed from a distance. The tragedy of conflict and failure, of individual versus society, exists in sociability as in serious life, but as material for play, and hence no longer dangerous and uncontrolled. The conversationalist emerges victorious in his world of symbols.

Simmel's sociology ranged much wider than drawing rooms, to include the serious realms of power, money, and historical change. As always, this material yields insights to Simmel's eye as he abstracts out the formal properties of diverse situations. His analyses of the effects of group size are classic, demonstrating that a group too large for all its members to converse together will have a different structure than a smaller one.

The point is drawn even more sharply when he compares two-person groups with three-person groups. The dyad's fundamental reality is its perishability, for it will dissolve whenever one person decides to leave; this gives each partner a particular hold on the other. The triad, however, has a basic independence of its members, for it will still exist if one person leaves. The individual thus becomes less significant to the group. Moreover, new configurations open up here, as it becomes possible for two to form a coalition against the third, or one to play the other two off against each other. In short, the whole realm of organized society and its power relations opens up through shifts in numbers and in the resulting geometry of social relationships. Simmel thus develops the meaning of Thoreau's remark, "I have three chairs in my house: one for solitude, two for company, three for society."

Simmel had other insights, some of them brilliant, on the structure of group conflicts, on the social relationships created by secrets, on the way in which the variety of groups in modern society gives each man a distinctive set of social ties and hence produces modern individualism. But Simmel never really carries these ideas far enough to produce a comprehensive sociological theory. Unlike Durkheim, he does not try to test causal propositions against empirical evidence, but only to display a philosophy of the forms that flicker across the human landscape. At bottom, Simmel, the lonely outsider, hated society. He wrote that men in groups are ruled by the lowest common denominator and that the higher forms of intellect and morality are always individual products. This personal disposition contradicted Simmel's own insights on the ways in which man is a product of society, and it kept him from pressing on to the breakthroughs that came to Durkheim when he realized that men's moralities and ideas have their origins in groups and their rituals.

But if Simmel, the outsider of the German intellectual world, could not produce a genuine sociology from the leads it offered, there were others who would. The American universities had been reformed in the 1870s and 1880s along German lines, and American intellectuals were shaking off the stupor of the era of petty religious colleges. The new American sociologists, full of the same German philosophy that sustained Simmel and impressed by the empirical approaches of the new experimental psychology, were to succeed where Simmel failed. In Cooley and Mead, the relationship between the invisible world of social symbols and the mind of the individual man was to become a theory of considerable power.

THE LIFE AND WORK OF COOLEY

Charles Horton Cooley (1864–1929) was born in Ann Arbor, Michigan, as the fourth of six children. His father was a migrant from western New York, who had a distinguished career as a justice on Michigan's Supreme Court. Charles was an introspective, imaginative, and ambitious boy, who read profusely. He prepared himself for college at age sixteen; however, ill health forced him to take seven years to graduate from Michigan in 1887. Before taking his doctorate in economics in 1894, Cooley studied mechanical engineering, worked for the Interstate Commerce Commission, and traveled abroad. For his doctoral dissertation he presented a theory of transportation relating a socioeconomic solution of the railway question to the study of territorial demography. This work remains a bench mark in "human ecology," a field that was to be fruitfully researched and developed by Roderick McKenzie, Robert Park, and Ernest Burgess in Chicago a generation hence.

Cooley's early inspiration came from Emerson, Goethe, and Darwin. From Herbert Spencer, whom he criticized subsequently for his subjectivity and lack of "culture," Cooley received his first broad outline of evolutionary knowledge. Franklin Giddings of Columbia University encouraged his aspirations to teach sociology as a university subject at Michigan. Cooley was a member of an academic clique that admired John Dewey, whose personality and lectures on political economy in 1893 and 1894 made a deep impression on Cooley's mentality. Dewey criticized and went beyond Spencer by maintaining that society was an organism in a more profound way than the latter had perceived. Dewey's analysis of language as the "sensorium" of society corroborated

Cooley's burgeoning interpretation of written language as the social medium of transmission par excellence.

While preparing his thesis, Cooley became intrigued by the "psychic mechanism"; he was especially concerned with the transmission and modes of recording language through space and time. He studied these processes in their historical and contemporary forms until he developed a conception of communication that was consistent with his organic view of society. In his lectures and studies he continually related his findings to such major aspects of the social process as conflict, survival, and adaptation. Cooley transcended the Darwinian climate of opinion by becoming a social psychologist. He came to the realization that he could never actually *see* the social life of man unless he understood the processes of mind with which society was indissolubly linked. He observed the mental-social development of his children as a method of organizing and expanding his theoretical insights. After beginning to teach, he read Walter Bagehot, William James, Gabriel Tarde, and Mark Baldwin and readied himself for his first book in 1902, *Human Nature and the Social Order.* Cooley preferred a life of contemplation and continued to teach at his Midwestern alma mater all his life. He turned down a professorship at Columbia, although he did consent reluctantly to serve as president of the American Sociological Society in 1918.

COOLEY'S SYSTEM

Cooley's social thought encompasses several interrelated dimensions: (1) His approach was organic; (2) his viewpoint was evolutionary; (3) his outlook was moral and progressive; and (4) his ideal was democratic.

His organicism rested upon the theoretical assumption of the reciprocity of the individual and society. In his first book he systematically debunks the alleged antithesis of the individual versus society on the grounds that the latter is a psychical whole of which the individual is a particular expression. As the separate individual is a myth, so is society an illusion when conceived of apart from individual members. For Cooley "society" and "individuals" are collective and distributive aspects of the same thing rather than empirically separable phenomena. Thus, society becomes a living whole, or organism, composed of differentiated members, each of which has a special function. A university, for example, is composed of administrators, faculty, and students, with each status group having particular roles to perform within the organizational structure. This approach was a predecessor of the emerging functionalist system.

Cooley's evolutionary viewpoint suffuses his system; yet it differs from the social evolutionism of Spencer and the leading nineteenth-century anthropologists in its emphasis on individual rather than collective aspects of development. He is more concerned with the evolution of the individual's social being (how the growing organism acquires a sense of the "I") than with grand historical sequences or stages of cultural evolution. His view encourages the student of human nature to believe in life as a creative process of which the human will is an integral ingredient. Far from being a passive element of society, each individual does his unique share in the work of the common whole. Cooley perceived each individual as a "fresh organization of life," which flows from the hereditary and social past. He envisioned each life history as containing a stream and a road; he discerned the stream as heredity, which comes through the germ plasm. He apprehended the road as "communication or social transmission," including language, interaction, and education. The road, which contemporary sociologists might call "culture," is a later development than the stream.

Cooley's moral outlook is expressed in his equation of rationality with the judgment of right. By rationality Cooley meant more than the product of formal reasoning; he pointed to the more profound rationality of conscience as an outcome of the social life of a person, including one's interactions with others and imaginary conversations with oneself. By locating society in the mind, Cooley, in his ethical treatise "The Social Aspect of Conscience," was able to explain the moral nature of confession as the opening of oneself to another, higher, more ideal person from whose vantage point one is able to obtain an outside view of oneself. Cooley's morality was thus rational, social, and progressive. While he did not feel, like some ethnocentric evolutionists, that twentieth-century culture was the apex of civilization, he did believe in the necessity for mankind to have a high and vivid image of personality that was morally edifying. Man's reach, so to speak, should exceed his grasp. He discerned three practically universal ideas of right: loyalty to the group, kindness to group members, and adherence to the customs of the tribe. Whereas his contemporary Max Weber understood the rationalization of the world in terms of continual disenchantment (for example, the recent demystification of the moon), Cooley stressed the possibilities for personal growth in a right (that is, rational) society efficiently organized according to democratic principles.

His conception of democracy embodied a philosophy of mind-enlarging consciousness. Cooley found the earliest forms of democratic unity in Western civilization among the pre-Roman Teutonic tribes, especially in the social units of the family, clan, and village group. Without indirect communications media such as the telegraph, telephone, radio, and television, people had to come together in face-to-face contact to experience the rising tide of social excitement that led to higher levels of consciousness. The men of old held feasts, games, and public assemblies and ceremonies as occasions for group exhaltation and as opportunities for the expression of public opinion. Modern-day Americans celebrate the astronauts' moon landing through the mass medium of television; the Romans fed Christians to the lions in stone stadiums; and the ancients chanted, sang, and danced festively around the campfire. The Woodstock, Altamont and Sky River rock festivals are contemporary examples of a return to primitive modes of togetherness, with the added thrill of amplified sound made possible by recent technological and cultural developments. Cooley stated that although "democracy as a spirit is spontaneous," it could only have a large-scale spiritual effect with the liberation of the creative faculties of the members composing the body politic. He saw in the present epoch the potentiality for a "higher and freer consciousness" and understood democracy as the general phase of that enlarged consciousness.

Cooley comprehended institutions as definite and established products of the public mind, which were the outcomes of the organization and crystallization of thought around the forms of customs, symbols, beliefs, and lasting sentiments. He perceived such institutions as language, the family, industry, education, religion, and law as continually responsive to the needs of human nature. He saw them as "apperceptive systems" of the public mind, which were inseparable from and unreal without relation to one another. Here again one can notice glimmerings of functionalism; Cooley, however, did not make the mistake of reifying the social system and locating needs in it rather than in the people who created it. Since *sociality* is mental, the institution is an individual habit of mind that is largely unconscious because of its commonality. The individual is not merely a passive effect of the social order, he is an effective cause as well.

THE LOOKING-GLASS SELF AND THE PRIMARY GROUP

In *Human Nature and the Social Order* Cooley presents his theory of the social self. Drawing upon Wilhelm Wundt and especially upon William James, he discusses the meaning of the "I" as observed in daily thought and speech. This "I" is the empirical self that can be verified by observation; it is neither an a priori Cartesian assumption nor a metaphysical entity. Cooley observed that this primal idea referred least often to the body and most often to either the "my feeling" or to the "looking-glass self." He regarded the self as a feeling state that is more or less consistent with ideas as they arise in our experience. The former "my" attitude refers to the individual's sense of appropriation toward various objects and people. He gives the example of gloating as a reflective self-feeling state in which the person who has either accomplished or acquired something that is pleasing thinks "mine, mine, mine" with a warm sensation. Cooley extends James' definition of psychology as the study of states of consciousness by establishing the sociality of selfhood as it relates to the thought of others. The social self emerges as an idea taken from the communicative life that the mind treasures as its own.

It was from this line of reasoning that the concept of the looking-glass self was born. In order to grasp this germinal idea, one should bear in mind Cooley's dictum: "The imaginations people have of one another are the solid facts of society." The dimensions of the looking-glass self are threefold: First, we imagine our appearance or image in the eyes of the other; second, we imagine some judgment of that appearance; and finally, we experience some sort of self-feeling such as pride or mortification. In other words, "I feel about me the way I think you think of me." For example, a person would be ashamed to appear ignorant in the presence of a learned man, or glad to be recognized by a celebrity. This phenomenon pervades our everyday existence in the social arena at even subtler levels than shame or joy. All the little looks and gestures that happen in daily encounters with others constitute the very fabric of society. This aspect of Cooley's sociology has been developed in the social thought of Erving Goffman, a man whom we shall meet in a later chapter.

In *Social Organization* (1909) Cooley introduced the concept of the primary group. Such an association is characterized by intimacy, face-to-face interaction, emotional warmth, and cooperation. These groups are the seedbeds of society in the sense that they are fundamental in forming the social nature of the individual and his primary ideals, including love, freedom, and justice. The outcome of a primary relationship involves a "we" feeling that makes for close identification of the self with the life of the group. Sociologically universal examples of this mode of association are the children's play group, the family, the neighborhood, and the council of elders. The basic experience of the primary group is the feeling of social unity with other members. In contemporary times primary groups have been emerging in the form of urban and rural communes, as people begin to band together with varying degrees of success for survival purposes and to re-experience a lost or shattered home life. For Cooley the self-governing, democratic village commune was the highest social form. He quotes Tocqueville: "It is man who makes monarchies and establishes republics, but the commune seems to come directly from the hand of God."

In contrast to the primary group the "secondary group" is impersonal, contractual, formal, and rational. Relationships are cool rather than warm. Professional associations, corporate bureaucracies, and nation-states are classic examples of this group type. But primary and secondary groups should not be taken as mutually exclusive categories. For example, primary groups may emerge within the secondary bureaucracies in the forms of boards of directors, academic cliques, circles of confidants, and like-minded associates.

CRITICISMS OF COOLEY

Cooley's methodology was one of "sympathetic introspection." By this he meant the process of the social scientist putting himself in touch with various sorts of persons, attempting to imagine how the world appears to them, and then recollecting and describing as closely as possible their particular feeling states. By this method Cooley essayed to understand the inner lives of rich and poor, criminals and children, conservatives and radicals, idiots and idealists. No phase of human nature was alien to him, so deep and wide were his sympathies. He took his own nature as a reflecting prism of the whole, and by examining his responses to others' presentations of self, he sought to pierce the invisible veil of society.

Since Cooley's methodology was analogous to Max Weber's *verstehen* and Pitirim Sorokin's "logico-meaningful" method, it may be criticized on similar grounds. A major canon of scientific method is that its statements must be intersubjectively testable; otherwise, reliability of results becomes impossible. Indeed, one of the scientific dilemmas of Western sociology has been the immense difficulty of agreeing upon uniform methods and procedures. Since Cooley depended primarily on his personal powers of observation and drew his insights by an imaginative reconstruction of society from his peculiar vantage point, there would be no way for objective social scientists to test his conclusions empirically. Mead himself took Cooley to task for locating society in the mind instead of in the social world out of which psychical experiences arise. However, Cooley was breaking new ground by locating the self in consciousness rather than in behavior and therefore felt free to unload his mind of positivist baggage. Methodological precision concerned him far less than breadth of comprehension.

Cooley was a sanguine and optimistic practitioner, whose small-town sociology is suffused with the mores and attitudes of Midwestern, white, Anglo-Saxon, Protestant liberalism. Cooley spent most of his life with his family and in the academic cloister at Ann Arbor, preferring not to venture into the flow of surrounding society. The prime advantages of this sheltered existence were the opportunities to meditate calmly and deeply on the quality of social life and to consolidate an expanding sociology department at the University of Michigan. The main disadvantage was Cooley's failure to come into direct or frequent contact with people of diverse modes of life. He understood the problems of social organization in terms of personal degeneracy; his analysis, while penetrating, was more speculative than empirical. His uplifting armchair sociology rings with a kind of idealization of the real, which disdained the painstaking task of data gathering.

Unlike Freud, Cooley was relatively out of touch with the world of unconscious wishes and motives. Cooley accepted Goethe's notion of man as a unified whole and rejected both biological and psychological determinism. The underlying theme of Cooley's theory of self was the metaphor of growth. His faith was in man's untapped potentialities, or what Dewey called "the infinite perfectability of man." Cooleyan sociology was a rationalistic blend of the provincial and the universal. The former attitude was a reflection of an isolationist America that had yet to be swept onto the international scene by a world war, while the latter pointed to the essentially Christian foundations of American civilization and the subsequent emergence of the national drive to "make the world safe for democracy."

THE LIFE AND WORK OF MEAD

George Herbert Mead (1863–1931) was born in South Hadley, Massachusetts, the son of a pastor. He studied at Harvard under the tutorship of Josiah Royce and William James. He traveled widely and took courses at overseas universities, mainly in Germany. In 1893 he was awarded a recently founded chair in philosophy at the University of Chicago, where John Dewey became a colleague and personal friend. Mead taught there until his death in 1931. He exercised a tremendous influence on several generations of students, principally through his oral teaching; his publications during his life consisted of scattered articles, notes, and critical studies in various philosophical, psychological, sociological, and pedagogical journals.

All those who knew Mead personally were unanimous in remembering him as a rare, high, and disinterested spirit. He was a professor who knew how to charm as well as interest his students. He had a manner well suited to the exposition of ideas; he reasoned in a spiral by returning to what he had already said and then integrating it at a higher level of understanding. He made a new point with each line of reasoning, weaving previous threads into a larger and more comprehensive fabric of thought. Colleagues and students admitted, moreover, that conversation was his medium; writing was a poor second best. Despite the pressure of the academic world to "publish or perish," Mead became chairman of the University of Chicago's philosophy department without having published a single book. Four volumes of lecture notes gathered by pupils and friends were issued posthumously under the titles of *The Philosophy of the Present* (1932), *Mind, Self, and Society* (1934), *Movements of Thought in the Nineteenth Century* (1936), and *The Philosophy of the Act* (1938). Like Georg Simmel, he was a philosopher turned social scientist, and in order to get a clearer portrait of Mead's social psychology within the history of sociological theory it helps to consider his philosophical perspective.

MEAD'S SYSTEM

Mead's social thought is relational, evolutionary, and pragmatic. Upon reading Mead one is struck with a sense of what Alfred North Whitehead called "the interrelatedness of things." As a philosopher of science Mead understood the mechanical and atomistic bias of the nineteenth century as an outcome of past systems of ideas. The chemists and physicists of the preceding century were mainly preoccupied with the notion of matter as composed of static, solid, self-sufficient particles. Their focus was on the structure rather than on the activities of the atom. With the recent emergence of relativistic theories in the natural sciences, atoms were perceived in terms of "eigen states" or "patterns of stability." This shift in emphasis, which provided a wider theoretical frame of reference for explaining physical events, was paralleled in Mead's social psychology by the dissolution of the implicitly atomistic image of man of much nineteenth-century sociology.

The sociologies of Comte, Marx, Spencer, and even Durkheim apprehended the relationship between society and the individual primarily in a deterministic manner. The locus for action resided almost wholly in the social or economic system such that "the invisible hand of society" totally controlled human behavior. The human individual was portrayed as a kind of self-contained molecule within the larger social organism. Mead's relationism consisted of his theoretical joining of self and society in the ongoing social process, such that the individual was neither isolated from his fellows nor wholly determined by any abstract system.

Mead's theoretical achievement was arrived at inductively by observation of what happens in the daily lives of human beings. For Mead the society in which we interact with one another in sundry groups constitutes an empirical reality. It is a product of evolution and is divisible into many modes of social reality, which are dependent upon variable definitions of the situation. He distinguished between Aristotelean and Darwinian ideas of evolution; according to the former doctrine, evolution is the development of the existing plant or animal species (which is the Latin word for the Greek term "form") without reference to the environment. In contrast, the theory presented in Darwin's *Origin of Species* is not concerned with the development of a particular species as such; rather, it is interested in showing how various forms evolve and survive in response to environmental pressures. Those forms survive that can best adapt themselves to changing life conditions. Behind this post-Aristotelean conception is the idea of a life process that takes on various forms (or species), which arise and decline through space and time. The human form is a relatively recent evolutionary development.

It was the German romantic idealists, culminating with Hegel, who formulated a philosophy relevant to the human life form in terms of the reflexive experience of ourselves as actors in the social world. According to this tradition the self is not a static unity that exists *in vacuo;* it is a dynamic, historical process that involves a subject-object relationship and arises as a result of interaction with other selves. The more we become aware of ourselves in the continuing social process, the more we increase our "species consciousness." In other words, we become more able to understand our human form as a consequence of life and social processes.

As a pragmatist philosopher Mead is heir to James and Dewey. Mead viewed modern research science with its mathematical and experimental methods as both a cultural outgrowth of the European Renaissance and Enlightenment and as an emergent evolutionary tool, whereby man might intelligently control his social institutions. He was in agreement with Dewey that scientific method applied to the problems of society was the key to the door of progress. Mead interpreted pragmatist doctrine as having three phases and two primary sources. The former included the following assumptions: (1) that a hypothesis is "true" if it works when tested, (2) that the process of knowing lies within human conduct, and (3) that knowledge is a process of acquiring the necessary "scientific apparatus" (including ideas, concepts, units of analysis, theoretical models, paradigms, equations, and so forth) to carry out the desirable task of social reconstruction in a democratic state. He understood the sources of pragmatism to be (1) behavioristic psychology, which enables the social scientist to apprehend intelligence in terms of human activity, and (2) the process of research or scientific method, which is self-revising and tests a hypothesis by how it works.

Mead recognized the French Revolution as the pivot of modern history; it built the principle of revolution into social institutions by incorporating the people's right to change or amend the constitution upon which the state was founded. The fundamental scientific problem that emerged in Mead's mind, then, was how we become selves in a rapidly changing and seemingly chaotic world. How to preserve order and at the same time accommodate change was Mead's perennial question.

The Social Self

That the human being has a self is the major supposition of Mead's theoretical framework. It is no mystical conjuration but an empirical exercise to observe that human beings make indications to themselves in the course of everyday life. Mead defined these "self-indications" as anything of which one is conscious, such as a ringing telephone, a friend's remark, the lyrics of a song, a thought, the recognition of a familiar figure, and so forth. The importance of discerning the existence of these self-indications is twofold: (1) An object (physical, abstract, or social) may be extricated from its setting and acted upon; and (2) the fact of human self-indication enables the individual's action to be constructed rather than simply released.

Mead distinguished between the *stimulus* and the *object*. The former does not have an intrinsic character that acts upon individuals. In contrast, the meaning of the object is conferred upon it by the individual. Human beings *react to* a stimulus (for instance, an unexpected pin prick), but they *act toward* an object (for example, the determination not to flinch at an injection). The individual is not surrounded by a world of preexisting objects that coerce him; rather, he builds up his environment of objects according to his ongoing activity. From a myriad of prosaic everyday acts, such as getting dressed or preparing food, to major life decisions such as choice of vocation or mate, the individual is making self-notations of objects, assigning them meaning, assessing their utility in reaching various goals, and then deciding what to do on the basis of such judgments. Mead understood this interpretive or self-conversational process as acting on a symbolic basis.

Mead made fuller sense of Dewey's notion of language as the sensorium of society by delving into the symbolic processes of human communication. He distinguished between gesture and symbol, deriving his concept of the former from Wundt's *Völkerpsychologie* and from Darwin's psychological classic *The Expression of the Emotions in Man and Animals.* By the term "gesture" Mead meant a social act that operates as a stimulus for the response of another form engaged in the same act. He presents as an example of a "conversation of gestures" the dogfight, in which the forms interact with one another on a nonsymbolic basis by growling, baring the teeth, and nipping the flanks. In such a situation each dog does not stop to ascertain the meaning of the other's aggressive behavior. One dog's response of growling to the other's baring of teeth is not made on the basis of what that gesture stands for. The first dog does not respond to the *meaning* of the second dog's gesture, because it does not indicate to itself the hostile intentions of that gesture. The adjustive behavior (that is, the ensuing fight) is called forth by the character of the stimulation, without any intermediary process of interpretation of meaning.

Human beings respond not to the gesture but to its meaning; thus, human language or communication is symbolically interactive. Take, for example, the baseball situation of "at bat." The pitcher peers down from the mound to receive the signal from the catcher as to what type of pitch to throw, while the batter checks with the third-base coach for hitting instructions relayed from the manager in the dugout. The catcher may indicate a curve ball by extending, say, two fingers, and the third-base coach may order a bunt by touching his ear and tipping his cap. Thus, before the delivery of the pitch, the situation has been structured according to prearranged signal systems, which have a common meaning (that is, evoke similar responses) for the actors involved. That the pitcher has the option of calling for another pitch and that the batter might be guessing that a curve will be thrown mean that the players are not merely reacting like dogs to gestures; they are interpreting symbolically the meaning of the signs, thereby organizing their activity to act intelligently toward the situation confronting them. When the gesture evokes the same attitude in the receiving as well as the sending form, it is a significant symbol. When the bodily or vocal gesture (speech) reaches that stage, it has become what we call "language."

What enables human beings to interact meaningfully (that is, symbolically) with one another in the ongoing social process is the primary mechanism of role-taking. As the human being becomes an object to himself and learns to act toward himself in various ways, he also learns to assume the roles of others in constructing his behavior. He learns to cast himself imaginatively into the other person's frame of reference and to assume an attitude toward himself that reflects this sympathetic understanding. For example, the parole-board officer attempts to ascertain the prisoner's fitness for parole on the basis of his moral and sympathetic judgment of the prisoner's current attitude toward the law. The self is reflexive in the sense that it coils back upon itself in the communicative process, and it is social in the sense that it is built up continually in the course of daily encounters with other human beings. The social self is a product of a series of defining situations, which arise in the life of the individual. In addition, the social self is an emergent process within society, which Mead construes as the fitting together of individual lines of action in human groups via role-taking.

The social self is neither a static intellectual monad like Descartes' cerebral "I" nor a defense structure such as Freud's executive "ego"; rather, it is a dynamic and changing transaction between the individual and others. Mead described the contents of the social self in terms of "I" and "me" aspects. The conception of the self as binary rather than unitary was mentioned by James and developed by Cooley, but it found its fullest expression in Mead. Mead understood that the social act itself is phasic in that the human being delays his action toward other forms. In preparing his act, the individual can consider the possible responses of the other in lieu of reacting wholly on impulse. Furthermore, the self that organizes its behavior within the social act in relation to other forms is composed of conditioned and spontaneous phases. Mead identifies the former as the "me" and the latter as the "I."

The "me" represents the organized set of group attitudes that the member assumes. It is the conventional, habitual, and routinized aspect of self that is always there. The "me" determines our self-consciousness insofar as we are able to take the role of others within the larger community of selves. Each member of a choir, for example, knows the score he or she is supposed to sing, and the resulting harmony of sound is a product of cooperation among the sopranos, tenors, and basses. The "I" stands for the response of the individual to the organized attitudes of others. It is aware of the social "me" in the sense that the "I" of one moment is present in the "me" of the next. In other words, the "now" or what Mead called "the present" is the sphere of the "I," while the "me" consists of the organization of past attitudes. Mead's "I" accounts for such phenomena as novelty, spontaneity, artistic creativity, and social change in relation to social situations, which function as occasions for the emergence of a creative self. The "I" as construed by Mead is the sociological analogue to Werner Heisenberg's indeterminacy principle in physics. Mead's formulation cracks the ideological edifice of determinism by allowing for the element of chance or free will in human affairs.

Mead developed an original theory of social change from the "I" concept. He understood institutions as social habits that are necessary for the maintenance and preservation of social order. Social control rests ultimately on the exercise of self-control, whereby the individual feels inwardly obliged to respect the rights of others within the community. This relationship of the individual to society becomes highlighted when persons of great mind and moral character emerge and make the wider society a different one. A genius's behavior is as socially conditioned as that of the ordinary person, with the exception that the genius's response to the organized attitude of the group is unique and original. Einstein, for example, lived a relatively simple life; however, his response to physics' universe of discourse was such that the consequences of his theoretical synthesis changed society at large. The lives of such world teachers as Jesus, Buddha, or Socrates are symbolic in the sense that their personal relationships represented an emergent order that was implicit in the institutions of their respective communities. They were deviant with respect to particular public moralities, but conformist in giving complete expression to such central principles of the larger community as rationality, neighborliness, truthfulness, and brotherly love. They were manifestations, so to speak, of higher beings, who, as religious personages and as charismatic leaders endowed by their publics with spiritual authority, approached the social realm from the standpoint of the spiritual plane and were enabled thereby to effect major social change.

The generalized other

Mead's second major contribution to sociological theory was the concept of the "generalized other." In the growth and development of the self the generalized other represents the stage at which the individual Is finally able to relate to himself according to the attitude of the whole community. Prior stages in the genesis of this truly social self are the pre-play, play, and game stages. In the earliest phase of self-genesis the child's baby talk is a reflection of his inability to make an object of himself through which he can approach himself. Mead objected to Tarde's theory of direct imitation because it failed to explain the manner in which the individual learns to make an object of himself, a process that is inherent in the evolution of human selfhood.

During the play stage of socialization, children assume roles segmentally and arbitrarily. They play in a quasi-theatrical way at being mother, father, doctor, television star, or astronaut. During this interval children have a rich fantasy life and begin to take on roles in a rudimentary manner by assuming the vague personalities that populate their minds in a McLuhanesque environment, which has become increasingly electrified since Mead's day. The successive radio and television generations of American youth have derived their symbolic worlds and their role models increasingly from the entertainment media, in-

cluding comic books, movies, and record albums, rather than from literature or personal contact. The mind begins to develop during this
formative stage as the child stimulates his imagination by assuming
inwardly the attitudes of his heroes.

In the game stage the child no longer assumes the attitude of particular individuals toward himself; he ceases taking discrete roles. The
child who plays in a game must be ready to take the attitude of everyone else involved in that game and needs to understand how the different social roles are interrelated. The child is confronted by the
ongoing activity of others, which is organized and has procedural rules.
To grasp the group in terms of its activity is essential. The child learns
the rules of the game not by rote acquisition, but in anticipating how
others are going to act in the game situation and then adjusting his
behavior toward their lines of action and building up his own. According to the framework of symbolic interactionism, learning includes
role playing in a situation where the social self arises in the ongoing
group process.

The final stage of self-development, according to the Meadian schema,
is the generalized other. This concept parallels Durkheim's idea of the
collective conscience and Freud's formulation of the cultural superego.
What is significant about this phase is that the individual has transcended rule-following behavior by becoming conscious of his realization
of the rules. This ability of making an object of his consciousness, of
his own process of self-indication, enables the human being to take an
abstract role, which stands for a series of concrete roles. For example,
the president of an organization assumes an abstract role insofar as he
is aware of the particular roles that constitute the status network of the
hierarchy. Other instances of such complex roles would be those of the
peace negotiator, political ambassador, labor arbitrator, football coach,
United Nations representative, and presidential "troubleshooter." In
each case the individual must be aware of invisible, informal webs of
personal relationships in addition to the organizational loyalties of the
involved social actors.

Mead identified the generalized other with the organized community
or social group that gives the individual his sense of self-unity. The
generalized other entails the extension of role-taking into continuously
expanding social circles, from the Cooleyan primary groups to such
secondary associations as the workers' union, the university, the corporation, the political party, and the nation-state. The whole community,
from the small group to the giant bureaucracy, can express an attitude
only because it is represented in each man's mind as the attitude of the
generalized other. As the size of Spaceship Earth shrinks with technological progress in transportation and communication, a global consciousness begins to emerge in minds around the world. To Mead and those
who follow him in this train of thought, the League of Nations and the
United Nations appear as attempts to institutionalize a planetary gen-

eralized other in order to resolve national conflicts of interests by mediation and mutual understanding rather than by war.

The generalized other is an idea of high explanatory power, which has had considerable influence in the formulation of empirical social research. Herbert Hyman's derivative concept of the "reference group" has become one of the central analytic tools in social psychology. Robert K. Merton and Alice S. Rossi interpreted it in terms of a "social frame of reference," while analyzing the causes of varying degrees of dissatisfaction among World War II troops. Muzafer Sherif employed related concepts in experimental studies of individual conformity to group judgments. Further implications of the concept of the generalized other remain to be explored by future generations of social psychologists.

CRITICISMS AND ASSESSMENTS OF MEAD

A major defect of Mead's sociology is its failure to account for the phenomena of power and stratification. Since he was more concerned with developing a social psychology in which the whole (society) is prior to the part (individual) and in describing the complex process by which the biologic individual acquires a self in the social process, Mead tended to ignore the ways in which men dominate and manipulate one another in political, economic, and status hierarchies. His approach to society was discursive rather than rigorously structural, and his schema neglected to analyze social class and mobility. Although his philosophy was relatively apolitical, it did reflect an underlying liberal ideology of self-improvement through personal change. A radical element of Mead's thought that has not been fully appreciated is his theory of the social consequences of personal change.

Another problem with Mead's theory is the difficulty of operationalizing his concepts for research purposes. Such notions as the "I" and the "me" and the "generalized other" are too vague to quantify in an era during which hard research is measured by elaborate indices, matrices, and tests of statistical significance. Since Mead's universe of discourse lends itself neither to the data-accounting approach to sociology nor to a calculus of theoretical propositions, his social psychology is sometimes regarded as useless for social research.

But the argument may also be reversed. Mead's relational perspective contains a covert critique of positivistic sociology. This critique has been most succinctly stated by Herbert Blumer, one of Mead's former pupils at the University of Chicago. According to Blumer, the fundamental deficiency in contemporary sociology is that it operates with unrealistic images of human beings. Man is not merely a medium through which beliefs, values, norms, and roles work themselves out in behavior; the human being is an acting agent who takes these matters into account in construing his behavior vis-à-vis the situations in which he acts. To be faithful to the character of human group life, it is necessary to recognize human beings as acting organisms organizing their own activity, rather than as neutral entities pushed into action by forces allegedly working through them.

For Blumer the trend in contemporary sociology is to remove sociologists from intimate familiarity with the life and experience of people in society. To the extent that this occurs, they become naïve about the world they propose to study and accept abstract theoretical constructions or answers to a few short survey questions as a sufficient contact with empirical reality. The Medians thus turn the tables on their positivistic detractors. As we shall see in Chapter 12, recent developments in social phenomenology have opened up the possibility of closing the gap between the two perspectives, of bringing about a close analysis of subjective experience as the foundation for more arms-length research methods.

Finally, Mead may be criticized for being naïve in his equation of process with progress. He stressed consciousness and rationality, while paying little attention to the unconscious and irrationality. Indeed, for Mead the Freudian unconscious was a chimera, since whatever people fail to indicate to themselves are things of which they are unaware. Mead's optimism wears a bit thin in view of the violent holocaust that has unfolded since his demise. However, one must remember that Mead was at bottom an ethical philosopher, who, like Durkheim toward the end of his career, was struggling to enunciate what he called a "method of morality." In essays collected under the title *Fragments on Ethics* Mead portrayed man as a rational being, because he is a social being. By analyzing the philosophies of Kant and the utilitarians he arrived at a pragmatic position according to which the only rule ethics can present is that an individual should deal rationally with all the values that are found in a particular problem. Mead's analogue of the Golden Rule was to "act toward other people as you want them to act toward you under the same conditions." His method of morality would take into account the combined and interrelated interests of the individual and society.

Perhaps it is no accident that the discoverers of the invisible world of society were great teachers as well as scholars. As speakers they were spontaneous, subtle, sympathetic, and able to arouse in their hearers attitudes that corresponded to the out of sight world they were depicting. They were creative communicators in that they knew how to make the given problematic. For Simmel, Cooley, and Mead mind is a social process, rather than an isolated entity stuck inside each head like a hive of molecules. Although Mead did chide Cooley for locating self in the mind rather than in the social process, the trio would agree to the proposition that intelligence is social. In their concern for the forms that human relationships might assume in various associations and in their desire to orient their thinking toward a more righteous and just human society, they were above all moral philosophers.

PART THREE

THE VICISSITUDES OF TWENTIETH-CENTURY SOPHISTICATION

CHAPTER NINE

THE DISCOVERY OF THE ORDINARY WORLD: THOMAS, PARK, AND THE CHICAGO SCHOOL

The year 1918 marked the beginning of a new era in American sociology. It saw not only the end of World War I, the coming of women's suffrage, and the decisive dominance of a new urban America, but also the publication of *The Polish Peasant in Europe and America* by William I. Thomas and Florian Znaniecki. This five-volume work, running to 2,244 pages, was a monument in more ways than one, for it represented the first major American effort to study a theoretical question by empirical means. The age of systematic sociological research had just begun.

For its first few decades, such research had a very well-marked home. It was the University of Chicago, from whose medieval stone walls and picturesque courtyards the sociologists of the "Chicago school" sallied forth to investigate the surrounding urban slum. Although subsequently in mild decline, the university enjoyed an intellectual position during the first half of the twentieth century rivaled only by Harvard; Enrico Fermi's cracking of the atom and Robert Hutchins' famous educational reforms were only some of its better-known events. Founded in 1892 on John D. Rockefeller's millions, it sought preeminence from the very beginning. Its first faculty consisted of many of the top thinkers in America, pirated away from rival institutions by Chicago's dynamic president,

William Rainey Harper. The first department of sociology in the world was set up here at its outset, under the chairmanship of Albion W. Small, who had come directly from the presidency of Colby College in Maine.

THOMAS' LIFE AND WORKS

William I. Thomas (1863–1947) was one of the first graduate students in the sociology department. He was already in his thirties, having previously taken a Ph.D. in English, held a professorship at Oberlin College, and studied philology and ethnology in Germany. Within a year after appearing at Chicago, he had a position on the faculty. Although he was the son of a rural southern preacher, Thomas became very much the sophisticated urbanite and *bon vivant*. Known as a snappy dresser and a lady charmer, Thomas eventually talked a wealthy Chicago heiress into putting up $50,000 for the study of race relations. This was quite a sum for its day (1908) and indeed constituted the first big research grant in the history of American social research.

With this money Thomas embarked on a study of Polish immigrants in Chicago. He originally intended to study other ethnic and racial groups as well, but his sense of empirical thoroughness led him to limit his focus. The Poles, as the biggest immigrant minority in Chicago at the time, posed an important enough question in themselves, especially since the Chicago newspapers were currently full of alarm about "Polish crime": the unpredictable outburst of violence from otherwise stolid and acquiescent men. Thomas, who had fully immersed himself in the social thought of his day (see Chapter 4), was already critical of simple evolutionist or racist theories of behavior. He expected that neither automatic modernization nor hereditarily determined failure would be the fate of these transplanted Polish peasants, and his research was designed to find out exactly what was happening.

Thomas drew for his approach on the latest developments in social psychology, especially the dynamic outlook of James and Mead. Social life must be seen from the inside, as people actually experience it, Thomas felt. Social structures operate on individuals only as the individuals interpret them and feel them bearing down against their own attitudes and motivations. He later formulated a key element of the symbolic interactionist approach in the statement that has since become known as the "Thomas Theorem": "If men define situations as real, they are real in their consequences."

In accordance with this methodology Thomas learned Polish, read the local immigrant press, and observed daily life in the Polish ghetto. His most famous methodological innovation was the use of letters that Polish immigrants had written to relatives at home. Thomas hit on this method fortuitously. One day, walking through the ghetto, he jumped back quickly to avoid a bundle of garbage thrown out of a window. In the pile of garbage he spied a pack of letters. Since he could read Polish, he looked through them and found a vivid account of immigrant life "from the inside." Subsequently, Thomas advertised for other collections of letters in the Polish press and used these as a major part of his documentary materials. Apparently the garbage method was not sufficiently fruitful.

In 1913 while on a trip to Poland, Thomas met Florian Znaniecki (pronounced Znan-yet-ski), a young Polish philosopher, and they discussed Thomas' work. The next year the Germans invaded Poland and Znaniecki escaped to America. Completely unanticipated and uninvited, he showed up penniless at Thomas' house in Chicago. Thomas took him in and made him a collaborator in his research, especially in filling in the background on the peasants in Poland.

The completed work, which began appearing in 1918, had an immediate impact, at least within sociology. It established the superiority of large-scale systematic research over speculative and superficial approaches, and it at last brought theoretical issues down to where they belong—in confrontation with the real world. *The Polish Peasant* concluded, among other things, that crime was the result of the lack of mediating institutions to integrate the individual into the larger society. Accordingly, a strong Polish-language press, Polish parishes of the Catholic Church, and other immigrant cultural institutions were far from being alien and dangerous to the fabric of American society. On the contrary, Thomas and Znaniecki argued, it was just such institutions that integrated the Polish community around itself and hence provided the prerequisites for its eventual integration into the rest of society. Thomas and Znaniecki thus avoided the naïve positions—condemning the immigrants, or demanding immediate Americanization—and gave a more sophisticated analysis based on careful observation of the facts. Their work can be faulted, especially for its neglect of politics, but in general their view holds true and bears considerable relevance to the experience of other minority groups, including the black minority of today.

But at the very moment of his triumph, Thomas' career had a sudden shock. Early in 1918 he was arrested by the F.B.I. in a hotel room with a Mrs. Granger, the wife of an army officer on duty in France. The charges —violating the Mann Act and registering in a hotel under a false name— were thrown out of court, but there was a great public scandal. The arrest appears to have been politically motivated, since Thomas' wife was currently prominent in Henry Ford's peace movement, then anathema to the Woodrow Wilson administration. The University of Chicago, under an onslaught of unfavorable publicity from the Chicago *Tribune* and similar quarters, abruptly dismissed Thomas. There was scarcely a protest from the faculty; for all his eminence, Thomas had enemies.

Thomas spent the rest of his career traveling and writing under grants from the Carnegie Corporation, the Social Science Research Council, and various wealthy heiresses. Except in the flashiness of his life style, Thomas might well be called the first sociologist of the modern era of research grantsmanship. Znaniecki went on to become a theorist of some note. Ironically, with its founding spirit in exile, the Chicago school emerged in the 1920s as a full-blown movement in sociology. Its new leader was, appropriately enough a protégé of Thomas, Robert E. Park (1864–1944).

PARK AND THE CHICAGO SCHOOL

Park, too, had had a colorful nonacademic career. He also had come from a religious rural family. He studied philosophy with John Dewey at the University of Michigan and with William James at Harvard, and in between he spent twelve years as a newspaper reporter, based from New York and Detroit to Denver, Minneapolis, and Chicago. Like most other intellectually oriented Americans, he put in his sojourn in Germany, where he encountered Simmel and earned a Ph.D. from Heidelberg in 1904. Park then became secretary of the Congo Reform Association and wrote a famous exposé of the barbaric conditions prevailing in the colonial regime of the Belgian Congo.

The racial situation in America attracted him next, and Park became a ghost writer and adviser to the black leader Booker T. Washington. Indeed, it has been urged that Park was the "power behind the throne" in Washington's movement. In any case it seems fair to say that the two men shared the same gradual, assimilationist, up-by-your-own-bootstraps philosophy of change. It was at Washington's Tuskegee Institute in Alabama that Thomas discovered Park in 1914, and brought him to Chicago. After 1918, with Thomas gone from the scene, Park took over the leadership of the Chicago school. The ex-newspaperman gave just the impetus that was needed. The growing city was the big story of the day, Park exhorted, and he sent his students out to find "the big sociological news" in the everyday world around them. Before the 1920s were over, the Chicago school had produced a series of studies such as Nels Anderson's *The Hobo* (1923), Frederick M. Thrasher's *The Delinquent Gang* (1927), Louis Wirth's *The Ghetto* (1928), and Harvey W. Zorbaugh's *The Gold Coast and the Slum* (1929).

Park himself, with his colleagues Ernest W. Burgess and Roderick D. McKenzie, produced an overall picture of the city, with a perspective derived from animal ecology. Although their model may have been unduly shaped by Chicago's position on the shores of Lake Michigan, it gave an elegant picture of the city as a set of concentric rings: a downtown core where the very rich and the very poor lived nearby (if in drastically different conditions), surrounded by neighborhoods beginning with slums and becoming progressively better as one reached the suburbs. As the city grew and new immigrants arrived, the best-off inhabitants moved to the outskirts. Their previous places became filled by the more prosperous members of the next inner ring, who in turn vacated spaces for the ring inside them, and so on until we reach the center, where the newest immigrant groups found the poorest places from which to begin.

This model of ecological succession was elaborated theoretically in several ways. In the 1930s researchers began to map rates of suicide, mental illness, crime, and other deviance onto such ecological diagrams and found they were concentrated in certain areas of the city. These were called "disorganized" areas and were believed to generate deviance. Another variation was Park's famous "race-relations cycle," which bears a metaphorical as well as a substantive relation to his ecological model. All groups, claimed Park, struggle for domination of available resources, both economic and territorial. After initial contact between alien groups, there is conflict. This stage is followed by the stage of accommodation, in which the boundaries between groups become clearly marked and respected on both sides (that is, the stage of segregation). Finally, there is assimilation, as the subordinate group adopts the ways of the dominant group and eventually disappears into it.

These theoretical models were fruitful in stimulating considerable research, but in the end they were not substantiated. The ecological picture of deviance suffers, we have discovered, from numerous flaws: the fact that people can move into an area after becoming deviant, rather than becoming deviant because they are there; biases against reporting crime and other deviance by inhabitants of the more respectable areas; and the "ecological fallacy" in statistical inference (of which Durkheim was frequently guilty) of supposing that the average characteristics of the people in an area can be taken as reliable evidence of how particular individuals are being affected. (For example, we cannot conclude anything if the area with the lowest average education has the highest suicide rate, for it may be the highly educated persons in that area who are committing suicide.) Similarly, Park's model of the race-relations cycle turns out to be purely speculative as far as the crucial stage— assimilation—is concerned. The experience of such groups as black Americans has shown us that assimilation may occur in language and politics without occurring in the economy or in personal relations. Nor is there an inevitable trend from conflict to accommodation; indeed, events can run in the opposite direction (as in the 1960s), and the theory does not tell us when or why this may happen.

In general, the principal shortcoming of the Chicago school turned out to be the thinness of its theorizing, and this in the end was to be its downfall. It has since lapsed into a preoccupation with statistical methods and descriptions, in the virtual absence of explanatory theory. Park's ecological model was merely an approach to describing the city and lacked any real substantive or predictive power. The naïve optimism of his theory of race relations is obvious today. Missing from Park's theory—and missing as far back as Thomas' The Polish Peasant—were clear ideas of stratification, of power, and politics. An approach to these things, however, was developing at the very heyday of the Chicago school, but rather far from its granite walls.

EMPIRICAL STUDIES OUTSIDE CHICAGO

The first man to revive effectively the themes of Karl Marx in American sociology, strangely enough, was a young theologian from Princeton Theological Seminary. This was Robert Lynd, who, with his wife Helen Merrill Lynd, was preparing to set out on missionary work in Africa when he received a grant from a religious foundation to study religious behavior in the United States. The Lynds chose Muncie, Indiana, a prospering industrial town in the Midwest. Their approach, influenced by anthropological studies of primitive tribes, was to take up residence, to participate and observe as widely as possible, and to interview local informants. The Lynds soon concluded that the gap between white-collar (middle-class) and manual (lower-class) workers was by far the most crucial element in determining people's life styles, and they proceeded to produce the first study of a community's stratification. After eighty years Marx's fundamental sociological ideas began to receive some systematic empirical verification. The studies, reported under the pseudonym of *Middletown* (1929), with a follow-up study during the Depression (*Middletown in Transition*, 1937), were immediately recognized. Robert Lynd became a professor of sociology at Columbia in 1931 and thus helped found a second major center of empirical research. Lynd became something of a spokesman for a liberal-left position in sociology; his son, the historian Staughton Lynd, became a prominent antiwar leader in the 1960s.

At about the same time as Lynd was working in Muncie, the anthropologist W. Lloyd Warner was finishing a study of Australian aborigine tribes (published under the title *A Black Civilization*) and deciding to apply his techniques to a study of the natives of the modern United States. He chose the staid old town of Newburyport, Massachusetts, which was to appear in the research reports from 1941 onward as "Yankee City." New England struck back in defense with a satirical novel about an anthropologist who comes to study a seacoast town, *Point of No Return* by John P. Marquand. In the end Warner had the upper hand in this exchange. His research has been criticized in various ways, most notably for its overemphasis on a supposedly rigid status ranking of the populace, but Warner's analysis of the religious and patriotic rituals of the Newburyporters (in *The Living and the Dead*, 1959) is a brilliant application of Durkheim's perspective to a modern society. Only a man with the detachment of an experienced anthropologist could have carried it off.

Warner went on to study a Midwestern town, national business leaders, and large-scale organizational trends in America, with increasing emphasis on surveys and statistics. This methodology has become increasingly popular throughout sociology. The percentage of articles reporting statistics in the major sociological journals increased from 10 percent during the period from 1915 to 1924 to 60 percent during the period from 1955 to 1964. This trend represents the self-conscious effort of sociologists to become "scientific." The effects of this change have been both good and bad for the discipline. In his presidential address before the American Sociological Society in 1929, the Chicago sociologist William F. Ogburn announced sociology's scientific coming-of-age and the exclusion of mere social do-gooders. This was also a personal confession for Ogburn, who had begun his career as a socialist and had gradually shifted to an emphasis on detached quantitative research on population and technological trends.

Questionnaire surveys became the order of the day. George Gallup began his preelection polling in the 1936 presidential election, and in 1940 a Columbia research team began the first serious effort to study the determinants of people's votes. In the 1940s and 1950s survey research became the dominant mode of research and was applied to everything from political attitudes to religious beliefs, school achievement, social mobility, and sexual behavior. Great improvements were made in the collection of reliable data and in methods of analysis. By 1960 every major university had its buzzing computer center, surrounded by hosts of researchers, programmers, interviewers, coders, and statisticians. Research had become a large-scale enterprise, and sociologists had to become adept at securing grants from foundations or government agencies to foot the bills.

On the positive side sociology began to acquire a basis of hard knowledge. The old racial theories of behavior were among the first victims of this collection of facts as sociologists documented the influence of social conditions on social success and social deviance. By the 1930s it was demonstrated that the range of intelligence is about the same among blacks as among whites. The biasing effect of social conditions on the IQ scores of people in deprived environments was also documented.

This effect on theory was a negative one—the destruction of the biological-evolutionist model. The collection of data also tended to corroborate some theories—especially the general sociological positions of Marx and Weber on the importance of stratification in social behavior, although this theoretical connection was long unnoticed by American sociologists. Quite without premeditation, researchers found that social class was the best predictor of behavior of all sorts, from political preferences to religious beliefs, marriage and child-rearing patterns, media participation, life styles, and types of deviance. It is not the only determinant, and the effects of other dimensions of stratification, Weber's cultural status distinctions, education and religion, on all of these behaviors was also demonstrated.

American sociology was not exactly rushing forward in elaborating these theories, however. Indeed, a pronounced tendency toward foot-dragging was apparent as far as theory construction was concerned. The methods for collecting data gradually became more sophisticated as sociologists learned how to achieve a reliable sample of the population, how to ask questions that did not bias the respondent, how to apply the proper statistical test to show when results were not due merely to chance. The best of the survey researchers evolved a method known as multivariate analysis, which takes account of the fact that behavior usually has multiple causes and shows how to control each factor in relation to the others so that the effect of each might be assessed. But in general this approach tended to concentrate more and more on its own technical problems and to forget about using its data to build general explanatory theory. Not only did technique tend to become an end in itself, but the survey researchers began to make a fetish out of numbers, to the point where they came to regard "empirical" as meaning quantitative data only. Where taken as an absolute requirement, this has restricted research to a few tightly structured loopholes on the world, missing most of the action and struggle in which things actually happen.

The same sort of limitation could be found in the research in experimental social psychology that has grown up since the 1940s. The founding figure in this movement was the German gestalt psychologist Kurt Lewin, in exile in America since the 1930s, like so many of his colleagues. This research has made impressive demonstrations on such topics as how groups influence individual conformity in perceptions and beliefs and how groups solve problems. But although there have been long strings of cumulative experiments on particular topics, such research has been as yet little related to any of the major theories in sociology. Experimental social psychology is on the borderline of sociology and psychology and more often than not has proceeded from purely psychological (individual) perspectives, with a corresponding behaviorist-inspired emphasis on methodological purity to the exclusion of all else. Experimental study of small groups has nevertheless accumulated a fair amount of knowledge that potentially holds some important contributions to sociological theory.

THE SOCIOLOGY OF ORGANIZATIONS

The missing link seems likely to come through yet another modern area of research, one that occupies a strategic position in sociology, the field of organizations. Organizational research got its real start in the 1930s with a pair of contributions emanating from Harvard Business School. In 1927 the industrial psychologist Elton Mayo began carrying out a long series of experiments on worker productivity at the Hawthorne Works of the Western Electric Company in Chicago. The researchers began with a conventional industrial-engineering approach, treating workers as part of the machinery to be manipulated by an efficiency expert; their initial experiments varied the lighting in the factory to observe its effects on production.

But no matter whether they turned the lights up or down, production seemed to increase. Mayo's associates hit on the idea that the workers were responding to being studied: Instead of treating them like cogs in a machine, someone was interested in them personally, and the workers appreciated the attention. To test this so-called "Hawthorne effect," the Mayo team set up further experiments in the factory, in which they paid attention to the personal reactions of the workers. These results were not interpreted entirely accurately, and the Mayo group tended to over-state their new philosophy: that management must concentrate on "human relations" (and implicitly ignore the economics of workers' pay, which is actually quite important). Nevertheless, the Hawthorne studies took organizations out of the hands of the purely technologically ori-ented engineers and "management scientists" and placed the emphasis squarely on the dynamics of the "informal group" of workers.

This work was complemented by the publication in 1938 of a book entitled *The Functions of the Executive,* by Chester I. Barnard. Barnard, then lecturing at Harvard Business School, was the former president of the New Jersey Bell Telephone Company. (Incidentally, Western Electric is the manufacturer of telephone equipment for the Bell system. It appears that this is a very research-oriented company. The Bell Tele-phone laboratories in New Jersey continue to be the leading non-academic and nongovernment research center in the social sciences in America.) Barnard argued from his own experience that the lines of authority in an organization chart are a myth. The president of a company is like a politician, not a puppeteer, declared Barnard; his subordinates are the ones who run the organization, and his job is merely to create the right climate in which they will get the job done. Barnard's shrewd observations on organization politics at the top and middle ranks fitted nicely with Hawthorne studies that showed that the workers enforced an informal norm over each other, so that no one man would work too hard or show up the others in the eyes of management. Organizations were suddenly transformed into living things; they were no longer abstract charts or inert machines.

Since the 1930s a great deal of research has been generated on organizations. Much of the best of it came from Chicago, where Park's student Everett Hughes guided an enormous number of studies of various occupations "from the inside," ranging from undertakers, jani-tors, and policemen, to physicians, lawyers, and scientists. By the 1960s the field of organizational research had accumulated data on a wide range of topics and had arrived at a fair degree of understanding of the ways men struggle for control or to evade control in organizations, on the way an organization's goals and outputs are affected, and on the determinants of different sorts of organizational structure. Although far from completed, a genuine explanatory theory has evolved in the field of organizations. This theory is the product not only of sociologists, but of researchers in business administration and political science, as well as in economics, psychology, and history.

Perhaps more than any other area of research, the field of organiza-tions ties together and develops the great sociological theories, especially the stream proceeding from Weber on through Michels and Mannheim (see Chapter 11). By no means have all of the researchers in this field been aware of this connection. For sociological research as a whole, the contributions of empirical research to theory building have remained more potential than actual.

This is not the full story, however. It is impossible for research to proceed for very long without some guiding questions being asked. American sociology got its start from the evolutionary and social-problems orientations of the nineteenth century. The wave of research since the 1920s has destroyed most of the old beliefs, but American research sociology as a whole acquired no new theory to replace what it had rejected. As a result, the old social-problems sorts of questions continued to guide research for a long time after they lost their original significance.

For example, sociology was agitated for decades by the question of whether social mobility had declined in America, of whether the society was becoming more rigid or "closed" since the supposedly wide-open frontier era. By the late 1950s, after thirty years of speculation, argument, and research, it was possible to give a definitive answer to the question: The amount of social mobility in America had changed very little, at least during the twentieth century. (It was not so very great in the first place.) In the process of answering this question, sociologists had overcome a large number of technical difficulties entailed in accurately measuring and comparing mobility rates. But there has been little effort to ask the general theoretical question: What determines the amount of social mobility in a society? The latter sort of question requires a larger perspective, and the last decade has seen a revival of comparative and historical studies and an accompanying theoretical orientation that should eventually correct this deficiency. But this illustration shows just how much our highly technical research depends on old, perhaps forgotten, debates over social issues. The old river-bed goes on even though the water has dried up.

Remarkably, all this has gone on after the time of the great intellectual revolution described in Part II of this volume. What happened in the twentieth century was that sociology split into a "high tradition" and a "low tradition." The latter has dominated America, where characteristically the most engrossing issues have come to be methodological debates, even though it should be apparent that the advance of sociological knowledge depends on integrating the data generated by various methods around the construction of an integrated explanatory theory. This split should not be exaggerated, however. The intellectual revolution of Durkheim, Weber, Freud, and Mead has sent out its shock waves rather slowly, but the twentieth century has seen its gradual penetration into the far-flung territories of sociology. The following chapters take up the various streams of its progress.

CHAPTER TEN

THE CONSTRUCTION OF THE SOCIAL SYSTEM: PARETO AND PARSONS

"Who now reads Spencer? It is difficult for us to realize how great a stir he made in the world. . . . He was the intimate confidant of a strange and rather unsatisfactory God, whom he called the principle of Evolution. His God has betrayed him. We have evolved beyond Spencer." Professor Brinton's verdict may be paraphrased as that of the coroner, "Dead by suicide or at the hands of person or persons unknown." We must agree with the verdict. Spencer is dead. But who killed him and how? This is the problem.[1]

Talcott Parsons (1902–   ) entered the sociological arena in 1937 as a detective investigating the demise of the culminating system of liberal rationalism. Spencer died with the optimism of the nineteenth century. He was the last of the great system builders, explaining everything—why people act, why institutions exist, why history moves in certain directions. Talcott Parsons has been the only man of the twentieth century to attempt the same with any success while living up to the new standards of sophistication. His detective work was aimed at finding out why systems no longer seemed possible, not to gloat on the fact, but to overcome the new obstacles.

Parsons was the first man to see clearly the breakdown of nineteenth-century rationalism

[1] Talcott Parsons, *The Structure of Social Action*, Vol. 1, p. 3. Published in 1968 by The Free Press Division of The Macmillan Company. Reprinted by permission.

and the great breakthroughs of Durkheim, Weber, and Freud. His system is an effort to synthesize these breakthroughs. He has been only partly successful. His position is unmistakably more derivative of Durkheim than of Weber, and he overlooks the achievements of Mead and his tradition entirely.

Parsons also marks the schism in American sociology between the high tradition and the low tradition. Many sociologists have stuck with the concerns and issues of the nineteenth-century reformers—individual mobility, deviance, social disorganization and its cures—merely casting them in more behavioristic terminology and going ahead with empirical studies only loosely related to any explanatory theory. Parsons represented an era in which general theory was largely divorced from detailed research, a split that has been slow in healing. Parsons himself was limited by the Anglo-American tradition whose grand theories he tried to revive, especially by a rather behavioristic interpretation of Freud, a patriotic naïveté about politics, and a propensity to elaborate too many abstractions. But more of this later.

First we must turn to a man very different in temperament from the optimistic Parsons—Vilfredo Pareto (1848–1923), probably the most cynical social thinker of modern times. Pareto, more than anyone else, represented the attack on the liberal rationalist tradition, and from him Parsons derived his sophistication about how to build a system in an era when no truly modern mind thought it still possible.

PARETO'S LIFE AND WORKS

Pareto's life coincides with the events that soured liberal positivist hopes in Europe to the point that they scarcely survived into the twentieth century. Born in Paris of an Italian father and a French mother, he grew up in Italy during the heroic years of Garibaldi. He studied science and engineering and began his career almost simultaneously with the newly united Italian constitutional monarchy of 1871. Like many another young man, he was an ardent, idealistic democrat. He worked for a railroad company and then as a superintendent of iron mines in the booming industrial north. At age thirty-four, Pareto received an inheritance that enabled him to retire and devote himself to research and writing. His field was economics, the classical science of British liberalism. In this field one plots the results of men's acting as rational decision-makers, following their independent interests in the network of contractual exchanges that creates a nation's wealth and measures out the common good with an invisible hand. Pareto soon distinguished himself as one of the great rigorists who introduced sophisticated mathematical methods into economics. His position in the discipline is still marked by his name on the concept "Pareto optimum." His efforts brought him a chair of economics at the University of Lausanne in 1892, when he was forty-four.

But Italian democracy was not going well. The old enemies had not given up; the noblemen still kept the peasants in poverty and near-serfdom in the Italian south; the priests still reconciled the faithful to their lot and warned against the godlessness of reformers. And new enemies arose: labor unionists, socialist agitators fighting against the sixteen-hour day, the thirteen-hour day, and the eleven-hour day in the factories of Turin and Milan. Anarchists appeared from the teeming slums, proclaiming property to be theft and parliamentary democracy to be a sham. In 1900 an anarchist's bomb took the life of the constitutional monarch King Humbert. Parliaments went through one deadlock after another; politicians did what they could for friends and supporters by getting them paid government jobs. Grinding poverty was the lot not only of the workers but of the underpaid lower-middle class, epitomized by the hardships of a young socialist schoolteacher named Benito Mussolini.

Nearing the age of fifty, disillusioned, Pareto retired to his villa above Lake Lausanne to think. He became a mysterious figure; the world began to call him "the hermit of Celigny." Shortly after the turn of the twentieth century he emerged with a book, but not on economics. The science of rational behavior had betrayed him. What he needed now was sociology. His first sociological book was an attack on socialism, which Pareto declared a new form of religious superstition. In the guise of reason it created utopian worlds without struggle, which the socialist and anarchist leaders used to inflame their followers against the upholders of democracy and of the nation. There was another long silence from Celigny as Europe plunged onward into World War I. In 1915, now an old man of sixty-seven, Pareto published his great work: the five-volume *General Treatise on Sociology*, to become famous under the English title *The Mind and Society*.

PARETO'S SYSTEM

Pareto's system may be summarized as follows:

(1) Societies have great stability. Whenever something happens to upset the old order—revolution, war, crime, natural catastrophe—there is a reaction, a conservative movement to restore order. After Robespierre came Thermidor and Napoleon; after 1848 came Napoleon II; after an assassination the nation recoils to the party of law and order. Most change is only apparent; new governments—republican, monarchist, Bonapartist, socialist—only change the ruling ideology, while underneath things go on much the same. In the formal terms of the economist, society is a system in equilibrium. A change in one direction is compensated by a change in the opposite direction. To the liberal faith in evolution and progress, Pareto answered with bitter wisdom: *"Plus ça change, plus c'est la même chose."*

(2) The economist sees men as rational decision-makers, choosing

among alternatives, seeking the correct path to maximize gain and avoid loss. By that criterion we must recognize that most action is not logical. The reasons people give for what they do cannot stand up under examination. They act first, then justify what they have done. The judge hands down his decision to fit the power interest of his associates, then cloaks it in high-sounding legal terminology. Moreover, men are easily taken in by false reasoning. All that one needs to make men accept slavery is to give it the name of freedom. Many actions cannot even be assessed by the standards of rationality; like the kneeling of the peasants before the priest, they are rituals. Except for scientists, stockbrokers, and a few others, most men are nonlogical most of the time. Thus economics must be superseded as the main science of human behavior.

(3) If one examines the reasons people give for their actions, one finds certain constant themes reappearing throughout history. These Pareto termed "residues," which may be interpreted as basic human motives. The main two residues are called the instinct of combinations (inventiveness or creativity) and the instinct of group persistence, or persistence of aggregates (conservative or security needs). There are also changing elements in human beliefs, which Pareto termed "derivatives," consisting of such ideologies as Christianity, democracy, and socialism.

(4) The basic forces in society, according to Pareto's hypothesis, are "sentiments." Sentiments can never be directly observed, since they are biological forces or instincts, presumably shifting with the genetic currents of the human race. One can only infer the sentiments from their manifestations, the residues and derivatives. Such inference is a risky business, but it is unavoidable if one is to capture the overall picture. Science solves complex problems by the method of successive approximations: Hypothesize a model of the forces at work; test it against the evidence; readjust the model where it fits badly; test it out on more evidence; and so on. This is presumably why Pareto needed five volumes to write his system. Moreover, his biological hypotheses were in the current scientific vogue of naturalistic explanations. Individual success and failure, crime, and mental illness were all attributed to racial or family heredity. Spencer's evolutionism had moved increasingly into a literal biological determinism.

(5) Not everyone has the same mixture of sentiments. In most people the strongest sentiments are the conservative and social ones. This is what one would expect from an evolutionary point of view; if strong group-preserving instincts were not predominant, it is unlikely that societies would survive. This fact accounts for the stability of societies.

(6) Some people, however, are cleverer, stronger, and more individualistic than others. In society, as in nature, there is a continual struggle for dominance. In this struggle the guileful people win out, both by using force and by appealing to the sentiments of the dull, conservative ones.

There is thus always an elite, and revolutions change only the leaders. But there is a certain pattern to the changes in dominance. The guileful people, whom Pareto calls the foxes, rise to the top. But if too many of them become concentrated at the top, the whole tone of society takes on too much originality, too much rationality, too much clever thinking, too many new ideas. Since the social order is built primarily on conservative instincts and feelings for security, the foxes eventually undermine their own position. Society is thrown increasingly into chaos —wars, revolutions, parliamentary strife—and a reaction sets in. The lions, the strong men who appeal to the conservative instincts of the masses, take over. Eventually the foxes begin to rise to the top again, using their guile against the stupidity of the lions, and the cycle begins again. In politics, as elsewhere in Pareto's system, the principle of dynamic equilibrium holds.

CRITICISMS OF PARETO

Pareto's theory is easy to criticize. It does not account for many of the observable changes in society. There may always be an elite, but why is it sometimes large and sometimes small, sometimes organized in a feudal system, sometimes in a patrimonial empire, sometimes in a mass party democracy? We may always fall short of equality, but what determines variations in the degree of concentration of wealth? Pareto's research methodology is sloppy, consisting mainly of analyzing and classifying what various classical authors (Plutarch, Cicero, Thucydides, and others) and miscellaneous newspaper clippings have said about the reasons why people act as they do. The biological explanation commits the fallacy of *obscurum per obscurius*—explaining something that is only dimly known by something completely hidden. The procedure results in explanations that cannot be tested. If asked why the people of Sparta were more easily regimented by their leaders than were the Athenians, Pareto would reply that the Spartans had more of the senti-ment of group persistences. It should be said in fairness that Pareto's method might have paid off if indeed his hypothetical sentiments had some attributes that might make them independently verifiable, like the genes in genetic theory later discovered in the cell. This they lacked, and Durkheim's logic tells us why such attributes of *individuals* would never be an adequate explanation of *society* in any case.

But to end with this critique is to miss Pareto's significance and per-haps to fault him for something he was not trying to do. At the very general level on which he worked, Pareto is mostly right. People do have sentiments, not just practical interests. Economic man and liberal rationalism are false leads. Deviations from rational social exchange are not merely due to a lack of information about full market conditions, and more education and better communications will not basically change things. Men often act in the service of nonempirical, purely symbolic ends, to which the standards of rational behavior cannot be applied at all. Furthermore, it is the rationalists who have the unworkable image of society; society is held together by nonrational sentiments, not by a deliberate social contract. On the last point Pareto's theory converges with Durkheim's argument for the necessity of precontractual solidarity.

Parsons was to make much of these elements in Pareto's thought plus his logical sophistication about the procedure of successive approximations and his concept of society as an abstract system of interacting parts in dynamic equilibrium. (The last concept is itself justified as something postulated under the method of successive approximations.) The more cynical side Parsons left out, ignoring Pareto's emphasis on force, deceit, and struggle in politics and substituting for Pareto's conservative pessimism a new evolutionary model of progress within the social system. But here Pareto was more perceptive than Parsons. Most politics most of the time certainly fits his general description. Observers who cannot (and do not want to) see through political ideologies are simply acting with that concern for social belonging that Pareto saw as such a widespread motive. In 1922, seven years after Pareto's treatise appeared, Mussolini came to power in Rome. Fascism, an innovation inconceivable to the nineteenth-century liberal mind, proved in fact what Durkheim, Weber, Freud, and Pareto had already proved in theory: that the naïve positivistic theory of man was inadequate to reality.

PARSONS' LIFE AND WORKS

It is a long jump from Fascist Italy and the morose Pareto to the sedate halls of Harvard University in the 1930s. But there is some slight continuity in our theme, for here Talcott Parsons was carrying out one of the great coups of academic politics. A young economics instructor, he had studied with the great anthropologist Bronislaw Malinowski at the London School of Economics and had learned the functionalist theories of Durkheim before they appeared in English. He went on to do his doctorate at Heidelberg on Weber's economic history and translated *The Protestant Ethic and the Spirit of Capitalism* for American publication. Arriving back at Harvard, he soon joined the sociology department, newly founded in 1930.

As the citadel of American scholarship, Harvard had waited thirty years to see if this new discipline would prove respectable. When it was finally decided in her favor, the usual search was made for the most eminent man in the field to head the new department. This man was judged to be Pitirim Sorokin. Sorokin was a Russian, formerly secretary to Kerensky (the head of the Provisional Government of 1917), once sentenced to death by the Bolsheviks, and later exiled. Like most Russian intellectuals he was full of grand ideas, none of which had emerged from the nineteenth century. He had published a notable book on social mobility, which marshaled all the statistical evidence of the day to embellish the theory that people owed their class positions largely to their hereditary ability. Then came his great work, the four-volume *Social and Cultural Dynamics,* a cyclical theory of world history, elaborately documented from the *Encyclopaedia Britannica,* which made much of a trend from spiritualism to materialism and back again. Like most cyclical theories, it rested mostly on the single case of the fall of the Roman Empire, and showed scanty acquaintance with non-Western history.

Within a few years Parsons had displaced Sorokin as the dominant sociologist at Harvard. Through a strategic alliance with functionalist anthropologists and clinical psychologists and with good support from far reaches of the Harvard faculty (Parsons was always a master of ecumenical movements), Parsons eventually had the sociology department replaced with a new, interdisciplinary department of Social Relations with himself as chairman. Sorokin found himself in exile for a second time, this time to his research institute for the study of altruistic behavior. But the coup was more than a purely local affair. Parsons brought the new European sociological theory into America at a famous university where many of the major theorists of the following decades were to receive their training. The dominance of the Chicago school was broken at about the same time, symbolized by the displacement of the Chicago-based *American Journal of Sociology* as the official journal of the American Sociological Society by the new, more theoretically oriented *American Sociological Review.*

The times were propitious for a general change in the orientation of sociology; it was not merely a matter of Parsons' intellectual and political brilliance alone. The old evolutionist and social-disorganization theories had degenerated into a form of biological racism that offended the awakening social conscience of the Depression era. Pareto's lions and foxes and Durkheim's anomie provided some explanation of the Fascist movements of Europe and their smaller American reflections in Huey Long and Father Coughlin. At the same time the newly imported sociology offered some answer to the increasing popularity of Marxism among intellectuals; Weber in particular offered a rival theory in the very heart of economic sociology. What Parsons so successfully offered was a revived liberal sociology at a time when liberalism seemed to be breaking down on both sides.

Parsons' theory has changed somewhat from his first great attempt to synthesize Pareto, Durkheim, and Weber in 1937 in *The Structure of Social Action,* whose opening words head this chapter. In the 1940s he grew increasingly interested in Freud and less interested in Weber. This period culminated in Parsons' major systematic work, *The Social System* (1951). At the same time, Parsons was engineering an interdisciplinary movement to establish a common ground for all of the social sciences (possibly even all the sciences), a project expressed in *Toward a General Theory of Action* (1951). In the 1950s it became clear that Parsons had overstepped himself in his emulation of Spencer's encyclopedic system (recall that Spencer's *Synthetic Philosophy* ran all the way from cosmology to ethics), that his efforts to comprehend everything drove him to elaborating extremely abstract categorizations that did not constitute a workable explanatory theory. By the 1960s Parsons had apparently lowered his sights again. He began to revive the Weberian historical sociology with which he had started out and to offer new theories on political movements. Parsons' intellectual highway is by now clearly marked, but it continues to turn up new surprises.

PARSONS' THEORY OF SOCIETY

Parsons' writings are usually quite complex, abstract, and difficult to read. C. Wright Mills, a bitter opponent of Parsons' abstract theorizing, charged that if Parsons' works were translated into plain English, no one would be impressed. He then proceeded to translate four paragraphs of Parsons' prose into one succinctly worded paragraph of his own. Nevertheless, there is a comprehensive theory to be derived from Parsons' writings, a theory of great sophistication and sometimes of considerable power.

Society as a system

Social causality is very complex, since all institutions (politics, economics, family, culture, and so forth) influence each other. There are chains of causes, vicious and benevolent circles; history is a seamless web. The nineteenth-century thinkers were naïve enough to think that one factor could be isolated as basic: heredity, environment, or economics. Parsons knows that this is impossible. But the very interconnection suggests a solution: Society is a system of interrelated parts. The model is analogous to an economic system, in which many individuals acting independently nevertheless contribute to a few predictable results (for example, prices go up or down) under the direction of an invisible hand that no one controls. The task of sociology is to search for the laws guiding the invisible hand in all of society. Parsons' major work is thus entitled *The Social System*.

Functionalism

Like Durkheim, Parsons believes that the causes of social structures must be found in their relations with other structures, not in smaller units such as individuals. The various parts of a society (polity, economy, education, religion, and so on) all serve functions for the other institutions, and they exchange these contributions for mutual support. For example, the schools train citizens and workers and in return are supported by state and industry; the church upholds family morality, and families are the bulwark of church membership, and so on.

The basic idea goes back beyond economics to the old biological analogy (which Adam Smith had updated to begin modern economics) in which society is one large body, with the king as the head, the soldiers as the arms, the priests and counselors as the eyes and ears, and so on.

Parsons has attempted to classify the basic functions that must be carried out in any society if it is to survive. With these tools it becomes possible to analyze all societies in the same way, even though they may not have the same institutions. What we call politics, for example, Parsons calls the "goal attainment" function, by which the group makes decisions for collective action. War is the most obvious example of such community action; regulating the monetary system would be another. (This may seem a rather limited view of politics, but we will discuss that criticism later.) But not all societies have anything that could be called a state; a primitive tribe, for example, may be organized only as a large kinship network. Using Parsons' concepts, we look for the *function* of collective action instead of for something that looks like a modern state, and we find it as one of the things that the kinship system does, in addition to what we ordinarily think of families as doing.

Parsons is fond of cross-classifying various distinctions to arrive at a related set of concepts, and his set of basic functions (there are four of them; almost everything in Parsons comes in sets of four) can be presented in that way. Everything can be classified as either a means or an end and also as either internal or external. Cross-classifying these factors, we get the table shown.

	Means	Ends
External	A (adaptive)	G (goal attainment)
Internal	L (latent pattern maintenance)	I (integrative)

We begin to see (and this is the simplest of Parsons' classifications) why he has such a reputation for abstruseness. At any rate, the initials A-G-I-L (or L-I-G-A) can be used as a convenient mnemonic device. Any social organization must fulfill all of these four functions: maintaining basic cultural patterns (education and family socialization do this for the larger society), integrating its members into harmonious participation (religion and the legal system do this), attaining community goals (performed by the polity), and adapting to the environment (performed by the economy). The need to fulfill these functions is one of the main limitations on any social organization and, therefore, one of its prime determinants.

The functional method can also be used to explain particular institutions. For example, in his paper "The Theoretical Importance of Love,"

William J. Goode gives a functional analysis of romantic love in American society. Goode begins by noting that societies vary a great deal in their attitudes toward romantic attachments: Some, like modern America, view it as a good thing (in fact, a required norm, since people are not supposed to admit to marrying for any other reason). Others, like traditional China, view love as a foolish infatuation that interferes with the serious business of negotiating links between families through marriages of their children. Other societies, such as Japan, view love as neither particularly desirable nor particularly undesirable. Goode goes on to note that these differences in love norms are related to differences in the kind of kinship system: The extended kinship system in China, linked with a patriarchal household economy and a patrimonial form of polity, contrasts with the segmented nuclear family in the United States, which carries out virtually no functions other than child rearing and recreation. Thus, love is frowned upon in China because it is dysfunctional for the system, and it is virtually required in the United States because there are no other bonds except emotion to hold the family unit together and thus get the children reared.

This functional explanation is not the whole story, of course; to say that something is needed does not tell us why it comes to exist. There is also a historical side to it—the creation of the romantic ideal by the medieval troubadours, the perpetuation of the ideal in the Christian church and in the marriage ceremony—and also a social-psychological side, as individuals arrange their own feelings toward each other. But Goode's functional analysis puts the question into the larger structural context, even if it does not answer all the whys and hows.

Social integration

The organic analogy suggests an equilibrium model, and many of the facts seem to fit: As Pareto noticed, societies recover after wars and disasters, people are aroused to punish deviants, and so on. How can we explain this? The old social-contract ideas of the nineteenth-century theorists, who thought that men rationally decide to uphold the rules because it is in their self-interest, were demolished by Durkheim's critique. Other theories—those of Sorokin, Spengler, and even Marx—never confronted the question at all, but assumed that societies were somehow held together. Parsons, in the forefront of mid-twentieth-century thought, could not evade the issue, which he called "the Hobbesian problem of order." This referred to Thomas Hobbes' seventeenth-century proof that the natural (that is, logical) state of self-interested man is not social harmony but "war of all against all."

Parsons' solution was to accept Durkheim's collective conscience, the nonrational feeling of solidarity that all ongoing societies have. Parsons renamed this the "value system," following the anthropologists who had come to talk about the cultural values that a society passes down through the generations. But how explain the coercive power that the value system (or collective conscience) has over individuals? Parsons threw out Durkheim's crowd psychology and substituted Freud. The collective conscience can be found in the individual conscience, that is, in the superego. Thus Freud's view of socialization —the child identifying with the punishing parent and internalizing the parent's commands—becomes the basis for society's influence over the individual. With this stroke Parsons draws the link between the psychological level and the social level, and the core of his system is complete. At last the age-old question of social order is resolved on a sound basis.

It follows from this that societies are different because they bring up children to hold different basic values. Parsons classifies these values into what he calls "pattern variables," or basic choices people are called upon to make when they encounter other people. For example, one can judge other people in terms of either what they do (achievement) or what they are (ascription). American society places a great emphasis on achievement, whereas medieval society was more concerned about whether a person was born an aristocrat, a peasant, a Christian, or a Jew. Another basic choice is between treating people according to abstract and general rules like the law (universalism) and treating them according to personal relationships like friendship (particularism). Societies can thus be described according to their combinations of basic values. For example, Parsons believes that the United States can be summed up as achievement-oriented and universalistic; Imperial China was achievement-oriented but particularistic; Germany is ascriptive and universalistic; and Latin America is ascriptive and particularistic. In the tabular form:

	Achievement	Ascription
Universalism	United States	Germany
Particularism	China	Latin America

Social change

The social system changes by either "differentiation" or "de-differentiation." This means that the division of labor can increase, with structures becoming more specialized in their functions, or decrease, with structures taking on more functions. The idea is a familiar one in economics: The self-supporting family farm is part of a system with little division of labor, whereas the modern economy of specialized food producers, clothing manufacturers, railroads, and so forth has a high division of labor. Extending the idea to the entire social structure and bearing in mind the functions that are served by the family, the church, and so on, one can place societies on a continuum from undifferentiated to highly differentiated. At the low end of the spectrum are primitive tribes, in which the kinship system is the only social structure, filling all the various functions itself. At the other end are the complex set of specialized social organizations found in the modern United States.

In sociology we find this idea worked out with increasingly greater sophistication in Comte, Spencer, Durkheim, and Parsons. As the division of labor increases, societies increase their efficiency and their productivity, just as the mass-production factories produce more with less cost than the old handicraft industries. Following Durkheim, Parsons notes that the cultural system changes along with the social structure; as societies become more complex and differentiated, the culture becomes "upgraded"—more abstract, more generalized. This is Parsons' explanation of the trend (described in Chapter 6) from particularistic, local, nature gods in primitive religions to the universalistic world religions and, finally, to the modern, transreligious, ethical universe. But differentiation also creates problems. Especially, the more division of labor between the specialized parts, the more pressure there is for integrating the system. In economics this means that the industrial division of labor has to be integrated by a new monetary and credit system. In societal change increasing differentiation creates problems that must be solved by political means—by state-supported education, welfare, old-age insurance, and so forth.

What causes societies to change, to move from one level of differentiation to another? Science, for one thing; economic growth, for another. New technological inventions, like the steam engine, the gasoline-powered automobile, and the radio, have changed the ways in which people produce and move goods, transport themselves, and communicate and have thus set off changes in human organizations that ramify out through the interconnected web of the social structure. Economic growth brings more and more of the world into one large division of labor, promoting greater specialization at all points and calling forth new agencies to coordinate things. Another cause of change is imperfect integration of the parts, due to prior change. Thus, as the Parsonian sociologist Neil Smelser has shown, the early industrial revolution in England put a great strain on the old family system; since workers in factories could no longer appropriately keep their children with them and have them help while they worked, the state eventually had to take over responsibility for the children by setting up schools and prohibiting child labor. The family was thus transformed into its functionally appropriate modern nuclear form.

These are all short-run changes, which come into play only once the processes of scientific discovery and economic change have begun. To explain the long-run changes Parsons draws on Weber's theory of history (presented in Chapter 6). The main difference is that Parsons omits political struggle, which was the main engine of change for Weber, and concentrates instead on changes in religious beliefs. Since Parsons sees societies as determined by their fundamental value systems, changes in values are the prime movers of social change, and charismatic leaders—the great prophets of antiquity, St. Paul, Martin Luther, John Calvin—are the key figures who set forth new values. But the cultural tradition is in the long run more important than the individual leaders, since they can only develop the potentialities already inherent in the tradition.

PARSONS' RELIGIOUS SOCIOLOGY

Parsons' students can remember him lecturing on the sociology of religion to a room full of Catholic nuns, Buddhist priests in their saffron robes, bearded rabbis, and Harvard undergraduates in Levis and tweed jackets, capturing the cultural history of the world into one long sequence: from the animistic religions of remote antiquity to the "instrumental activism" of the Hebrew prophets and their vengeful almighty God; on through early Christianity and the medieval struggles to separate church from state and thence to Martin Luther's abolition of the monkhood, which upgraded the obligations of Christianity and made monks of us all; to Calvin's Puritanical insistence that the world be as righteous as the kingdom of heaven, carried to the new world by the Calvinistic settlers of Massachusetts Bay who laid down the value system of the United States; the gradual secularization of that Protestant ethic into an achievement orientation that tolerated all religions and set loose the economic and social changes of the mightiest nation in the history of the earth; until at last one could see cultural history devolving down through the ages to the very man standing before us, this son of a Calvinist preacher and heir (his very name told us) to a long line of preachers, holding our rapt attention with the culminating system in which cultural history at last comes to full self-understanding. Spencer was dwarfed by the performance. It called to mind the visionary giants of the past: Hegel, Dante, and Thomas Aquinas.

Indeed, Talcott Parsons' sociological system is an adaptation of the traditional Christian world view to the sophisticated requirements of modern secular thought. Unlike most contemporary social scientists, Parsons believes in free will—a voluntaristic conception of man in society, as he put it in *The Structure of Social Action.* To this extent he breaks with the hard-nosed positivistic attempt to bring man under the deterministic canons of physical science. At the same time he holds that social order and predictable behavior are not only real but necessary, just as Christian theology maintains both that man is free and that God is nevertheless all-determining.

Parsons solves the religious paradox in sociological terms: Men are free to choose, but they always choose in the presence of other men who are also free. They can act together in harmony because they develop values that tell them what things are worth pursuing and norms that set the rules under which they pursue those ends. Men do not have to live up to the values and norms of their society, but they find it best for themselves, as well as for others, if they do.

The norms that develop always must have some rewards built into them, so that men reward each other for doing what they must do. Like the utilitarians on back to Adam Smith, Parsons sees the world as held together by an invisible hand, a system in which men exchange things with each other. The exchanges are sometimes economic—pay for work, money for goods—but Parsons adds a Freudian dimension to make the exchange a moral matter as well as a material one. Men trade not only goods but human contact and emotion—approval and disapproval, feelings of belonging, a sense of social solidarity. Thus, men who live up to the norms reap the rewards of feeling that they belong and are respected; those who do not conform punish themselves by isolating themselves from human society. Parsons incorporates the old moral lesson into his sociology: one can find happiness in being good, while evil is its own punishment—to be cut off from God (or society).

The functional imperatives of society thus take the place of the Christian God. Men do not have to live up to them, but if they do not, retribution swiftly follows as their world crumbles around them. Durkheim, the ultrapositivist, had debunked religion in the name of science by showing that God is but a symbolic representation of the moral order of society. Parsons, the American secularized theologian, turned up the other face of the argument with his claim that society is fundamentally a spiritual order. All men basically acknowledge the claims of social order, no matter how much they rebel against its claims on them personally; individuals may steal, cheat, lie, and fight, but no one would want a world in which everyone did so, for then society would not exist. God in the end is stronger than the devil, and the devil himself knows it. Even force and violence ultimately contribute to this order. Like Dostoevsky's Grand Inquisitor, Parsons sees that power is necessary to enforce the claims of society on the individual. The wielders of power—the kings and the generals and the politicians—may personally profit a great deal, but without them society would crumble into a chaos that no one would want. Thus men are selected to do God's will, whether they know it or not.

Parsons incorporates not only the traditional Christian moral vision, but its optimistic nineteenth-century adaptation, liberal evolutionism. Society has not only been becoming more productive and more powerful as it develops, it has also been becoming more just. As the value system has shifted from ascription to achievement, from particularism to universalism, men have been becoming more humanitarian. Torture, public executions, cruelty to the insane, the burning of witches—all these have gradually disappeared in the more modern societies. The sense of universal brotherhood has spread—from a society in which one trusted only one's relatives to the rise of feelings of national identification and now (optimistically) beyond nations to all mankind. Politics, too, has become increasingly participatory and just. In a list of evolutionary stages through which societies must pass if they are to become increasingly differentiated (and thereby more modern and more powerful), Parsons rather ethnocentrically includes democracy as a necessity for all truly modern systems. Whether or not some men want to allow democracy, it is the price they must pay if they want progress. In politics as elsewhere, Parsons' God manifests himself increasingly throughout history.

PARSONS' CONTRIBUTIONS

Parsons' liberal optimism betrays its weaknesses most clearly in his treatment of politics. Fascism, Parsons felt, was a transitional phenomenon caused by the struggle of a rationalized economy and a tradition-breaking scientific culture against an old world of family, community, and politics that had not yet adjusted. Parsons has never taken seriously Durkheim's fears that an extremely rationalized society would destroy social solidarity nor Weber's warnings that modern bureaucratic organizations eliminate responsible social leadership and condemn us to a world of bureaucratic drift. Like the early British liberals, Parsons holds far too gentlemanly a view of politics, closing his eyes to the realities of power struggles where the interests of the various factions by no means coincide with the interest of the collective system. By concentrating entirely on the functional aspects of society, Parsons is powerless to explain the vast realm of phenomena that are not functional. Like his predecessors, Parsons has his gaze too much on the heights to fully understand what goes on in the mundane world below.

The major fault in Parsons' method is overabstraction. When Durkheim identified the collective conscience, he was talking about something that real groups of people feel when they come together, not about a big invisible balloon in the sky neatly covering the boundaries of the United States or China or some other country and labeled "value system." In the same way, Parsons reifies the very general idea of a social system and identifies it with whole states, not noticing how many different, relatively nonconnected groups there are within every state, oblivious of or in conflict with each other. His error is in jumping from some aspects of reality that fit the metaphor to the assumption that they all do. Societies sometimes draw themselves together after a war, but quite as often they break up into new societies; the fundamental assumption of dynamic equilibrium is a variable to be explained, not a universal process to be taken for granted. The path forward from Durkheim's insight is not to make it more abstract, but to examine particular groups of people as they create the various kinds of collective conscience found at a tea party, a diplomatic reception, in the corridors of a mental institution. Erving Goffman, as we shall see in Chapter 12, is the man who took up this latter task.

Parsons' major contributions to sociology have been to uphold the high theoretical tradition and to ask the fundamental questions in an era when few social scientists were even aware that they were there to ask. He has carried out part of the crucial integration of the great insights of Durkheim and Freud and showed some of the places where Weber fits into the emerging grand pattern. If functionalist explanations fall far short of incorporating the realities of human conflict and explaining the links between the functions an institution serves and the fact of its existence, they nevertheless sometimes cast a spotlight on the manifold interconnections of the social structure. Finally, not the least of Parsons' contributions is one for the twenty-first century: He has preserved our knowledge of free will and human consciousness as facts until the time that our theories become adequate to explain those mysteries.

HITLER'S SHADOW: MICHELS, MANNHEIM, AND MILLS

The decade of the 1930s posed the biggest shock to popular world views since the French Revolution of the 1790s. The unimaginable happened: Fascism came to power in Germany. An authoritarian, antimodern, antiscientific, antirational, and antidemocratic movement, it negated all the ideals men had thought were in the ascendant for almost 200 years. Moreover, Fascism was not simply a conspiracy of a few backward aristocrats, but a popular mass movement with literally millions of enthusiastic followers, and it sprang up in one of the most advanced industrial nations in the world.

The 1917 revolution in Russia that brought the Communists to power for the first time had already made a dent in the complacency of Western liberal beliefs, but not so great as the Fascist success. After all, at least one sector of Western thought had been predicting such a revolution for quite a while, and in any event it could be brushed off as a modernizing effort in a backward country. One way or another the Russian Revolution could be assimilated to existing modes of thought, but Fascism! Until it happened, no one would even have thought it possible. And having happened, it posed the question of explaining it, which has dominated our attention ever since. The inferences drawn have not all been sound, but we have been thinking in Hitler's shadow for forty years.

Fascism did not appear out of nowhere, of course. Currents of anti-Semitism and antirationalism had been welling up since the later part of the nineteenth century. In 1922 Benito Mussolini, a former Socialist leader, took power in Italy after marching on Rome with his black-shirted followers, promising an end to economic and political disorder. And in 1923 Adolf Hitler began his slow climb to prominence in an abortive *Putsch* organized in the beer halls of Munich. Fascism built up strength slowly and in full public view before Hitler was named Chancellor in 1933. Men of reason had plenty of time to listen to it and react to it, but for the most part, they found it so incompatible with their assumptions that they dismissed its importance.

The Marxists, especially after the onset of the world-wide economic Depression of 1929, made an effort to explain Fascism as the death agony of capitalism entering its final crisis. But why *this* death agony, so unlike what Marx seemed to predict? Moreover, the issue seemed not so much an economic one—Hitler was successful enough in restoring economic prosperity once he took power in Germany—as something more deeply rooted in man's social nature that made him respond irrationally to crises, whether economic or otherwise. Marxism had shared the rationalistic assumptions of the nineteenth century, but these seemed no longer to apply.

Marxism was breaking down in other ways as well. The Russian experiment in Soviet utopia was going badly. The power struggle between Stalin and Trotsky had turned into a reign of terror by the 1930s, and the world was treated to the spectacle of most of the old revolutionary leaders being tried and executed on charges of treason and finally of the exiled Trotsky lying dead in his villa in Mexico with an assassin's pickax through his brain. Stalin's dictatorship wiped out most of the optimism of the left; Hitler's brought the rest of the world to its feet in shock. Science and industry were moving onward toward the innovations of television, the jet plane, and the atom bomb, but the old hopefulness was gone. The world had suddenly lost its meaning, and modern man found himself wandering amid his material creations like a character in the novels of Franz Kafka.

World War I already had begun to foreshadow this disillusionment with human rationality. It was a war that everyone, after the first spasms of patriotic enthusiasm, agreed was senseless—begun over a trivial issue in diplomacy, unstoppable once the mammoth machinery of warfare was set in motion, dragging on in the trenches of the Western Front at the cost of millions of lives, and ending by having settled nothing. It was during and after World War I that the characteristic disillusionment of modern literature became the universal outlook of thinking men, spread by the Dadaists, T. S. Eliot, Ernest Hemingway, and the rest of the "lost generation."

Disillusionment had been particularly acute on the left, for the Socialists had explicitly hoped to be able to prevent such wars. Wars are fought for the benefit of the ruling classes, they asserted, but it is the workers who die in the ranks; hence it would be absurd for the workers of one country to kill their class brothers for the benefit of their bosses. The Socialist movement, grown to considerable strength among the workers of Germany and France, was counted on to maintain peace. But when war was declared in 1914, after the assassination of the Austrian Archduke Ferdinand in Sarajevo, the Socialists for the most part fell in line with the prevailing mood of chauvinism. The Social Democrats in Germany, the strongest working-class party on the Continent, threw their support squarely behind the kaiser by voting for the emergency war funds for the army.

MICHELS' IRON LAW OF OLIGARCHY

At least one man was not surprised by this unprincipled turnabout. He was Robert Michels (1876–1936), a young historian who had been unable to get a job in the German university system, despite the recommendation of Max Weber, because he was a member of the Social Democrats. Michels had participated extensively in party activities and had come to the conclusion that the Socialists did not live up to their own ideals. Although the party advocated democracy, it was not internally democratic itself. The revolutionary Marxism of the speeches at conventions and on the floor of the Reichstag was just a way of whipping up support among the workers, while the party leaders built a bureaucratic trade union and party machine to provide sinecures for themselves.

Michels' analysis appeared in 1911 in a book called *Political Parties*. The phenomenon of party oligarchy was quite general, stated Michels; if internal democracy could not be found in an organization which was avowedly democratic, it would certainly not exist in parties which did not claim to be democratic. This principle was called the Iron Law of Oligarchy, and it constitutes one of the great generalizations about the functioning of mass-membership organizations, as subsequent research has borne out.

The Iron Law of Oligarchy works as follows: First of all, there is always a rather small number of persons in the organization who actually make decisions, even if the authority is formally vested in the body of the membership at large. The reason for this is purely functional and will be obvious to anyone who has attended a public meeting or even a large committee session. If everyone tries to have his say (as happens especially in the first blush of enthusiasm when a new, democratically controlled organization is created), then in fact nothing gets done. The discussion goes on at great length without even covering all the necessary issues, until finally most people leave or keep quiet and let a few persons present their plans. Before long, the group has delegated to a few of its members the authority to prepare plans and to carry them out, while most members confine themselves to formally selecting and approving plans presented to them.

Second, says Michels, the leaders who have this delegated authority tend to take on more power than the members who selected them. Once in power (whether this is an elected office or a purely informal leadership role), they tend to remain there for a long time and become relatively impervious to influences from below. New leaders enter their ranks primarily by being selected or co-opted from above by the old leaders, rather than rising on their own from below. The reason for this is partly functional and partly because of the way resources of power are distributed in an organization.

The leaders are a much smaller group than the rank and file, but they have the advantage of being better organized. The members as a whole come together (if at all) only at occasional meetings or elections, but the leaders are in constant contact with each other. The leaders tend to form a united, behind-the-scenes, informal group, for it is much easier for them to make plans, carry out programs, and hassle out disagreements in private personal negotiations than under the parliamentary rules of open meetings. But since the leaders operate in close contact with each other, out of the sight of the general membership, they tend to develop their own ways of looking at things. They are "insiders" who have a sophisticated view of how things are done, how bargains are struck, how strategies are formed. They know the ropes, and new leaders must become initiated into their world; hence they are selected from above, rather than projected from below.

Third, the leaders gradually develop values that are at odds with those of the members. Michels here applies the principle of Marx and Weber that men's outlooks are determined by their social positions. The social positions of party leaders are fundamentally different from the positions of mere party members, since their experiences of participating in the organization are different. For the ordinary member the organization is something he belongs to and participates in from time to time, but it is not usually the center of his life. He expects his party or his union to fight for his interests and his values, but that is about all.

The leader's position is different. For him, the organization is usually a full-time job, or at least a major part of his life. Especially if the organization is big and powerful enough to have paid officials, these officers receive money, power, and prestige from their positions, and often a chance to belong to a higher realm of other elites. The union leader gets to associate with corporation officials; the socialist deputy sits in the legislature with other men of power. It is not surprising, says Michels, that the values of such leaders become subtly corrupted. The leader becomes less concerned with the interests of the rank and file or the ideology of the party and more concerned with keeping himself in office. He becomes conservative, in the sense that he wants only to preserve his organization and not jeopardize it on risky ventures, even if the organization's ideals call for it.

But doesn't this corruption of the leaders bring them into conflict with their followers? It sometimes does, says Michels, but the leadership has the upper hand in such struggles. Unless the membership is extremely upset about something—and maybe not even then—they are unlikely to mobilize their numbers to displace the leadership. For power in the organization goes to those who control its administrative resources, and these are in the hands of the leaders. They are better organized than the membership. They are better informed, for they are in constant contact with latest developments both inside and outside the organization, and they can use this knowledge, which is usually kept secret among themselves, to attack their opponents as ill-informed and unrealistic. They control the communications within the organization: distributing its newsletter, calling its meetings, setting its agendas, making its official reports. They have full time to devote to organization business and organization politics, whereas their opponents are usually part-time amateurs; the leaders also have the finances, the staff assistance, the contacts, and the know-how.

And finally, they have the legitimacy of being the existing leadership who can claim to represent the organization, whereas their opponents can be called "factions" and "splitters" who represent only themselves and who aid the organization's enemies by creating internal dissension. The united leadership, then, can wield power out of all proportion to its numbers because it controls the material and ideological resources of the organization. Michels provides a sort of mini-Marxism of class conflict and the weapons that enable one class to prevail, only his setting is a single organization rather than the whole society. But Michels had no hopes that history would ever reverse this distribution of power resources. As long as we have large-scale organizations, these consequences are inevitable. "Who says organization," stated Michels, "says oligarchy."

Michels' analysis was remarkably perceptive. Subsequent research has revealed that the dispersion of power away from the membership and into the hands of the leaders who control the administrative apparatus occurs in all sorts of formally democratic membership organizations—in political parties all over the world, trade unions, clubs, legislatures, charities, P.T.A.'s, and professional associations ranging from the American Medical Association to the American Sociological Association. The Iron Law of Oligarchy is not, of course, an outright declaration that members never have any control of their organizations. Theories that state such absolutes are usually wrong, for reality is more complex and variable than that. Properly understood, Michels' theory tells how the different positions in an organization shape the interests of their holders and give them certain organizational weapons that they can use in the struggle with others for control of the organization. It does not state that the leaders are always completely corrupted or that they always have their way.

The history of political parties in America illustrates the point nicely. The Republican and Democratic parties in America, especially the latter, have always been strongly influenced by party bosses and professional politicians, from the spoils system of Andrew Jackson through the 1968 presidential nomination of Hubert Humphrey. The techniques of organizational control that Michels describes are well illustrated in almost any political campaign. Nevertheless, some reforms have occurred from time to time; some politicians occasionally arise who make more than a token appeal to popular demands; and long-entrenched party bosses are sometimes displaced. Michels' theory, then, is not a matter of absolutes, but of variations, of which he described the most typical outcome. Subsequent research has shown us that the threat of organizational oligarchy, although always present, varies with the type and setting of the organization. The most oligarchic associations are those that have a very numerous and dispersed membership and large-scale centralized administrative machinery for the leaders to control. The less oligarchic organizations are those that depend on frequent participation by their members and that compete with other associations for their members' support. Michels' position on the chances of real democracy is pessimistic, but we have since seen that there are at least some possibilities of overcoming oligarchy.

Michels' theory has been fruitfully applied in yet another direction. The American sociologist Philip Selznick has shown that the same sort of processes can be found in government agencies in his classic analysis of the New Deal's TVA (Tennessee Valley Authority) project to help the poor farmers of Appalachia. Such bureaucracies are not like political parties, of course, since they do not claim to be controlled by their membership, but rather by the elected officials who head the government. But there are similar processes in both. The bureaucracy's members come to take on distinctive interests and outlooks from running the organization, which begin to cut them adrift from the official purposes of the legislators who originally created it. Like party officials, the bureaucrats become more interested in having the organization survive and prosper than in meeting any particular ideals. The TVA, for example, soon gave in to powerful conservative interests of the wealthier southern farmers and neglected the poorer farmers and the public as a whole. The liberal rhetoric of the organization's ideals continued, says Selznick, but only as a protective cover, analogous to the radical speeches of Michels' German party leaders.

The overall picture is of a world of organizations that control their own members, rather than vice versa. Bureaucracies and political parties alike operate according to the principle of self-protection and self-aggrandizement, regardless of what happens to the interests of the larger society or to the organization's own enunciated goals. Such ideals float over the surface, but serve only to cloud our eyes to the organizational realities below. We think the social world is rational and purposeful, but the appearance is deceptive, and things are not really under any individual's control.

His pessimism confirmed by the Social Democrats' support of World War I, Michels finally took a university position in Italy. The German academic system would not accept him in any case. When Mussolini's Fascist movement arose, Michels gave it his support. For Michels, its open disavowal of democracy was at least a sign of honesty, and he was convinced that if democracy was impossible, the only answer lay in strong leaders.

MANNHEIM'S THEORY OF SOCIAL RELATIVISM

Michels thus disappeared from the intellectual scene, but the questions he raised did not. Their implications were drawn out most thoroughly by another German, Karl Mannheim (1893–1947). Trained in sociology and philosophy, Mannheim became a professor of sociology at Frankfurt University in the late 1920s. Nearby was the first research institute for sociology to exist in Germany. Its funds came from a millionaire manufacturer, the father of one of the university students. It is doubtful that he knew quite what he was endowing, for the Frankfurt Institute became a crucible for the ideas of Weber, Freud, and a new revival of Marx. Around it gathered a remarkable collection of men, known as the "Frankfurt school," most of whom were to make their marks on social research in America after the Nazis forced them out of Germany. They included Theodore Adorno, the guiding spirit of the research for *The Authoritarian Personality;* the prominent neo-Freudian Erich Fromm; the leading sociologist of literature Leo Lowenthal; Karl Wittfogel, who reformulated Marxist analysis of Eastern societies in *Oriental Despotism;* the Marxist philosopher Max Horkheimer; and Herbert Marcuse, the chief neo-Marxist prophet of the mid-twentieth century. In this atmosphere appeared Mannheim, the most conservative figure on the scene and the most eminent.

Mannheim first stated his position in 1929 in *Ideology and Utopia.* His stance was essentially that of a liberal, trying to find a place for his values in the modern world. These were the beliefs that reason and democracy were the best defenses of human welfare, freedom, and culture. But these values were threatened, and Mannheim squarely faced the threat: Nothing was truly believable anymore. No values were certain; no truths were sure.

What had happened was that men had penetrated beneath their old assumptions—first, of religious dogmatism, then, of secular humanism— to recognize the social relativism of ideas. Mannheim did not invent this relativism himself. Its most popular expositor in the 1920s was the German philosopher Max Scheler, but it went back through Nietzsche, Marx, and Hegel and ultimately had its roots in the Enlightenment effort to bring all assumptions under the test of scientific reasoning. To paraphrase Mannheim, we have come to see that there is no such thing as "truth" or "value" all by itself, but that these are always *somebody's* ideas. Moreover, the men who think these ideas do not confront the universe in the abstract; rather, they occupy particular positions that shape their outlooks. We can trace these influences on men's ideas more easily, says Mannheim, if we realize that most men do not originate any ideas at all, but just repeat what they have heard from others. The basic ideas of any social period come from a few elite groups of thinkers. If we look at the social positions that these intellectuals occupy, we can see the determinants of their thought.

For example, the only intellectuals of the European Middle Ages were priests and monks. They were organized in the Catholic Church, which claimed universal spiritual domination throughout Europe. Accordingly, their ideas took the form of a universal system of theology and philosophy, which claimed to reduce the entire world to order and which was dogmatically asserted to be true. This ideal was found, for example, in the *Summa Theologica* of Thomas Aquinas. This age of absolute faith began to break down when the Church began to lose its monopoly over the livelihoods of intellectuals. This came about first from the various reformations and schisms in the Church, then from the industrial revolution, which created a new, literate, middle-class audience. Intellectuals could now make a living by selling books and articles on an open market. This in turn meant that there was a competition of ideas, leading eventually to the recognition that there were innumerable points of view on the world. The free market of ideas created the philosophy of relativism.

But then is nothing true? What about the methods of natural science, which slowly build up a body of knowledge, verified by experiment and refined by generations of critical reasoning that holds good irrespective of time and place? Mannheim paid little attention to scientific knowledge, it is true, but this was because he considered it irrelevant to his main concerns. He was interested in thought about society and especially about politics, and it is for such thought that social relativism is especially crucial.

Political beliefs always combine our analysis of what exists in the world with our values of right and wrong. Concepts like "democracy" or "freedom" have this twofold nature; they state not merely how things work, which is the aim of natural science, but how they *ought* to work. The question of what the right political system is, then, is not amenable to the methods of natural science—at least not in any simple fashion. But this was what the liberal tradition of the Enlightenment had proposed to do—to find the right way to conduct human affairs through the use of reason, rather than by relying on dogma or force. As we shall see, Mannheim did not want to give up this hope of the eighteenth-century thinkers, but his reason told him that the issue of relativism must be faced before it would be possible to say if anything of this hope could be salvaged.

Political thought, says Mannheim, falls into five main camps: bureaucratic conservatism, traditional (historical) conservatism, bourgeois liberalism, socialism, and Fascism.

1. *Bureaucratic conservatism* is the position taken by administrators. Its principal tenet might be formulated as "Don't rock the boat." It declares that there are no issues other than technical questions of how to get things done and does not want to take the trouble of asking *what* should be done and *why*. It simply wants to continue as usual with existing operations. Bureaucrats, says Mannheim, try to reduce all questions of politics to questions of administration. This attitude is found among administrators and technical experts everywhere; it deals with questions of value by denying that they exist, although of course it contains the implicit value of keeping the bureaucratic machine running, and as such constitutes the ideology of the bureaucrats.

2. *Traditional conservatism* is the viewpoint of privileged aristocrats, wealthy landowners, and established churchmen. It declares, contrary to the bureaucratic ideology, that history cannot be controlled by plans or decisions. Such conservatives are fond of naturalistic metaphors: Society develops over the centuries like a spreading tree or a flowing river, and nothing anyone can do will have much effect on the natural course of events. Needless to say, this argument for respecting tradition is made by those who are most favored by what the past has wrought up to now; it is those who are sitting in the highest branches of the tree who extol its supposedly harmonious growth.

3. *Bourgeois liberalism* declares that men do have the power to reason, to plan, to decide their fate. It points out the flaw in the conservative argument: that not everyone benefits equally from the traditional opinions on what is good for all; accordingly, the best form of government is that in which all the people, or their representatives, assemble to decide their common policy. Truth is not found merely in dogma and tradition, but is something that men may arrive at by rational discourse.

4. *Socialist thought* goes one step further and points out that men not only have intellectual disagreements but have real conflicts of interest. Government, even democratic government, is not just a debating society in which men decide on the best interests of all; it upholds the laws and property of an economic system that favors certain men and enchains others. In short, socialist thought exposes liberalism as an ideology averting men's eyes from their material situation, at the same time that material advantages determine who will be able to take part in the government debate. Truth, then, can be revealed only by the revolutionary class, the workers, who can strip away the bourgeois ideology because they have nothing to gain from it.

5. *Fascism,* finally, emerges after the lessons of socialism begin to sink in. Liberal democracy is unmasked as ideology, but socialism soon undergoes the same fate. There is nothing transcendental or compelling about the values of socialism, it is soon discovered. They represent

only the interests of one more class or one more set of politicians, and all their talk about history being on their side is revealed to be a purely ideological claim. Fascism, says Mannheim, emerges from this sort of total relativism. Its reasoning is: If you can't be right, you can at least be on the winning side. Cynicism about the possibility of attaining political truth leads to opportunism and the worship of power for its own sake. Fascism is the ideology of the unsuccessful, the marginal politicians and intellectuals. It finds its followers among those who, for whatever reasons, want to return to dogmatic certainties; in a time of chaos, there are many who would sacrifice everything for guaranteed law and order.

If each of these positions is determined by the social interests of their respective social groups—bureaucrats, aristocrats, middle-class entrepreneurs, workers, and opportunistic ideologues—which position is right? How can we decide among them? Mannheim gives two answers. First, he points out, these philosophies were largely formulated by intellectuals, who then peddled their ideas to the classes most favorable to them. The intellectuals themselves were a motley group, recruited from many classes of society. This shows that the position of the intellectual is a distinctive one, detached from any social class and hence potentially attachable to any. Marx, for example, came from a bourgeois family but attached himself to the camp of the workers. The "free-floating intelligentsia," then, is in a position to transcend any particular class interests. If they can attach themselves to any class, they can also attach themselves to none and devote themselves to synthesizing the insights gained by each of the above ideologies. Out of their particular positions, the intellectuals should be able to formulate a general one.

But what can this position be? Mannheim's second answer derives from a historical view of values. No values are absolute, he says. What is believed in one age will not be believed in another, and each group has its own interests and outlook on life. Any group that tries to impose its values on others by declaring them universally valid is committing both an intellectual error and an exercise of coercion. The dilemma arises because we are always making choices of action, and hence we cannot do without values, be they explicit or implicit. But at least it is possible, says Mannheim, to be aware of this and to avoid beliefs that are inappropriate to the times. For example, the traditional conservative ideology which spoke of the world as a God-ordained order, in which nobles controlled and protected their serfs like fathers their children (and God his world), had some relevance to a medieval society. It becomes an ideology only when the modern landowner tries to keep down the wages of his farm workers by using the same arguments, even though he now operates in a market economy in which his main concern is profit.

Mannheim's criterion, then, is that ideas should be in harmony with historical development. We cannot have absolute truths and absolute rights and wrongs, but we can at least demand that ideas be realizable in action in the world as it currently exists. Mannheim makes a partial exception for those political ideas he calls "utopias," which he sees as preparing the way for a new stage of society. Thus, the Rousseauist ideals of freedom were a utopia of the eighteenth century, but they foreshadowed the bourgeois society of the nineteenth century and hence could be seen as serving some function in the light of history.

If we look back at Mannheim's list of the five main political ideologies, we see that with one exception, they form a historical sequence. The exception is bureaucratic conservatism. Ever since bureaucracies began to develop in the seventeenth century, they had taken an anti-ideological, antipolitical stance: Times change and reasons for action change too, but bureaucracies go on and on. The other four ideologies fall into a historical progression: First, traditional conservatism reigned in the premodern society of aristocrats and priests. This was challenged by the bourgeois liberalism of the rising businessman, which accordingly became most salient during the formative years of the industrial revolution. Advancing industrialism created the working class and its characteristic ideology of socialism. And, finally, modern society went into a period of crisis, caused by the failure of the previous ideologies to correctly express the nature of the modern world, and the result was Fascism.

But Fascism was not the end of history, at least from Mannheim's standpoint. It was rather the ideology of chaos and frustration, and it simply embraced the crisis rather than pointing to a way to resolve it. What was still lacking was a politics appropriate for modern society, and this Mannheim himself proposed to provide. This was the aim of his next book, *Man and Society in an Age of Reconstruction* (1935).

MANNHEIM'S POLITICS FOR MODERN SOCIETY

Mannheim begins with an idea that has become familiar in modern liberalism: We have come to the end of laissez faire in economics. Economic freedom for businessmen was important during the nineteenth century as they struggled to free the market from traditional restrictions and thus to build up modern industrial society. But now that the free-market system has won out and industrialism is an operating system, it must be controlled to keep it from destroying us. A planned economy, directed by the government through monetary and fiscal controls, has become necessary to avoid catastrophic depressions, inflation, unemployment, and other ills.

Similarly, says Mannheim, we have had a laissez-faire philosophy in social and political matters. This has been the characteristic ideology of the bourgeois period, when the model of the individual businessman and his private property influenced men to think of themselves as independent and self-sustaining individuals, fashioning their own fates and requiring nothing of society except the freedom to go their own ways. But when the interactions of men in modern society produce seemingly irreconcilable conflicts (for example, class conflict, whether in unionized or revolutionary form), the individualistic philosophy provides no way out. We are left in chaos until people begin to turn to Fascism, which promises to impose order by sheer force. But Fascism does not solve the underlying problem; it only buries it under totalitarian repression. Just as a sort of Keynesian strategy must be applied in the economic sphere, Mannheim declares that we can have the benefits of modern society only by the creation of planning in the social sphere.

The social and political ills of modern society, as distinct from its economic problems, Mannheim finds to be caused by two major trends: the principles of fundamental democratization and of increasing interdependence.

There has been a seemingly irreversible trend to include more and more of the populace in political life. Alexis de Tocqueville noticed this in the 1830s, and by Mannheim's time it was becoming taken for granted, just as today we automatically assume it will happen in the new nations of the Third World. But, says Mannheim, fundamental democratization in the sense of political participation does *not* automatically lead to increased freedom and an improved political life for everyone. This impression was given by the first stages of democratization in the early nineteenth century, when the industrial revolution brought the well-educated and business-trained middle class into politics. As they won the vote and the right to hold office, they brought with them their characteristic rationalism. This gave a sense of improvement over the old traditionalism, an optimistic feeling that public affairs were now to be settled with intelligence and humaneness.

The later period of industrialization, however, mobilized the rest of the populace, and their entry into politics began to reverse the earlier effects. As urbanization, transportation, and the mass media made the lower classes (the small businessmen, workers, and farmers) a political force, they too won the franchise. But the effect was to lower the level of political debate to demagoguery: appeals to the emotions rather than to reason, to those who want quick, simplistic solutions rather than intelligent understanding of problems. Whereas the earlier phase of democracy enhanced the sense of freedom and rationality, the later phase of mass politics opened the way to potential dictatorship.

At the same time, the different sectors of modern society have become increasingly interdependent. We now have a national economy rather than a set of local economies, an increasingly powerful national government, nationwide transport, and nationally centralized mass media, all of which bring people functionally together in very large numbers. One result of all this is that crises and conflicts in one part of society can no longer remain isolated, but quickly affect the rest of the system. By becoming more interdependent, we have become more vulnerable. Men are affected by financial affairs, political decisions, or cultural fads in far-off places; they become haunted by things they can neither see nor control.

As things become more interdependent, the bases of power in society become more concentrated. The economy becomes dominated by a few far-flung corporations and by agencies of the central government that regulate money, credit, and trade. As society comes to depend on the smooth functioning of a complex and gigantic system of exchanges, the organizations that can regulate this activity become necessarily more important and more powerful. Our lives are thus affected by the decisions made in large bureaucracies, and those bureaucracies in turn are controlled by their technical experts and managers, who alone understand the complexities of the system. Thus, at the same time that the mass of men achieve the formal trappings of democracy, the situation puts real power in the hands of only a few.

The same shift in power occurs in the military sphere with the rise of modern weapons. In earlier times, says Mannheim, sheer numbers had some weight; one man was worth one gun. But this equality of force disappears with modern tanks, airplanes, and bombs, which make one centrally controlled military organization more powerful than large numbers of individually armed men. In short, power necessarily becomes more concentrated in modern society, thus increasing the chances of dictatorship.

One might think from this argument that, at any rate, the centralized organizations arising in response to the increasing interdependence of the parts of society would provide the coordination necessary to prevent catastrophes. But no, says Mannheim, we can have large-scale organizations, with all their dangers to individual freedom, without gaining intelligent direction of social policy. This, in fact, constitutes the crucial problem of modern society, for which mass democracy and institutional interdependence provide only the background. Bureaucratic organizations provide rational control, says Mannheim, but there are two kinds of rationality.

On the one hand, there is *substantial rationality*, "an act of thought which reveals intelligent insight into the interrelations of events in a given situation." The model of substantial rationality is a man thinking realistically, calculating so that his actions reach their intended goals. On the other hand, there is *functional rationality*, "the fact that a series of actions is organized in such a way that it leads to a previously defined goal, every element in this series of actions receiving a functional position and role." Here Mannheim is talking about an industrial or administrative organization rather than a single man. The crucial difference is that whereas the individual man's rationality involves his understanding of all of his actions, the organization's rationality consists in reducing most of its members to cogs in a machine. Substantial rationality, then, is found only in the man at the head of the organization, whereas his subordinates are made functionally rational by disciplining them to carry out orders, not to reflect on them.

These two kinds of rationality, then, are not the same thing. Indeed, substantial rationality can undermine functional rationality, as when the organization's members or outsiders foul up its operations by standing back and criticizing or offering competing plans as to how things should be done. The conflict of these two principles is shown in World War I, says Mannheim, in the dispute between the German army and German diplomats and political leaders. The latter soon saw that Germany could not win the war because it was isolated against the rest of the world, and hence the only (substantially) rational course was to negotiate for peace. The army, however, was organized as a highly efficient bureaucracy, and its members were trained to think only in terms of how to carry out war operations. They exhibited what Mannheim calls bureaucratic conservatism, the outlook that denies all policy questions in favor of "getting the job done." In the conflict between the two forms of rationality, the functional rationality of the military carried the day. Germany did not attempt to negotiate and eventually was crushed militarily. The same pattern, of course, has been seen many times over, most recently in the American military's attempt to treat the Vietnam War as a purely technical question, quite apart from its moral or policy implications.

Mannheim's theory comes down to this basic issue. Modern industrial society will necessarily consist of powerful, centralized bureaucracies, run by their elites. The only question is: Will it be an intelligent and humanistic elite or a short-sighted and irrational elite? Mannheim views advanced industrial society through the lenses of Weber's and Michels' theories, which see supposedly rational organizations blindly drifting, following the imperatives of their internal functioning regardless of their consequences for the larger society. Business corporations, government bureaucracies, political parties, the military, the police, all follow their own patterns of self-aggrandizement, regardless of the disasters they may lead us into. Thus, we come into the modern era of enormously concentrated social power, controlled by blind and irresponsible elites who cloak their irrationality with the outdated ideologies of liberalism. The result, says Mannheim, is bound to be crisis—economic depression, senseless war, domestic disillusionment, and panic. Here two other possibilities open up: Either the Fascists will gain control, with their irrational glorification of order at any price—and this will, in the end, lead to enormous oppression and destruction—or, and this was Mannheim's hope, the organizations of modern society will be gotten back under control by a new elite, trained in social science, who will provide a planned society.

Mannheim gives no clear idea of what such a plan would be, but presumably it would take into account the interdependence of all the parts of society, the consequences of organizations that their own members could not see, and the ways in which individuals' emotions are channeled into aggression or sublimation. But if no plan yet exists, we must get to work on it, for these are the only choices: bumbling along in our network of powerful but unguided organizations and risking Fascism whenever a crisis arises, or instituting planning.

But what happens to freedom in a planned society? This was a key question for Mannheim, since freedom was the main value he set out to defend against the forces of modern society. His answer invokes the perspective of historical relativism. It is useless to talk about freedom in the abstract, says Mannheim. Each age has its own conception of freedom, based on its particular problems and possibilities.

Earliest human societies are in the "stage of chance discovery." Their methods of dealing with the world consist of traditions, accidentally adopted and maintained because they work. This notion is like Sumner's concept of folkways. On this level of society, freedom means spontaneous physical action—the freedom to go where one pleases, to do what one wants when one wants to do it. The limitations on this freedom come primarily from the environment—wild animals, the weather, diseases, lack of food—which may keep man from being able to do everything he wants.

More advanced civilization has reached the "stage of invention." Men have learned to reflect on their world, to develop tools, crafts, machines, businesses, factories, organizations. The new techniques and organizations free us from the hardships of nature, but in return we must give up much of our physical spontaneity. The self-discipline of work with tools and in cooperation with others gives us much control over the physical environment, but it forces us to change our concept of freedom: It is no longer physical freedom of movement that is important, but the freedom to make one's own fortune by using tools and building one's business. It is the freedom of the inventor and the entrepreneur.

But if the stage of social inventions gives us control over the physical environment, it puts us at the mercy of the social environment. What good is formal freedom to choose his own work, says Mannheim, to a worker who is at the mercy of the shifting trends of the labor market? Accordingly, we find ourselves at the dawn of the "stage of planning," in which we give up the free activity of each entrepreneur and inventor to go his own way regardless of the consequences for others in return for a new sort of freedom: the freedom to control our social world instead of being controlled by it. Democracy can be preserved in planning by incorporating the safeguards and procedures of democracy into the plan itself. At least, such was Mannheim's hope. He had to be optimistic about planning, for he felt there was no other acceptable choice.

What can we say about Mannheim's ideas in the light of the thirty-five years since they were written? The Nazi regime, predictably enough, turned an enormous bureaucratic efficiency to the service of such irrational goals as destroying "the Jewish menace" and conquering the world and eventually perished from the response to its ill-calculated policies. Most modern societies have instituted economic controls, be they socialist or Keynesian, which apparently serve to prevent the kind of economic crisis that brought the Nazis to power in the first place. But there remain other crises besides economic ones, especially those involving internal social conflicts and foreign wars, as well as society-wide issues of the quality of life. In regard to these matters things remain much as they were in Mannheim's day.

MODERN APPLICATIONS OF MANNHEIM'S THEORIES

C. Wright Mills (1916–1962), the controversial, motorcycle-riding sociologist from Columbia University, made the most serious application of Mannheim's perspective in his analysis of power in America. Mills was a big, burly Texan, so full of energy that he even wrote standing up; he went through three marriages and wrote six major books before dying of a heart attack at the age of forty-six. His key work, *The Power Elite* (1956), gathered together the evidence to show that power has become highly centralized in all sectors of American society.

The American economy, according to Mills, is dominated by a few hundred giant corporations, whose top executives and owners make up a national upper class. In politics the national government far outweighs state and local governments as the locus of crucial decisions, and within the government the executive branch initiates policies that the elected representatives in Congress have only the power to rubber-stamp. Mills felt that the military had become a third major power center, going its own way in carrying out a world-wide policy of war preparation and finding its own allies, especially in its suppliers in the corporate economy. Mills documented the "military-industrial complex" before that notion became popular.

Mills' picture of America was widely challenged, especially his relegation of pluralistic competition to the secondary levels of local patronage politics and his conclusion that high government officials, military officers, and the corporate rich form a united power elite ruling America in their own interests. Much of this criticism was based on value judgments that saw nothing wrong with a state of affairs that Mills found reprehensible. Most of his critics were supporters of the cold-war policies of the 1950s that Mills felt were based only on the self-interest of a coalition of businessmen guarding their privileges and the military inflating their own importance and that threatened the world with nuclear catastrophe. Opinion has shifted more toward Mills in the 1960s. The Vietnam War has given a concrete example of how the momentum of a military bureaucracy is scarcely controlled by the rest of American society. We have discovered that the moral shock of the Eichmann trial, with its defense of concentration-camp slaughter as "just following orders," is not merely a historical relic of Mannheim's day, for Americans have faced the same issue as the same sort of functional rationality is applied to the extermination of Vietnamese peasants.

If we understand what Mills was saying in the light of Mannheim's larger picture of modern society, many of the disputes centering around just what Mills meant by power fade into triviality. Mills was documenting Mannheim's theories of interdependence and centralization in American society and the resulting transfer of power from local politics and political parties to a set of bureaucratic elites. In this perspective it is of little importance just how united those elites are or how consciously they try to manipulate our society (although even on this point, recent research has documented the disproportionate influence of a socially coherent upper class on national politics). Indeed, of the three alternatives Mannheim provides for modern society—the bumbling planlessness of organizations' functional rationality, the irrationality of a Fascist dictatorship, or planning by an intelligent and humanistic elite— Mills clearly put America in the first category. He was not, as some of his critics charged, hankering romantically for the bygone days of agrarian democracy. He accepted the concentration of organizational power in America as historically inevitable and only wanted it put under the control of men who were aware of its dangers and responsible to the people at large.

In this perspective it appears that we are still more or less in the situation that Germany was in prior to the 1930s—bumbling through the Vietnam War on the momentum of military organizations; drifting through our race conflict on the momentum of entrenched business interests, political parties, and government bureaucracies; allowing the police to exploit superstitions about psychedelic drugs and the new youth culture for their own self-aggrandizement. Our situation remains what Mills called "organized irresponsibility"—and in the background, should current compromises fail too badly, are the incipient Fascist demagogues, with their slogans of nationalism and law and order. Only the existence of a controlled economy keeps at least the catalyst of a major depression from being a continuous danger.

What about Mannheim's solution—planning? Mannheim was rather vague about exactly what to do, and since Mannheim few thinkers of independent stature have addressed the question. It is true that a group of social scientists, jealous of the success of economists in achieving a policy voice through the Council of Economic Advisers, have been clamoring for a Council of Social Science Advisers to offer policies on the overall state of society. Although the general theme is within the compass of Mannheim's hopes, these men have little of Mannheim's substantive insights into modern society or indeed of the knowledge accumulated by the major thinkers of the last century. Their proposals consist of little more than the old social-problems philosophy that has guided American sociology, without striking success, since its inception (see Chapter 4): Keep a survey team trained on ghetto "hot spots," and pour in a few more welfare dollars when the riot temperature is rising. This philosophy sounds much more like a well-known political strategy for domestic counterinsurgency than anything based on sociological knowledge. The mentality of the would-be planners at this point resembles that of the bureaucrat, who as Mannheim said, reduces all policy questions to questions of technique and administration and blindly accepts and maintains the implicit values of the status quo.

Indeed, Mannheim correctly pointed out that the greatest dangers to modern society come not from rebellious individuals at the bottom of the social structure, but from the irresponsible momentum of military, business, and government bureaucracies. If we are to have any sort of successful planning to preserve our freedoms, it must be directed first of all at controlling the military, the police, the corporations, the mass media, the self-inflating educational system, rather than being controlled by their blind self-aggrandizement. It is here that the advances of sociology can have their most important application. Only if all of us— politicians, bureaucrats, and ordinary citizens alike—become aware of the intrinsic dynamics of our organizations will we ever stand a chance of getting them under our control and giving the world, at last, a semblance of substantial rationality.

ERVING GOFFMAN AND THE THEATER OF SOCIAL ENCOUNTERS

Sociology today bears a surface resemblance to many of the dominant ideals of modern America: It is hard-nosed, quantitative, scientific, and practical-minded. Like the technical experts behind the hydrogen bomb and the cost-accounting system, sociologists seem immersed in their statistics and their computer programs, oblivious to the human realities behind the numbers and abstractions. Yet it would be a mistake to take the obvious, publicly visible side of sociology for the whole of the discipline, just as it would be wrong to conclude from the overwhelming impact of modern technology that we have become a nation of robots. The robots are here, to be sure, but the human element keeps reappearing alongside them. In American society there is a youthful generation pushing for a cultural revolution in political ideals and in personal behavior; and in sociology, the movement of radical empiricists whose most representative figure is the enigmatic Erving Goffman.

Goffman's sociology might well be called the sociology of the forgotten man. Embarrassment, uneasiness, self-consciousness, awkward situations, faux pas, scandals, mental illness—these are his subjects. His colleagues and students have begun to map out the whole underside of society: drug users, delinquents, con-men, suicides, flying-saucer cultists, prisoners, topless dancers, and policemen on patrol. But the new sociology is more than a peek into the hidden and the bizarre. It follows one of the great strategies of the sociological method, first laid down by Emile Durkheim: Since society is ordered by norms that are usually unnoticed because they are taken for granted, the sociologist should concentrate on cases where the norms are broken in order to see clearly what they are and what forces act to uphold them. It is this strategy of revelation through disruption that Goffman has adopted: to look at the places where smooth-functioning public order breaks down, in order to see what normally holds it together. The method has produced insights that have begun to restructure sociological theory from top to bottom; we have come to see how social reality itself is constructed out of tacit understandings among people meeting face to face, and even death has a meaning only from the way it is enacted in the omnipresent human theater.

THE LABELING THEORY

The first elements of the new approach to become popular in sociology appeared in a new theory of deviance, called the "labeling theory." The sociologist of juvenile delinquency David Matza illustrates the theory and its predecessors with a set of parables. How does one become a delinquent? One theory points to a stressful environment: Sally's parents fought bitterly and finally were divorced; her mother took a job and was rarely at home; Sally underwent a great deal of stress, became pregnant, and in due time became an unwed mother and thereby a delinquent. A second theory is that there are delinquent subcultures, so that an individual need not be individually disturbed to become deviant but may merely belong to a group In which deviance is "normal." The parable thus reads: Sally's family lived in a lower-class neighborhood; Sally began to hang around with a "tough" gang, and as a result she became an unwed mother and a delinquent.

The third theory, the labeling theory, argues that not even a majority of persons in supposedly delinquent areas become delinquent, that persons in "nice" neighborhoods may be just as likely to commit infractions but are less likely to be arrested or officially punished for them, and that it is the process of getting caught that transforms trivial offenses into the beginnings of a full-scale delinquent role. In terms of the parable: Sally was in a parked car with her boyfriend one evening. After a few embraces she struggled free and insisted that it was time to go home. The boy was about to start the car when a police car rolled up, and a searchlight caught Sally buttoning her blouse. This was followed, through the rest of the night and the following days, by brusque commands, a ride in the squad car, fingerprinting, a personal search, a medical examination, calls to parents, charges of curfew violations and statutory rape, and lectures by police sergeants, juvenile court officials, probation officers, school administrators, and the family. As a result, Sally went out at the next opportunity and got pregnant.

Goffman gave much of the impetus to labeling theory with his analysis of the inner workings of a mental hospital, reported in his book *Asylums*. Mental hospitals are supposed to cure mentally ill persons. Goffman decided to look at the matter from the inside and got himself into a large state-run institution for a year—not as a patient (he felt the role would confine him too much to just one section of the hospital), but as the next best thing, recreation assistant, with his true identity known only to the hospital superintendent. Once inside, attracting attention neither as a patient nor as an authority-wielding attendant, he blended in so closely that his comings and goings were hardly discernible. "I could have sworn there were only fourteen in this room a minute ago," a puzzled attendant would say. Through his brilliantly enacted plan Goffman collected the evidence for a radically unconventional insight: that mental illness is a social role just like any other and that the mental hospital is a place where people learn how to be properly mentally ill.

The theoretical underpinnings of Goffman's analysis hinge on his model of the self. The self is a social product, Goffman asserts, taking up G. H. Mead's insights. A person is not an isolated thing, but an image carved out of the whole life space of his interactions with others. A man alone is an animal; only in the society of others does he acquire his essential humanness. Each person's self is a reflection of the responses of others, and each person gives others parts of their selves in return. Society is like holding hands in a circle, says Goffman, in which each one gets back on the right hand what he gives with the left.

Ordinarily, one derives one's feeling of self from acting with a variety of people in many contexts. But a mental hospital greatly simplifies the conditions of life: In place of a network of different relationships, one finds himself in a world of only two social categories: patients, all of whom are considered basically flawed and incompetent, and staff, all of whom have freedoms patients are denied and the authority to control patients in major and minor ways. The hospital is large; bureaucratic exigencies require that large numbers of patients be fed, clothed, rested, exercised, watched, and—because of their lapses from ordinary social behavior—sometimes forced to bathe, dressed, restrained from violence and destruction, and generally treated as persons whose selves carry no dignity or autonomy.

Moreover, the hospital, as a place to keep patients away from normal society, is necessarily a "total institution"—the patient spends every hour of the day within the same walls, subject to the same monolithic controls, and facing the abiding scrutiny of a regular staff who keep permanent records of his behavior. The social sources that reflect his self, then, are not only degrading, but monolithic; they offer him no escape into privacy or to alternative audiences who know nothing of his shortcomings. Much of the bizarre behavior of inmates, including such acts as slobbering, cursing, defecating in their clothes, fighting, and withdrawing from any contact, can be seen as desperate devices out of an impoverished repertoire of actions to give some autonomy to the self. The formal organization of a mental hospital, then, by its very nature, creates many of the symptoms that it is designed to cure.

The foregoing does not do justice to the many subtle and complex ways in which being mentally ill has been analyzed, by Goffman and others, as a social role rather than as inexplicable, random, and exotic behavior.[1] The general form of analysis has been applied to many areas: to showing how agencies, subject to organizational exigencies, make "blind men" out of people who have trouble seeing, by teaching permissible roles for recognized blind men to follow; to showing how in ghetto schools the self-fulfilling prophecy makes children into failures by treating them as potential failures; and most notably, showing prisons, officially operating to rehabilitate prisoners, instead operating to socialize the novice lawbreaker into a subterranean inmate culture that furnishes him with a new self as a full-fledged criminal. This perspective lends itself to a cynical appreciation of institutional ironies and considerable skepticism about well-intentioned efforts to rescue deviants and unfortunates back into the dominant society that defined them as deviant in the first place.

But the labeling theory and its correlatives are only a small part of the revolution in world views that Goffman and his colleagues are bringing about in sociology. The marks of this larger perspective can be gleaned from the above. First, this revolution entails a radical empiricism that is not satisfied with statistical accounts or abstract theorizing either about individuals or society, but that looks in detail at exactly what happens in the situations its subjects are living through. Second, it demands that all acts and social statuses be viewed as the products of social interaction among persons; thus deviance is not to be explained merely in terms of the "deviant," but in terms of the workings of the groups that label him as such. Finally, it is based on a radically new view of social reality: not as something "out there" that is always fixed and need only be described and taken account of, but as something that men *construct* as they go along out of an infinite set of possibilities that may be realized in contradictory ways at different times and places. This plural, *enacted* view of social reality is the essence of the revolutionary breakthrough, and Goffman's conception of life as theater provides us with a key for building our understanding of it into a new sociology.

[1] Current research on the biochemical bases of some mental illness only adds to the complexity of the analysis, rather than eliminating social factors. Whatever the physiological process involved, all men live in a social world, and even a person with a malfunctioning body shapes a self in relation to the social world around him. Later in this chapter we will discuss Goffman's suggestion of just what it means *socially* to define someone as mentally ill.

GOFFMAN'S THEATRICAL MODEL OF SOCIAL LIFE

Shared staging problems; concern for the way things appear; warranted and unwarranted feelings of shame; ambivalence about oneself and one's audience: these are some of the dramaturgical elements of the human situation.[2]

Since we all participate on teams we must all carry within ourselves something of the sweet guilt of conspirators. And since each team is engaged in maintaining the stability of some definitions of the situation, concealing or playing down certain facts in order to do this, we can expect the performer to live out his conspiratorial career in some furtiveness.[3]

When do people become uneasy? The answer provides Goffman with a key that opens up the everyday social encounters comprising virtually the whole of experienced society. Embarrassment, Goffman notes, occurs when one's claims to present a certain self are contradicted by the situation: When a purportedly well-to-do person asks an acquaintance for a loan, when a date is refused, when status unequals avoid each other's eyes in an elevator. Uneasiness also occurs when persons show themselves to be less than fully and spontaneously involved in a conversation: by self-consciousness, which communicates to others that one is more concerned with how one is presenting himself than with the conversation itself; by "interaction-consciousness" brought about by an overmanipulative hostess or by uneasy pauses in the conversation; by "other-consciousness" caused by persons whose obvious affectation or insincerity draws attention to themselves and away from the flow of talk; and by preoccupation with things outside of the conversation. Conversation creates a little capsule of reality of its own, and those who violate its standards are the villains of ordinary social life. Correspondingly, there are heroes of sociability, as in the legend of Sir Francis Drake's refusing to be distracted from his backgammon game by the approaching Armada.

In general, then, social interaction is a kind of performance with its own guiding rules. Persons are expected to maintain a consistent social face and to help others in maintaining theirs. Living up to the latter rule is called tact. The rules of politeness serve these functions. Thus, conversationalists avoid threatening topics and contestable claims about themselves or overlook such gambits on the part of others and thus avoid insulting them; there is an effort to stay out of uncontrollable disagreements, to avoid lulls and unresponsiveness, which would suggest a lack of interest in the other's conversation, and to end the conversation in a way that seems natural and does not communicate that one has gotten tired of the other's talk.

Goffman works up such observations into a full-fledged theatrical

[2] Erving Goffman, *The Presentation of Self in Everyday Life* (New York: Doubleday Anchor Books, 1959), p. 237.

[3] *Ibid.*, p. 105.

model of social behavior. Behavior has an expressive element as well as a practical element; it is designed to communicate a definition of reality as much as to carry out tasks. Social performances are often put on by teams, such as the husband-and-wife combination entertaining guests in their home, the car salesmen convincing a customer, the factory workers putting on a show of diligent effort for the superintendent's inspection. Accordingly, it is possible to view the social world as divided up into frontstage and backstage regions; in the former a group project the optimal definition of their situation; in the latter the performers can let down their standards and relax under the cover of a carefully guarded privacy. As Goffman notes, social bonds are strongest between individuals who share common backstages, since they must trust each other to guard the secrets of their common strategy of presenting themselves to outsiders.

Why is life like a theater? Goffman implies two main reasons. First, being able to control the reality that other people see is a prime weapon, available to almost everyone in some degree, for raising one's status, power, or freedom. Thus, aristocrats and upper-class people use their wealth and leisure to put on shows of grandeur and dignity which give them deference; middle-class people put on a show of respectability to set them above the working classes; managers try to enhance their authority by putting on an impressive demeanor before their subordinates; and workers protect their autonomy from the bosses by restricting their encounters to carefully guarded frontstages.

There is a second reason why life must be like a theater: performances are *necessary* if there is to be a clear, consistent, and recognizable social reality. Situations do not simply define themselves; they must be constructed by symbolic communication, and hence social life must be expressive, whatever else it may be. Goffman thus advances the viewpoint of Durkheim as well as that of Mead. Durkheim's concept of the collective conscience was a way of pointing out the existence of a shared consciousness as the essence of society. Goffman brings this notion down from the heights of abstraction, so that we no longer find ourselves trying to imagine a big balloon of consciousness hanging over France or England or the United States and making up the collective conscience of those societies; rather, we think in terms of millions of little social realities that come into existence whenever people are together.

Situations have a power of their own, transcending the individuals who make them up, just as Durkheim noted that the individual contributes to the collective conscience but is often powerless against its overwhelming force. The power of symbolic realities is found everywhere, from the deafening silence of a church communion or a public ceremony, which keeps individual observers from opening their mouths and gives novice speakers stage fright, to the tacit rules dividing the acceptable from the impermissible in polite conversation. By analyzing situations as processes of social theater, Goffman shows how collective consciences are created and have their powerful effects.

Our worlds, Goffman is saying, are full of abstract notions about what is real, both for ordinary members of society and even more so for sociologists. What we know firsthand is always something in the present time, in some particular place and situation; what we believe to be real is something inferred from this situation. We meet someone and infer from what he does and says his character (trustworthy or insincere, amusing or dull) and his status (an important personage or an ordinary guy). Thus, we are always presenting a self to other people, and we control our acts for their effects in expressing what we would like others to think we are like when we are not with them: We take care not to get to a party too early lest it seem that our lives are otherwise empty; we entertain guests in the cleaned-up frontstage of a living room and guard the bedroom backstage.

We not only construct characters and statuses for others to see as the permanent realities floating above any immediate here-and-now; we also construct the large organizations that we think of as the permanent, supraindividual structures of society. As we may recognize with some shock, organizations are invisible. No one has ever seen an organization. What we have seen are buildings, which *belong to* an organization, and organizational charts, which are symbolic representations in geometric form of the formal rules relating the members of the organization. As we can see from a little mental experimentation, an organization could still exist if its buildings were taken away; it could also exist without any of its present members, since it is made up of invisible positions that can be filled by new people when the old ones leave. Our world, then, is populated by entities (General Motors, the Pentagon, the University of California, the city of San Francisco) that exist only in people's minds; we are misled into thinking of them as physical things because the people who enact these symbolic entities are usually found in specific physical places. As long as some people believe in them, organizations are real in their effects, and people who do not accept their rules are punished as criminals, madmen, or revolutionaries. But to keep these organizations in existence, they must continually be enacted; when someone succeeds in changing the script of the play, the form of the organization changes, and we say that a power play has occurred.

Society, in a very important sense, is a theater, and its performances —symbolic social ceremonies—are crucial in maintaining it. Durkheim, sixty years earlier, had argued as a general theory that society is held together by ceremony and ritual; Goffman shows society-sustaining rituals at every point in daily encounters. As Goffman puts it:

. . . In so far as the expressive bias of performances comes to be accepted as reality, then that which is accepted at the moment as reality will have some of the characteristics of a celebration. To stay in one's room away from the place where the party is given, or away from where the practitioner attends his client, is to stay away from where reality is being performed. The world, in truth, is a wedding.[4]

This is a radical way of looking at reality. Social reality is what people say it is, and Goffman is suggesting that instead of trying to focus on some independent things that people seem to be talking about, we should watch them as they are talking about it. The ultimate reality is a puzzle, sometimes a myth, and the "realest" thing we can catch hold of is the behavior of the people constructing reality. A movement of radical empiricists calling themselves ethnomethodologists has taken up just this problem: how people go about constructing in their own minds and conversations a view of the social world around them. This movement, led by the U.C.L.A. sociologist Harold Garfinkel, builds on the insights of the German social philosopher Alfred Schutz (who in turn was influenced by Max Weber's concept of *verstehen*) and on modern logical and linguistic philosophy and carries out the more radical implications of Goffman's style of sociology.

THE ETHNOMETHODOLOGISTS

The ethnomethodologists go beyond Goffman in their minute analysis of how people construct an everyday reality. Their main finding has been that people act as if reality were solid, given, and unambiguous, but the social world they communicate about is actually fluid, highly subject to interpretation, and not easily discoverable.

In Garfinkel's terms, social communication contains a large quotient of "indexical expressions"—terms that cannot be defined, but can only be tacitly understood in the concrete situation by the particular people involved. Words like "this," "now," or "you" are simple examples of indexical expressions; whole systems of ideas can be more complex cases when they contain (as they usually do) concepts and connections that people understand well enough as long as they are in the swing of reading or talking about them, but about which, when pressed for a precise account, they must eventually respond, "You know what I mean!"

Garfinkel uses the method of revelation through disruption to high-light these facets of people's "practical reasoning."[5] His long-suffering students perform exercises in which they get into a conversation and then ask for full clarification of meanings:

Subject
    Hi, Ray. How is your girl friend feeling?

---

[4] *Ibid.*, pp. 35–36.

[5] "Ethnomethodology" means the ethnography (anthropologically detached description) of people's methodologies for dealing with everyday reality.

Experimenter
    What do you mean, "How is she feeling?" Do you mean physical or mental?
(S) I mean how is she feeling? What's the matter with you? [He looked peeved.]
(E) Nothing. Just explain a little clearer what do you mean?
(S) Skip it. How are your Med school applications coming?
(E) What do you mean, "How are they?"
(S) You know what I mean.
(E) I really don't.
(S) What's the matter with you? Are you sick?[6]

The point is not simply to show that people communicate mostly tacitly, taking for granted that their conversational partners know what they are talking about. These experiments also show that people eventually become angry when pressed to explain their statements and that the source of their exasperation comes from a growing recognition that this line of questioning is, *in principle,* endless. There are indexical expressions contained in virtually everything one says, and the effort to make such expressions objective, to reduce the statement to one in which "You know what I mean" is *not* ultimately necessary, is impossible.

People act as if the world has this objective character, and they expect others to act in the same way, even though this is not a true description of reality. Garfinkel's findings are that people can carry on social relationships and carry around a patchwork, invisible, and ambiguous social order in their heads precisely because they act as if there were something solid there all the time. People do not usually ask each other to clarify their statements, even when they are patently ambiguous; they give each other the benefit of the doubt and assume that there is a solid meaning that will be forthcoming in due time.

The social world, then, is really quite a flimsy thing, but since people do not generally realize this, it can take on a considerable amount of solidity. People confronting a representative of an organization do not usually ask for the precise basis of his authority or whether there are rules that require what is being demanded of them. Instead, they assume that what is ordinarily done is proper and necessary, and they accept roles as docile customer, client, or employee that are not necessarily enforceable upon them. Garfinkel illustrated this by having his students go into a department store and offer a small fraction of the marked price for some item. The students found themselves approaching the task with considerable apprehension, since people do not bargain about prices of shaving cream or toothpaste in American stores. But they discovered that once they actually began to bargain—to offer twenty-five cents for a ninety-eight-cent item—it was like breaking through an invisible barrier. With sufficient assurance they gained command of the situation,

---

[6] Harold Garfinkel, *Studies in Ethnomethodology* (Englewood Cliffs, N.J.: Prentice-Hall, 1967), pp. 42–43. © 1967, Prentice-Hall, Inc.

and the salesperson became flustered and ill at ease; they often felt that there was at least some chance of success of having the bargain accepted. It is an explicit rule in most American stores that things must be bought for their marked price, but the rule has force only because everyone expects it to be followed; most of its force comes from the fact that it is never challenged.

The ethnomethodological viewpoint is potentially revolutionary in its implications. Social structures exist only because people believe that they exist, and those beliefs can be successfully challenged by people with sufficient power or self-assurance to override attempted sanctions. The whole fabric of daily interpersonal ceremony, deference, politeness, and authority exists because it is taken for granted, usually backed up by nothing more than potential social disapproval of its violators by those who believe in its solidity. The person who sees social structure as social myth can puncture the bubble; his equanimity in refusing to accept a conventional definition of the situation gives him the psychological advantage, for the power of the upholders of these conventions rests on their self-assurance that their reality is objective rather than a matter of definition. The hippies have led a cultural revolution against constraining formal definitions of situations precisely by their capacity to "blow people's minds" with a well-enacted expression of a counter-definition of everyday realities.

Of course, not all enacted invisible social structures are so easily challengeable. A business organization is a network of rules and roles that exists only because people agree that it exists, but short of a general siege of amnesia, the people who run it are not likely suddenly to deny its existence. After all, there are material and psychological advantages to playing this symbolic game—those who do, make a living, gain some status and authority, and so on. The state, a police force, an army —all of these exist only because their members (or at least a sufficient number of them) agree to act as if their rules and positions were real things; but if they can act as such, they can coerce others into believing, too.

But even with the advantages of power, comfort, and wealth that human organizational play-acting brings, such organizations are not as stable as they appear on the surface. The formal organizational chart rarely corresponds to the actual arrangements of power and cooperation; generals are often at the mercy of master sergeants, bosses may exercise less influence than their secretaries, and little-known politicians and bureaucrats can dictate to Presidents. Reality is negotiable, even in organizations in which a total denial of the ultimate validity of the organization would be impossible, and how people negotiate it determines what will actually happen within it. Moreover, even an organization that can back up its claims to reality with coercive violence is sometimes subject to a crippling wave of disbelief. Revolutions occur when everyone comes to doubt the power of the state, much in the same way that a bank is destroyed when there is a run on its funds.[7] From the merest encounter of strangers avoiding each other's eyes on the street, to the mightiest empire, human social order is ultimately a symbolic reality that exists only as long as it is generally believed in and changes as people struggle to shift those beliefs to their own advantage.

GOFFMAN'S CONCEPT OF FUNCTIONAL NECESSITY

Goffman's position is more conservative than this. He is neither a revolutionary nor a hippie. Rather, he stands squarely in the Durkheimian functionalist tradition, a more empirically oriented Talcott Parsons. Life is full of nonpractical ceremonies, but Goffman sees ceremonies as functionally necessary to maintain social order. He explores the underside of life, but he is not really sympathetic to the underdog. *Asylums* does not condemn hospital personnel for destroying the selves of mental patients, but explains their behavior in terms of the exigencies of a necessarily bureaucratic total institution. In the same vein Goffman's analysis of the rules of politeness and social ceremony is carried out without irony. In his view individuals who do not live up to the rules of polite interaction are justly punished by embarrassment, self-consciousness, or ostracism, for such rules are functionally necessary for social reality to be kept alive. Indeed, Goffman defines mental illness as the incapacity or unwillingness to perform well and to obey the rules of social encounters. Social justice is harsh; if one does not live up to such rules, one is punished by one's fellows; and since one's self is derived from others, one may well be stuck with a permanently spoiled identity as a faulty social interactant or a mental patient. But all this is necessary to uphold society, to preserve symbolic reality for those who can participate in it.

Like most functionalists, Goffman is too ready to see things as necessary simply because they exist. His descriptions of traditional middle-class politeness are becoming outdated. Although he argues that such formalities are necessary to protect the boundaries of the self and to maintain a clear definition of reality, the increasing informality and frankness of interpersonal manners in the most modern sectors of American life illustrates how flexible people can be. They are tougher than Goffman supposes, capable of more honesty, and willing, at times, to put up with an ambiguous, and freer, reality. In the end Goffman is not willing to follow through his own radical realism to the point of seeing how men struggle to impose their own definitions of reality on

[7] Some organizations, of course, are much more flimsy than this. Most voluntary associations, such as new political parties, social clubs, softball leagues, and stamp collectors associations, go through a period of initial enthusiasm about the organization's objective reality. Then most of them find themselves sliding back down into nonexistence through an acceleration of doubt of the organization's survival, as its believers desert the invisible sinking ship of its reality.

others, and the potentially liberating effect when people begin to realize just how this operates. To be sure, the ethnomethodologists for the most part also fail to carry through their social implications. They confine themselves to analyzing in great detail the rules that seem to govern people's everyday behavior—in effect, turning the speculative philosophical field of epistemology into an empirical research enterprise.

GOFFMAN'S INFLUENCE ON SOCIOLOGY

The potential effect of Goffman and the ethnomethodologists on the field of sociology is enormous. For the first time there opens up a real possibility of sociology's becoming a science—a precise and rigorous body of knowledge that explains why people act as they do in relation to each other and why the symbolic products that we call organizations, institutions, cultures, and societies take their particular patterns. This was not a real possibility as long as sociologists remained at arm's length from the observable reality they were trying to explain, dealing with it either through vague abstractions or through the static and secondhand accounts of what people do by asking them survey questions about their attitudes. Human social behavior has finally become the central focus of attention, not in unrealistic laboratory situations, but in the real-life encounters that make up the substance of society. Furthermore, Goffman's model of social performances provides us with a tool for fruitfully organizing this material, simultaneously pointing to the series of events that mold and express an individual personality, the actual dynamics of cooperation and authority that make up an organization, and the negotiation of bonds of sociability and intimacy that knit together social classes and endow them with a status and a group culture. The combination in Goffman of Durkheim and Mead foreshadows a new and powerful social psychology, in which Freud's paradoxes of the conscious and unconscious begin to yield to explanation. Goffman and the ethnomethodologists offer an approach to the empirical realities of organizations and classes that, applied through the heritage of Weber, can pinpoint the dynamics of the larger structures that link together face-to-face groups into a world society.

From this vantage point in time we are beginning to see a new vision of man, which was only dimly and partially perceived by the thinkers of the past. In the work of Freud, Darwin, and Spencer, of Durkheim, Weber, Mead, Goffman, and many others, we are reminded of man in the long perspective of biological evolution: a distinctively gregarious and aggressive animal, linked to his fellows by elaborate emotional interactions, capable of symbolic communications that evoke unseen and unseeable realities, putting on collective symbol plays before the audience of his fellows and recapitulating them inside his own head as symbolic thought, and thus filling our bare physical planet with that invisible world we call society. We struggle like animals for domination in a group that we need too much to wish to destroy; our weapons are not only teeth and nails and their mechanical extensions in man-made tools of violence, but rituals and communications that play on others' emotions and guide them by the images before their eyes and in their minds. Through these efforts groups are created and other men are excluded from them; organizations are formed and their control disputed; vast industries are produced; art and science and the rest of our symbolic culture arise, forming an invisible network that dominates even the dominators and comprises the spiraling complexity of human consciousness in the face of the inert chemical universe.

Our own realization of these processes is gradually taking shape into a sociology. And if the sociologies of the far past—of the times of Marx, Spencer, and Sumner—have helped to create the popular world views of our day, we may expect the popular awareness of the future to take on a new sophistication and a new tone from the sociological advances of today: a new sophistication about the dilemmas and intricacies of a world in which men are free to conflict with each other, even as the chains of interdependence lock them in; and a new tone resulting from a new image of man. Thinkers of the past have seen man as a creature of his heredity or of his history of rewards and punishments, a thing of blind trial and error, or a cog in a larger structure or environment. All of these models contain elements of truth, but the best sociology gives yet another image of the fundamental nature of man: a creature who *creates* his own actions and their meanings and constructs new realities where none existed before. Constrained as we are in what we can easily or are likely to create, nevertheless the social world is our own product. The solid world dissolves, opening up a universe of possibilities.

EPILOGUE

THE SOCIOLOGY OF PAST AND FUTURE

We have brought the history of sociology up to the present. But what of the future of sociology? In principle it appears that sociology may be moving toward becoming a powerful explanatory science. Weber laid out the basis of a theory of stratification, politics, and social change capable of comprehending the complex interconnections of human motives and social institutions; subsequent research on organizations, groups, and cultures goes a long way toward fleshing it out into a refined set of explanations. The diverse approaches of Durkheim, Freud, and Mead to the nature of human interaction and human consciousness have been advanced by many years of empirical and theoretical applications and brought toward an illuminating synthesis by the symbolic interactionists, phenomenologists, and individual theorists like Erving Goffman. The various theoretical and empirical pieces of the puzzle seem to be available, at least in rough form; it only remains to put them together.

This is not to say that sociology is about to become a successful applied science as well. As we have argued in the Introduction, there is a crucial difference between objective explanations of the world and the subjective values that motivate persons to control or change that world. Even if we achieve agreement on an explanatory theory, the differences in values and interests among persons in different social positions will still exist; hence there will remain sharp disagreements about how the theory ought to be applied. The achievement of a genuine sociological science could not usher in a technocratic utopia; but it would enable various factions to pursue their interests more intelligently.

But the question remains: Will the potential pure science actually be achieved? Numerous obstacles still exist. Exclusive attention to the practical and ideological issues of current social problems and political controversies have diverted many sociologists from the task of developing the basic science; concern for technical refinements in research methods has sometimes displaced the larger aims of the discipline. The theory-oriented sociologists themselves are often caught up in factional fights, which obscure the ways in which theories on different levels of analysis must be fitted together to achieve a comprehensive explanation. Thus functionalist and conflict explanations vie in highly abstract terms, and theorists of face-to-face interaction debate with theorists of larger social structure over the true locus of sociological reality. Only when these models are intelligently integrated as applying to different aspects of human society will the long-sought general theory be possible.

Doubtless, a synthesis will eventually be accomplished, if only because of the tendency for the natural selection of the theory that can generate the most successful lines of research. But the long run may be very long indeed; the history of sociology shows that much of its most promising material can be neglected for many decades.

It is possible to prophesy with at least a little confidence, however. If sociological theory is at all advanced, it must be possible to turn it upon itself and to ask the sociological questions: What conditions determine whether men will do good theorizing or bad theorizing, speculate or research, concentrate on politics, on social problems, or on a general theory of society? What, in short, are the social causes of social thinking in all its varied forms? If we can answer these questions for the past, we will have a guidepost into the future.

As sociological theorists from Marx, Weber, and Durkheim through Goffman and Garfinkel have shown, men construct their ideas of reality from their immediate social circumstances. Each man lives in his own world of commonsense practicality, encased by the social rituals that tell him what is right and wrong, ordinary and sacred. Men can occupy as many different subjective worlds as there are different social situations. Furthermore, very little of these worlds need have any objective truth to them. Beyond a certain amount of practical understanding of the physical world and the practices of the social groups right around him, the individual can—and does—live in a murk of distortions and downright myths. And even more: Since some men derive political and religious authority and social status by manipulating other men's beliefs, there is a built-in bias *against* the discovery of objective truths about society.

This has been the case for most men throughout most of history. Primitive societies, for example, saw the social world entirely through the veil of fantasy built up around the religious rituals that permeated all aspects of life. In order for objective social knowledge to develop, several things had to happen. First, societies (or at least parts of them) had to become rationalized—in Weber's term, disenchanted. This began to occur in the agrarian empires of antiquity, in which the practical matters of government administration and commerce created a more matter-of-fact attitude toward the world. But practical necessities by themselves are a small aid to social thought, for it is possible to develop practical know-how without having it lead to a conscious understanding. Most of human history up through the present day shows that practical skills can coexist with all sorts of social myths and misconceptions. The second condition, therefore, was the rise of a group of intellectual specialists who could create a social community of their own—an intellectual community—within which the search for knowledge for its own sake could receive social support. From a sociological perspective, it is the social structure of such an intellectual community that determines the ideas of reality its members construct.

Only occasionally in world history have such communities of intellectuals been independent enough to create much in the way of knowledge judged by its own standards of truthfulness rather than by the larger world's standards of practicality or ideology. One such community flourished briefly in ancient Greece before being reabsorbed into the political and religious establishments. The foundation period of the European universities in the High Middle Ages provided another period of semi-independence, but it was confined largely to philosophers who prepared students to study theology.

The modern intellectual community of social thinkers began to take shape In the seventeenth and eighteenth centuries in Western Europe as intellectuals found independent bases of operations in political movements and in the leisure activities of parts of the affluent upper classes. The result was the outburst of creativity that intellectuals of the day called the Enlightenment. A second base for this kind of community came with the rise of modern government bureaucracies, which employed intellectuals to collect information for administrative purposes. A third and ultimately crucial development was the rise of the modern research-oriented university, beginning in Germany in the late eighteenth century and spreading to France, England, the United States, and elsewhere toward the end of the nineteenth century. Upon these various social bases the social sciences—history, economics, psychology, anthropology, sociology, and political science—began to split off from the general intellectual role of the Enlightenment philosopher. It is in the interaction of intellectuals finding their homes in these different institutions that the changes in modern sociology are to be explained.

THE DEVELOPMENT OF SOCIOLOGY

Sociology is the general science of social phenomena, and it has the most diverse roots of all the social sciences. It derives from the materials of historians and from the generalizing attempts of philosophers of history, from the concerns of institutional and historical economists and the fact-gathering of public administrators and reformers, from the work of socially minded psychologists and philosophers, and from the studies made by anthropologists interested in primitive culture and man's evolution. But each of these areas of research has crystallized into a scholarly community with its own focus (history, economics, psychology, anthropology), rather than concentrating on the development of generalizations about society itself.

Sociology got its independent identity toward the end of the nineteenth century as the ideology of liberal political movements. Accordingly, it was able to move toward a generalizing science only where academic systems existed in which liberal reformers were allowed to preach their doctrines. In this respect the social conditions for the establishment of scientific sociology were similar to those for economics, which began as the scientific justification for early British liberals. This has also meant that the main obstacle to the development of a genuinely scientific sociology has been its attachment to political ideologies more than to knowledge per se. The same holds true for the related discipline of political science, with the difference that the latter's attachment to ideological doctrine has until recently been so strict as to exclude any "science" in its concerns for the "political."

Sociology and political science were largely indistinguishable in the eighteenth century and before, when they made up two segments of the amorphous intellectual scene: On the one hand were the social philosophers, such as Hobbes, Locke, Montesquieu, Rousseau, Turgot, and Condorcet; on the other were the German professors of administrative science, with their collections of legal philosophy and descriptive "statistics." For most of the nineteenth century these two traditions continued, but with the difference that the intellectual world was becoming increasingly specialized and organized into distinct groups. History, economics, psychology, and anthropology gradually split off.

At the same time the industrial revolution and the democratization of governments in the West produced the beginnings of political movements and parties among the growing urban classes. This gave sociology a more strictly political focus than before. The first important sociologists were men like Saint-Simon, Comte, Tocqueville, Marx, Mill, Le Play, and Spencer, all of whom were outside the academic world and who addressed political audiences. We find in their thought the main formulations of most of the important ideologies that have since become popular: liberalism in both its laissez-faire and welfare-state forms, communism, socialism, and corporate conservatism. If we extend our focus to the second-rate thinkers, the group of nineteenth-century sociologists includes the founders of utopian movements like Fourier as well as early Fascist ideologues like Gobineau.

The most important of these men for the development of sociology were those who combined a university orientation with their political and popular interests. One of these was Comte, who was trained in the natural sciences at the *Ecole Polytechnique*. He hoped to take Saint-Simon's political ideology and build a social science out of it; his never-realized aim was to have a professorship established for himself at the *Ecole*. Another case was Marx, who lost an obviously successful career as a German philosophy professor because of his youthful political attachments and made up for it by making a comprehensive theory out of his revolutionary ideas. A third case was that of Le Play, who combined training in engineering with conservative politics to launch his meticulous studies of the working classes of Europe. Tocqueville stood apart from the others as a nonacademic politician who nevertheless combined original observation and historical scholarship with a generalizing outlook. He was really the last of the Enlightenment gentleman-intellectuals, combining the roles of historian, artist, and philosopher, in the manner of Montesquieu.

But as ideologists of political movements, these men's ideas did not become the basis for development by a community of researchers. This more strictly scholarly orientation would require an academic setting. Factual research was generated in the nineteenth century, but mostly by the practical administrators mentioned above. This kind of research had been carried out in Germany since the eighteenth century under the rubric of *Staatswissenschaft* (administrative science); it became prominent after 1872 through the efforts of a group of welfare-oriented German professors and administrators who formed the *Verein fur Sozialpolitik* (Union for Social Policy). In England the government investigating commissions, formed periodically since the inquiries into factory working conditions in the 1830s, performed a similar function, joined by various private philanthropists and reform organizations.

For the most part, this work remained completely descriptive, making no contributions to generalized theory. The nearest such work came to a theory was in the efforts of the Belgian astronomer Quételet in the 1830s. Quételet immersed himself in government statistics on births and deaths, suicides, crimes, and so forth, and emerged with a proposed science of "social physics." There was a flurry of interest in statistics across Europe and even in the United States. Unfortunately, Quételet's "laws" amounted to little more than the computation of a few simple probabilities and the demonstration that rates of population change or of crime could be predicted from the rates in previous years. The promises of statistics to produce great practical and intellectual benefits failed to materialize, and the field retired once more into the seclusion of administrative cubbyholes.

Sociology began to enter the universities toward the end of the nineteenth century. In the United States this happened at the time of the great academic revolution of the 1880s and 1890s. Many new universities were founded, and others were upgraded by the addition of research-oriented graduate schools and the inclusion of modern subjects in their curricula. The American universities were reformed on the German model, but they retained some distinctive traits. One of these was that control rested with a president rather than with the faculty. This meant that the American universities were much more receptive to new subjects than were the German universities, since approval was needed only from the president and not from the established powers on the faculty. American universities might have been under the autocracy of the presidents, but they escaped the autocracy of conservative professors guarding control of their fields.

The precarious financial position of the American universities made them oriented toward expanding their student bodies and attracting public support by any means possible. Increasing numbers of students meant increased income from tuition, alumni contributions, and state appropriations—the sort of benefits that European universities, supported by an autocratic state, did not need. American universities were thus growth oriented, which meant that the numbers of faculty in a field were continually expandable, unlike the European situation where a single full professor per field was often the rule. A by-product of these two conditions—presidential control and "market" orientation—meant that American universities alone were receptive to practical subjects, since administrative rather than scholarly interests dictated that the university should attempt to attract students by any means possible.

Because of these conditions the new American universities soon incorporated all varieties of social science and quickly achieved at least a quantitative leadership in most fields of research. (It should be kept in mind that the number of universities in America, even in the nineteenth century, was much greater than in any European country.) There had been numerous social-reform movements in nineteenth-century America: followers of Comte, Fourier, the British liberals, and many others. In 1865 these were amalgamated into the American Association for the Promotion of Social Science, which served as a lobbying organization to get its various subspecialties into the universities. History and economics managed this in the 1880s; sociology, anthropology, and political science in the 1890s; and psychology established its first departments separate from philosophy around 1910. The first department of sociology in the world was founded at the new University of Chicago in 1892, and others soon followed.

Like the other social sciences sociology achieved its place in American universities because its ideological and practical offerings were in keeping with the prevailing political atmosphere of liberalism and with the popular emphasis of American higher education. (Conversely, the least political and practical of the social sciences, anthropology, had the hardest time in the American universities; it drew much less interest than the other fields and generally remained a small area within sociology departments until the 1940s or even later. The opposite was the case in the intellectually oriented European universities, where anthropology was admitted early and sociology scarcely at all.) The resulting characteristic of sociology in America has been its overriding concern with social problems as seen from the point of view of liberal reformers; the elaboration and testing of general explanatory theory has been little pursued.

Insofar as a theory was needed to give intellectual justification to the field, early American sociologists picked it up from popularistic doctrines of evolution and from the social psychology found in philosophy departments. In these departments the German idealist philosophy, newly imported with the university revolution, mingled with the older British philosophy and the experimental psychology of the new psychologists, who had not yet acquired an independent department for their specialty.

The struggle between the old-style speculative philosophers and the new experimental psychologists produced two important developments: One of these—the ideology of the new psychologists, who were demanding a separate university department—was *behaviorism,* which denied the importance or even the reality of the philosophers' traditional concept of mind. The other, the defense of philosophers against behaviorism, was the social psychology formulated by such men as James, Mead, Dewey, and Cooley, emphasizing the symbolic and social nature of human thought and behavior. This "symbolic interactionism," as it has come to be known, is America's main contribution to sociological theory. It has remained the strongest (and often the only) theory in American sociology. One reason for its continuing popularity is that it does not raise the embarrassing questions about stratification or politics that a more structural theory would and hence guarantees that sociologists' research will not come into conflict wtih their underlying liberal ideology.

In Britain sociology scarcely made it into the academic world at all. The intellectually elite Oxford and Cambridge universities would not admit a discipline lacking in serious scholarly content, and British sociology found its home in private associations, in practically oriented research agencies, and in the London School of Economics, founded at the turn of the century by the Fabian Socialist Sidney Webb. A British sociological society was founded in 1908 under the leadership of city planners and philanthropists. At the London School of Economics sociology managed to pick up some scholarly clothing by associating itself with anthropology. British sociology has since reached a high level of practical and politically oriented research, most of it carried out by reformist Socialists in the tradition of the British investigating commissions. The situation began to change in the 1960s, however, with sociology beginning to win academic positions of its own.

The main theoretical breakthroughs in sociology came from the Continental universities, especially where sociology came in contact simultaneously with the generalizing style of philosophy and the traditions of scholarly research. But these theories were largely individual and tentative and did not pay off in the establishment of a continuing community dedicated to their development through further research. A number of sociologically oriented philosophies emerged after the 1870s, as philosophers in Germany, France, Belgium, and elsewhere reacted to the popularity of Spencer and Marx. Their first products were speculative models of society as an organism (Schäffle, Lilienfeld, Worms); their later models incorporated bits of Marx (Toennies) or neo-Kantian philosophy (Simmel).

Despite the fact that such reflections on society were a respectable part of the philosopher's role, found in philosophers from Kant and Hegel on up through Dilthey, none of these social theorists gained a solid foothold, even in philosophy, let alone a separate position for sociology. The primary source of antagonism to sociology came from the fact that it was associated with liberalism and positivism—the ideology that natural science could be used as a solution to social problems. This had been the philosophy of French and British intellectuals who championed the bourgeois era against the powers of the old regime, and hence it was anathema to official circles in authoritarian Germany and France. All the major sociologists of the period—Spencer, Durkheim, Weber, Simmel, Pareto, Toennies, the Americans—were liberals of either the laissez-faire or welfare-state persuasion. Where the government was antiliberal, sociology was not admitted.

Germany had the most productive university system for scholarly research of the nineteenth century, but it offered no entree to sociology. Simmel and Toennies were kept from promotion to full professorships in philosophy for almost thirty years (compared to an average of fifteen years for psychologists, whose field was nonideological). The greatest German sociologist, Weber, began in the research-oriented disciplines of legal and economic history. But he went beyond the narrower concerns of history by treating his data from a generalizing perspective derived from sociology and from a half-sympathetic but cynical interest in Marxism. Weber was instrumental in founding the German Sociological Society in 1908, and he spent much effort in trying to break the wall of academic political prejudice on behalf of leftist sociologists such as Simmel and Michels. Weber's campaign against value judgments was an effort to set aside the nationalist political standards that kept sociology from being recognized academically. He never succeeded, and the illness that forced his retirement from teaching during his most productive period may have been at least partially the result of his crisis of conscience over compromising with this state of affairs.

It was only during the short-lived Weimar Republic, when liberalism finally became respectable, that sociology found a place in the German universities. Its main research-oriented practitioners were led by the liberals Mannheim and von Wiese and the Marxists Lukacs, Horkheimer, and Adorno. The ideological standards of the Nazi period wiped out sociology again. (The Nazis did not much bother the by now ideologically acceptable subjects of economics and psychology, as long as their practitioners were not Jews.)

Weber's sociology balanced between the particularistic approach of German historical scholarship and the generalizing theories of sociological positivism. Durkheim, sociology's greatest general theorist, had no such compromise to make. As a liberal philosopher, after the replacement of the conservative French Second Empire by the liberal Third Republic of 1871, Durkheim was in a good position to get sociology accepted into the French universities. The new republic created a public-school system, taking over from the conservative Catholic Church, and the result was an expansion of the French universities to supply teachers. Along with this went an intellectual upsurge comparable to that following the establishment of a public-school system in eighteenth-century Prussia.

Conditions were thus favorable for sociology. The main obstacle was that the French university system, unlike the American, was controlled by an intellectual elite, and hence Durkheim had the task of making sociology intellectually respectable. He did this by combining his philosophically derived generalizing perspective with empirical materials that could test his propositions: first on the history of law, then with statistics on suicides, and finally with anthropological field data on primitive religion. His main academic rival was psychology, hence Durkheim's efforts to distinguish the sociological from the psychological level of analysis.

Durkheim was personally successful in getting a chair of sociology established for himself at the pinnacle of the French university system. But the extremely centralized structure of the French academic world prevented his work from being much followed up. There were few professorships, unlike in America. Moreover, anthropology was also fighting for a hold in the universities. Durkheim's alliance with social anthropology provided the latter field with an intellectual basis it had previously lacked, producing the functionalist school of anthropology. But it also caused a fusion between Durkheimian theory and anthropological research materials. The result was that empirical Durkheimian sociology has tended to become confined to the analysis of primitive society. Subsequent theorists in French sociology have generally produced new philosophical syntheses unattached to empirical research, as in the work of Gurvitch and of the post-World War II Marxists.

The fusion of theory with research on modern society forged by Durk-heim was thus largely lost. It has survived only in a mild degree, mainly in the United States, where it has served as one of the imports periodi-cally brought in to help fill the domestic theoretical vacuum. In the form of Parsonian functionalism a watered-down version of Durkheim pro-vides just the right underpinning of implicit liberalism to fit the political climate of American academe.

PROJECTIONS FOR THE FUTURE

Sociology today exists world-wide. The United States dominates the field by sheer quantity of sociologists and of research funds. Productive sociologists are found mainly in the bigger and wealthier universities of America's huge system of higher education, where research is the prime basis for promotion and a lively competition among universities for the most eminent researchers keeps everyone active. Sociologists at the minor schools have heavier teaching loads and less facilities for research, but the chance of promotion to a major university motivates some of them to research also. In addition, federal, state, and independ-ent foundation-supported agencies in the areas of education, crime, wel-fare, and mental health employ considerable numbers of sociologists and statisticians to amass figures and carry out policy-related research. A smaller group of sociologists are found in business, doing market and public-opinion research and, occasionally, internal organizational con-sulting. Finally, there are a small number of amateur sociologists (with some links to academic sociology) found in the sphere of intellectual magazines and the major news media and among popular authors.

Of these groups it is the top university sociologists who dominate, although sometimes precariously. It is their work that fills the profes-sional journals and makes up the landslide of books published for the huge textbook market. Top university professors do very well in incomes from publishing royalties and from salaries bid up by strong interuniver-sity competition and enjoy considerable freedom from rigid work schedules. Against this, the government or foundation-employed re-searchers have much less maneuverability and less income, despite their proximity to sources of research funds. They have the liability that how they spend their funds is subject to close administrative control. They must do research by the conceptions of their funding agencies, ordinarily within a bureaucratic ethos that emphasizes quantitative objec-tivity and practical relevance to the exclusion of any theoretically sig-nificant explanatory perspective on the subjects they investigate. Thus, although there have been thousands of practically oriented studies on education, poverty, and crime, they have brought little increase in our general understanding of these phenomena. Practical researchers in business are even more closely bound to produce results, and thus their work is factually minute and uncumulative. Such sociologists are really holders of minor staff positions for bureaucracies and carry little intellectual or social prominence.

The situation in the academic world has certain similarities to this. The large number of researchers has resulted in considerable specialization and an emphasis on the empirical details and technical refinements that distinguish one piece of research from another. The greatest prominence goes to "middle-range" theorists, who summarize previous studies in a particular area and point out questions for further research. This arrangement organizes sociology into communities, which ensure that a specialist will have at least some other persons who will be interested in his research and from whom he can get leads for further research. These research communities jealously guard their autonomy, with the result that American sociology tends to be a set of unrelated areas (research on social mobility, research on the effects of religion on students' performance, and so forth), each showing some cumulation, but cut off from any generalized explanatory theory. Needless to say, this has also tended to isolate most sociologists from the broadening perspectives of world history, which had been so important in the development of the great theories of sociology. The only feature of the academic environment conducive to general perspectives at all is the necessity for some sociologists to write textbooks for students, but even these tend to be summaries of research in disparate areas rather than attempts to integrate the research.

The basic cause of this situation is the large-scale, decentralized structure of American universities as compared with European universities. There are perhaps thirty to fifty American universities and colleges that can claim to be in the running for prominence in sociology, each of which has some ten to fifty faculty members engaged in their own research and teaching their own courses. The widespread support for sociologists makes it difficult for them to claim general prominence by virtue of their theorizing, since the others can easily ignore the claims of any general theory that has not been demonstrated to have immediate implications for their own research specialty. Thus, whereas in France a handful of Paris professors can claim to speak for sociology, and in Germany perhaps a few score can do this, in the United States there are many hundreds who could claim this role; hence almost none of them does, for the others are not likely to listen.

Theory in the United States is a more difficult path to recognition than is research. Consequently, much of American sociology is oblivious to the task of developing or testing serious theory; individual researchers can guard their autonomy if they can do their own specialized work without it. It is not surprising that virtually the only men in American sociology of the last half-century to claim general theoretical leadership —Parsons, Sorokin, perhaps Homans—were all at Harvard, the one

American university whose long-established intellectual and social prominence (and its wealth) gives it a social base that cannot be easily ignored.

Contacts between academic and nonacademic sociologists have varying effects on this situation. There has been an intermixture between academic and practical research, brought about especially in the 1950s and 1960s by men whose careers span both realms and by increasing funding of practical research in and around universities. This has reinforced the theoretical fragmentation of sociology by emphasizing factual data collection for limited practical purposes and by the bureaucratic emphasis on technique and on quantitative objectivity rather than on substance and explanatory understanding. This practical orientation is not entirely novel, however. Academic sociology began in the United States precisely because practically oriented social reformers got places in the universities, and the lack of theoretically related research is an old trait of American sociology. Nor has this emphasis been entirely without good effects. The growth of practically oriented organizational research in the 1930s (especially at the instigation of the Harvard Business School) produced a research field that has been exploited by theoretically oriented sociologists. In this area Selznick, Homans, Gouldner, Blau, Dalton, Etzioni, Goffman, and others have produced the most important advances in our understanding of social structure of the last half-century.

There has also been a small degree of contact between academic sociologists and the world of humanistic intellectuals. The most important contribution of this world to sociology has been David Riesman's work. In addition to producing a flow of popularizations from sociology to the outside (mostly of little originality or merit), this contact has also provided a reference group having perspectives and concerns that transcend the specialties of academic sociology. It may perhaps be credited with inspiring such men as Mills, Goffman, and Gouldner.

The patterns of American sociology have been set since the 1890s: a decentralized university system, lack of research-related general theory, emphasis on practical concerns. By the 1920s the increased numbers of sociologists began to produce intense specialization and emphasis on research technique. Most of these traits have intensified since then; as the educational system has become ever larger and more decentralized, research has become more bureaucratic, and practical research funding has increased. These conditions seem likely to prevail even more fully in the future. At the same time the social prestige and intellectual productivity of independent intellectuals has declined, and they have become less and less a source of ideas for sociologists. This pattern in American sociology seems likely to grow stronger.

The contrast with the rest of the world is instructive. The numerous universities of Asia (especially India) and of Latin America are unlikely to provide leadership; their positions afford little time or resources for research and are often appropriated as sinecures for members of personal cliques, rather than being given as rewards for intellectual competition. The "brain drain" of the most ambitious intellectuals to the West accentuates this situation. Japanese universities, perhaps the best of the non-Western nations, show an emphasis in sociology on quantitative description and narrow technicism reminiscent of the main trend in the United States. Soviet sociology is primarily descriptive and technical and almost totally devoid of intellectual content. This is the result of the elevation of Marxism from researchable theory to state dogma and the ensuing restriction of empirical sociology to practical work for government agencies. The situation is similar in Eastern Europe, but with a quasi-underground of political philosophy produced by contact with the West.

In Western Europe sociology is divided among the contradictory trends of technicism and philosophizing. Since World War II European states have set up a great number of bureaus and institutes to collect sociological data on public opinion, education, industrial relations, and so on. As in the United States the material produced by such practically oriented agencies has been primarily descriptive, rather than designed to test explanatory theory. It has risen steadily in technical quality but, except in the work of outstanding individuals like the French industrial sociologist Michel Crozier, has remained little integrated with the cumulative development of theory.

By the 1960s a sociological culture of technical specialists in administratively useful statistics had spread around the modern world. Nowhere has it paid off much in intellectual dividends nor, for that matter, in particularly significant practical results. But that is what one might expect, given the fact that sheer information, especially without theoretical understanding, can be useful only to justify the programs of one political power group or another. Since bureaucratic researchers, like any other government employees, usually develop great staying power once on the public payroll, their failure to be of substantial use will be no hindrance to their continued presence on the scene.

The main intellectual focus of Continental sociology is in the universities of Germany and France and in the intellectual communities of major urban centers like Paris. The latter groups are far more important in Europe than in the United States. They are also more politicized, mostly in the direction of the far left. They are the primary reference group for university students and thereby have some effect on the academic milieu and especially on sociologists. Their luminaries of the last decades have included such quasi-sociologists as Sartre, Merleau-Ponty, Marcuse, and Lévi-Strauss.

In France especially, chairs of sociology have been filled on political grounds, parceled out according to the strengths of political parties. This is true to a lesser degree in Germany, where the anti-Communist effects of the American occupation linger on in the older men. Thus,

French sociologists (who are found not only in the few chairs of sociology but also in philosophy) include Communists like Louis Althusser and Roger Garaudy and liberal ideologues like Raymond Aron. In Germany many leading sociological positions are filled by members of the neo-Marxist "Frankfurt school," which dates from the 1920s (see Chapter 11); its current eminence is Jurgen Habermas. The most prominent liberal sociologist is Ralf Dahrendorf, characteristically American-oriented in his research, who achieved a subcabinet-level post in the Brandt government. The theory-oriented university intellectuals, especially the radical ones, are largely cut off from the empirical research of the practical agencies, as the latter is regarded as a political sellout as well as lacking in intellectual substance.

Academic sociology on the Continent is highly centralized, as opposed to that of the United States. There are one or at most a few professors at each of a few dozen universities, and each has the responsibility to give an overview of the entire field in his lectures and to prepare students for comprehensive examinations at the end of their studies. By contrast, American professors give specialized courses (except to the introductory students) with their own separate exams. The result is to make European sociology very theoretical and generalized. All professors have a chance, indeed an obligation, to be theorists. To rest one's career on specialized empirical research, as is often done in the United States, is of distinctly low status. Practical research careers are given little weight, and there is often antagonism toward empirical research methods in the universities. The fact that the sociology professor is usually highly politicized and oriented toward the high-status intellectual community increases his emphasis on philosophical issues and his antagonism toward specialized research.

One result has been that few important advances have been made on the work of Weber, Simmel, Mannheim, Michels, or Durkheim in Europe. Weber's concepts of ideal types, *verstehen,* relativism, historicism, and value-free scholarship have been extensively discussed, and the question of whether his political writings were precursors of Fascism (a rather absurd allegation) has been analyzed at length. But Weber's efforts to explain the dynamics of stratification, politics, status cultures, bureaucracies, and world history have scarcely been touched, let alone tested and developed by subsequent research.

In the same way Durkheim's theories have largely given rise to speculative arguments in France about the nature of the collective conscience, the question of reification, and so forth, and to philosophical systems, such as that of Gurvitch, which elaborate similar elements. Only the anthropological researcher Lévi-Strauss has attempted to advance Durkheim's ideas as an explanatory theory, and he has done so primarily for primitive societies and with a sense of reviving a neglected theory.

Even Marx, the most popular theorist among current European sociologists, has given rise to virtually no empirical work. The philosophical and critical aspects of his thought have taken precedence over his explanatory theories of stratification and economic change, at which Marx made so promising a start before his thought was crystallized into dogma by his followers. It is not for lack of intellectual capital that European sociology does not produce advances in explanatory theory. Marx's work alone would be enough (as we can see when viewing what Weber built upon that basis), but the structure of the sociological world has kept it from being developed.

Recently, there are signs that things may be changing. The number of sociology professors has increased in the last decade as universities have expanded to accommodate more students. The result may be an overproduction of theorizing professors and a resulting shift toward more empirical research in the universities. (This is perhaps more likely to happen in pluralistic Germany than in centralized France, where an increased number of provincial professors does not change the situation of the Paris elite). A sign that this has begun may be the increased interest shown in such empirically related theories as Lévi-Strauss' structuralism and, more surprisingly, in Parsonian functionalism, even on the part of Marxists like Althusser and Mandel. It is ironic that European sociology, in search of explanatory rather than philosophical theory, should turn to a watered-down American version of European theories of the turn of the century. Weber, Durkheim, and Freud become accessible secondhand, after their firsthand value has been obscured by decades of philosophizing; unfortunately, the Parsonian version gives back all too little of what is really valuable in them. Nevertheless, a revival of the core tradition may be starting, and good results may be expected if a renewed theoretical orientation can be combined with the impressive historical scholarship that has never ceased functioning in Europe. The future impact of Goffman and the ethnomethodologists on European sociology may also be expected to be fruitful.

Much of the immediate future may thus depend on an international flow of ideas between the United States and Europe, which could make up for what is lacking in each. American universities have always stressed empirical research; what theories there have been in America have generally come from Europe. Small, Thomas, Park, and most of the other founding fathers studied in Germany, as did Talcott Parsons, and their theoretical ideas are mostly elaborations or syntheses of European theories. The main American innovation, the symbolic interactionism of Cooley and Mead, owes much to German philosophy, which it combined with the empirical orientation of early American psychology and sociology. Apart from this social psychology, American sociology was notably atheoretical until the 1930s, when it benefited from an infusion of German scholars fleeing the Nazis. Much of subsequent theory on the structural level derives from these men. We might mention the influence of Hans Gerth on C. Wright Mills; the importance of Reinhard Bendix for generating Weberian-style research on stratification, politics, and social change; the influence of Alfred Schutz on ethnomethodology. In a similar vein Erving Goffman derives his Durkheim-ianism from W. Lloyd Warner, who became part of the British school of social anthropology while doing research in Australia.

In a sense the classical theories are more alive in America, at least among particular groups of sociologists, than anywhere else. More-over, these theories are gradually becoming unified with empirical research. For example, work on organizations and stratification has gone far toward fleshing out the principles of Marx, Weber, Michels, and Mannheim, although the prevailing fragmentation of interests, plus per-haps a liberal bias against the political implications of such theories, has kept many sociologists from noticing it. Similarly, research generated around Goffman and his colleagues on social rituals and the social con-struction of reality offers much toward an elaboration of the most solid aspects of Durkheim's theory. If research on stratification can be taken out of its preoccupation with methodological technique and that on social interaction out of its narrow concern for social problems, the development of a genuinely explanatory theory uniting sociology may be at hand.

Whether this will come about or not remains subject to contending forces. One of these is the recent rise of an activist student body in the now mammoth American university system. Left-wing activism pro-vides a useful infusion of Marxism and related conflict theories and a healthy cynicism about popular functionalist and technicist ideologies. This may spur the younger and more sympathetic researchers, who come from the ranks of these same students, toward research de-signed to create a more adequate perspective on stratification and politics. The psychedelic culture, another wing of the student move-ment, may also have a catalyzing effect on theoretical views of individual consciousness, social interaction, and the enacted nature of institutions.

But such advance will occur only as long as there is a sustained tension between the research orientation of academic careerists and the ideological interests of student activists. If the anti-intellectual side of student culture, with its emphasis on pure activism or pure drug experience, were to prevail, research would stop or become chan-neled into narrow areas where dogma could be most easily confirmed. On the other hand, without the outside influence of radical politics and psychedelic philosophy, most American sociologists show every sign of becoming even more narrowly concerned with problems of technique and isolated areas of research.

The future, then, portends further conflict among the various factions in American sociology. It is possible that, given a not-too-unexpectable shift to the far right in American politics, the narrow technical research-ers would make an alliance with their counterparts in government bureaucracies, and sociological theorizing would be driven out of Amer-ica as effectively as it has been from the Soviet Union. Sociology would survive, but it would have nothing in common with the grand visions of Weber, Durkheim, Freud, or Mead. In this case the future of sociology would remain in Germany, France, and England, although the cutting off of Europe from the impetus of American research-oriented theory would slow down its development by many decades.

At the other extreme, the synthesis of classical theory with the existing tradition of research might be allowed to come about, and the result would be to set sociology on its feet at last as a powerful explanatory and predictive science. This would have enormously beneficial effects on social anthropology and on empirical political science, which would become unified into a general social science; on economics, which would derive a new basis on the institutional and historical sides and would be better able to solve its as yet intractable problems of explaining economic development and the distribution of wealth; on psychology, which would receive a new orientation putting the cognitive and emotional aspects of human communication into its center of focus; and on history, which is even now becoming a close partner of sociology in the understanding of society. We might even expect a renaissance in philosophy, provoked by a precise understanding of the social nature of morality and ethics and of the social construction of conscious "realities."

The future of sociology will probably not be as easy as all this, nor perhaps as bleak as the first alternative mentioned. In any case, the development of a genuine sociology will provoke political opposition, for it tears the veil from the ideological justifications of politicians and administrators of all stripes, exposing alike the ritual fantasies of the right, the utopian dreams of the left, and the subrational bureaucratic drift of the liberal center. The world view of a true sociology offers hopes about human potentialities, but at the same time it produces a mighty cynicism about contemporary institutions of all kinds and their likely transformations. With a theory in which conflict, ritual, plural group realities, and the supraindividual dynamics of organizations are inherent features, this is scarcely avoidable. For men of humanistic values the courses of action suggested under such a world view would probably amount to a libertarianism so thorough as to provoke a sizable and vicious reaction. Real knowledge about society would probably be considered not worth the price by most interest groups. It is conceivable that sociology, once attained to a powerful intellectual status, will be forced underground, after the fashion of the Pythagoreans, the Hermeticists, and other mystery cults of antiquity.

Societies of the future will be full of potential for making life thoroughly unpleasant for their members. Against this historical drift, sociology is working for liberation. The outcome will depend on the result of many struggles, begun long ago and likely to continue for a long time to come.

BIBLIOGRAPHICAL
SUGGESTIONS

There is no satisfactory overview of the whole development of sociology, but the scope of its history
can be gathered from Howard Becker and Harry
Elmer Barner, *Social Thought from Lore to Science,*
3 vols. (New York: Dover, 1961), which tells about
most of the main figures plus an extraordinary
number of minor ones, ranging from ancient Greece
to modern Afghanistan. Other texts, such as Nicholas S. Timasheff, *Sociological Theory* (New York:
Random House, 1967), and Don Martindale, *The
Nature and Types of Sociological Theory* (Boston:
Houghton Mifflin, 1960), share this lack of discrim-
ination between the important and the unimportant
and end up being catalogs. At the other extreme
there are books such as Raymond Aron, *Main Currents in Sociological Thought* (Garden City, N.Y.:
Doubleday, 1968), and Robert Nisbet, *The Sociological Tradition* (New York: Basic Books, 1966), which
treat just a few of the classical European thinkers.
These books are often insightful, but give the impression that social thought consists of the isolated efforts of great men and comes to an end
entirely when Max Weber died.

CHAPTER ONE   The Prophets of Paris:
Saint-Simon and Comte

The Enlightenment background of the early French
sociologists is made wonderfully alive by the
Frenchman Paul Hazard in *European Thought in the
Eighteenth Century* (New York: Meridian, 1963) and
is given a thorough German treatment by Ernst

Cassirer in *The Philosophy of the Enlightenment* (Boston: Beacon Press, 1955). The lives of Saint-Simon, Comte, Fourier, and others are found in Frank Manuel, *The Prophets of Paris* (Cambridge: Harvard University Press, 1963). A good selection of Saint-Simon's work in paperback is Henri de Saint-Simon, *Social Organization and Other Writings*, Felix Markham (ed.) (New York: Harper Torchbooks, 1964), and of Comte's work, *Auguste Comte: Sire of Sociology*, George Simpson (ed.) (New York: Crowell, 1969). Comte's lengthy *System of Positive Philosophy* is heavy going.

CHAPTER TWO   Sociology in the Underground: Karl Marx

Marx is still eminently readable, although this is least true of his masterpiece *Capital* (New York: Kerr, 1906). A good selection of his and Engels' writings is in Lewis S. Feuer, *Marx and Engels: Basic Writings on Politics and Philosophy* (Garden City, N.Y.: Doubleday, 1959). *The Eighteenth Brumaire of Louis Bonaparte* (New York: International, 1963) is a fine example of Marx as a historian of contemporary events. Erich Fromm's *Marx's Concept of Man* (New York: Frederick Unger, 1961) gives Marx's early humanist philosophy; Fromm's introduction is a useful guide to some rather difficult writing. Herbert Marcuse, *Reason and Revolution* (New York: Humanities Press, 1954), is the classic exposition of Hegel's system and its transformation into Marx's; Marcuse's *One-Dimensional Man* (Boston: Beacon Press, 1964) contains his revival of these themes, now popular with factions of the new left. The history of Marxism is most absorbingly told in Edmund Wilson, *To the Finland Station* (Garden City, N.Y.: Doubleday, 1953), beginning with Marx's eighteenth-century predecessors and continuing up to Lenin in 1917; Isaac Deutscher, *Trotsky*, 3 vols. (New York: Vintage, 1965), continues the story through the tragedy of Russia in the 1920s and 1930s. George Lichtheim, *Marxism* (New York: Praeger, 1965), gives a scholarly analysis of the Marxian system from the 1830s up to the present. Marx's economics is updated for current issues in Paul A. Baran and Paul A. Sweezy, *Monopoly Capital* (New York: Monthly Review Press, 1966), and Andrew Gunder Frank, *Capitalism and Underdevelopment in Latin America* (New York: Monthly Review Press, 1967). The continuing power of a sophisticated and nondogmatic use of Marxian sociology is illustrated by Norman Birnbaum, *The Crisis of Industrial Society* (New York: Columbia University Press, 1969).

CHAPTER THREE   The Last Gentleman: Alexis de Tocqueville

Tocqueville's *Democracy in America*, 2 vols. (New York: Knopf, 1945), is read everywhere; his *Old Regime and the French Revolution* (Garden City, N.Y.: Anchor, 1955) is even more worthwhile—short, concise, delightful in idea and expression. Tocqueville tells much of his own life story in his *Recollections* (New York: Columbia University Press, 1949). Tocqueville's work, as well as that of Saint-Simon, Comte, Durkheim, Sorel, and many others in this book, can hardly be understood apart from the history of France; Alfred Cobban, *A History of Modern France* (London: Penguin, 1957), outlines the story extremely well. George Pierson, *Tocqueville and Beaumont in America* (New

York: Oxford University Press, 1938), describes what Tocqueville saw and did not see on his visit to America. Tocqueville's ideas about mass society have been given modern currency by J. L. Talmon, *The Rise of Totalitarian Democracy* (Boston: Beacon Press, 1952), and Hannah Arendt, *The Origins of Totalitarianism* (New York: Harcourt, Brace & World, 1954).

CHAPTER FOUR   Do-Gooders, Evolutionists, and Racists

Of the Anglo-American tradition, the works most worth reading today are William Graham Sumner, *Folkways* (New York: Mentor, 1961), and Herbert Spencer, *Principles of Sociology* (New York: Appleton-Century-Crofts, 1884), Vol. 1. Spencer's work must be sampled selectively, as it is padded out to enormous length by all sorts of curious examples—but one must remember that he was being paid for monthly installments of magazine serials. The utilitarian tradition is described in Elie Halévy, *The Growth of Philosophical Radicalism* (Boston: Beacon Press, 1955). About all that anyone would ever want to know about early American sociology is found in L. L. and Jessie Bernard, *Origins of American Sociology* (New York: Russell & Russell, 1965), and in Roscoe C. and Gisela J. Hinkle, *The Development of Modern Sociology* (New York: Random House, 1954). Richard Hofstadter's *The Age of Reform* (New York: Vintage, 1955) and his *Anti-Intellectualism in American Life* (New York: Vintage, 1966) give the proper historical setting. The vogue of biological and racial explanations is hard to grasp from most modern histories, which leave this out because of their own bias as to what is important (and a good image) for the field. An exception is Pitirim Sorokin's *Contemporary Sociological Theories* (New York: Harper, 1928), which gives the full flavor of the pre-World War I intellectual milieu.

CHAPTER FIVE   Dreyfus' Empire: Emile Durkheim and Georges Sorel

Durkheim's major works are *The Division of Labor in Society* (New York: Free Press, 1964), *Suicide* (New York: Free Press, 1966), *The Rules of the Sociological Method* (New York: Free Press, 1938), *Socialism* (New York: Collier, 1962), *Professional Ethics and Civic Morals* (New York: Free Press, 1958), and *The Elementary Forms of the Religious Life* (New York: Collier, 1961). They are all well worth reading. Miscellaneous papers on and by Durkheim are in Kurt H. Wolff (ed.), *Emile Durkheim: Essays on Sociology and Philosophy* (New York: Harper Torchbooks, 1965). Talcott Parsons, *The Structure of Social Action* (New York: McGraw-Hill, 1937), Vol. 1, and Edward A. Tiryakian, *Sociologism and Existentialism* (Englewood Cliffs, N.J.: Prentice-Hall, 1962), give critical assessments. Major works in the French Durkheimian tradition are Marcel Mauss, *The Gift* (New York: Norton, 1967), and the writings of Claude Lévi-Strauss, to which the best introduction is his *Structural Anthropology* (Garden City, N.Y.: Anchor, 1967). Georges Sorel, in addition to *Reflections on Violence* (New York: Collier, 1961), wrote *The Illusions of Progress* (Berkeley: University of California Press, 1969). He and others in the *fin de siècle* generation in Europe are treated in H. Stuart Hughes, *Consciousness and Society* (New York: Vintage, 1961).

CHAPTER SIX   Max Weber: The Disenchantment of the World

Max Weber's works are voluminous and still of great value. His great (and uncompleted) lifework, the comparative studies of the world religions, is found in *The Protestant Ethic and the Spirit of Capitalism* (New York: Scribner, 1958), *The Religion of China* (New York: Free Press, 1951), *The Religion of India* (New York: Free Press, 1958), and *Ancient Judaism* (New York: Free Press, 1952). A short summary, based on his lectures, is in *General Economic History* (New York: Free Press, 1950). Weber's main generalizing efforts are found in *Economy and Society*, 3 vols. (New York: Bedminster Press, 1968); parts of this are in paperback as *The Theory of Social and Economic Organization* (New York: Free Press, 1964), *The Sociology of Religion* (Boston: Beacon Press, 1963), *The City* (New York: Free Press, 1968), *Max Weber on Law in Economy and Society* (Cambridge: Harvard University Press, 1954), and *From Max Weber: Essays in Sociology* (New York: Oxford University Press, 1946). The last also contains Weber's famous lectures "Science As a Vocation" and "Politics As a Vocation." Other writings are collected in *The Methodology of the Social Sciences* (New York: Free Press, 1959). Finally, Weber's *Rational and Social Foundations of Music* (Carbondale: Southern Illinois Press, 1958) is a tour de force in the sociology of cultural history. The major commentary on Weber is Reinhard Bendix, *Max Weber: An Intellectual Portrait* (Garden City, N.Y.: Anchor, 1962); see also Talcott Parsons, *The Structure of Social Action* (New York: McGraw-Hill, 1937), Vol. 2. Some applications of Weber's analysis from very different points of view are found in Reinhard Bendix *et al.* (eds.), *State and Society* (Boston: Little, Brown, 1968), and Talcott Parsons, *Societies: Comparative and Evolutionary Perspectives* (Englewood Cliffs, N.J.: Prentice-Hall, 1966).

CHAPTER SEVEN   Sigmund Freud: Conquistador of the Irrational

An excellent anthology of Freud's classic essays is A. A. Brill, *The Basic Writings of Sigmund Freud* (New York: Modern Library, 1938), which includes selections from *Psychopathology of Everyday Life, The Interpretation of Dreams, Three Contributions to the Theory of Sex, Wit and Its Relation to the Unconscious, Totem and Taboo,* and *The History of the Psychoanalytic Movement.* The *Collected Papers,* 5 vols. (London: Hogarth Press, 1953–1956), contains substantial and wide-ranging material for the serious student, while John Rickman, *A General Selection from the Works of Sigmund Freud* (Garden City, N.Y.: Anchor, 1957), is a topnotch sampler for beginners. The classic biography is Ernest Jones, *The Life and Work of Sigmund Freud* (New York: Basic Books, 1961); however, Maryse Choisy, *Sigmund Freud: A New Appraisal* (New York: Philosophical Library, 1963), is the most intimate, in-depth psychological portrait of the founder. Freud's views on religion and culture are amplified in *The Future of an Illusion* (Garden City, N.Y.: Anchor, 1957) and *Civilization and Its Discontents* (New York: Norton, 1961).

Outstanding secondary sources include Erich Fromm, *Sigmund Freud's Mission* (New York: Harper & Row, 1959); Philip Reiff, *Freud: The Mind of the Moralist* (New York: Doubleday, 1961); Paul Roazen, *Freud: Political and Social Thought* (New York: Knopf, 1968); Bartlett H. Stoodley, *The Concepts of Sigmund Freud* (New York: Free Press, 1959); and David Bakan, *Sigmund Freud and the Jewish Mystical Tradition* (New York: Van Nostrand, 1958). In *Life Against Death* (Middleton, Conn.: Wesleyan University Press, 1959) Norman O. Brown applies psychoanalysis to history in an illuminating manner. Herbert Marcuse's *Eros and Civilization* (New York: Vintage, 1962) explores man's potentialities for regeneration in terms of freedom from repression. Hendrik M. Ruitenbeek (ed.), *Psychoanalysis and Social Science* (New York: Dutton, 1964), selects eleven key essays that probe the integration of the social sciences and psychoanalysis in America. Paul Robinson, *The Freudian Left* (New York: Harper & Row, 1969), sums up the contributions of Reich, Roheim, and Marcuse. Finally, it should be noted that although Freud has been obscured by a series of successors, he is well worth reading in the original.

CHAPTER EIGHT   The Discovery of the Invisible World:
Simmel, Cooley, and Mead

Simmel's works are available in Kurt H. Wolff (ed.), *The Sociology of Georg Simmel* (New York: Free Press, 1950) and *Conflict and the Web of Group-Affiliations* (New York: Free Press, 1955). Essays by and about Simmel are in Kurt H. Wolff (ed.), *Essays on Sociology, Philosophy, and Aesthetics by Georg Simmel et al.* (New York: Harper Torchbooks, 1965), and Lewis A. Coser, *Georg Simmel* (Englewood Cliffs, N.J.: Prentice-Hall, 1965). On Simmel, see Nicholas J. Spykman, *The Social Theory of Georg Simmel* (Chicago: University of Chicago Press, 1925), and Lewis A. Coser, *The Functions of Social Conflict* (New York: Free Press, 1956).

The major works of Charles H. Cooley are *Human Nature and the Social Order* (New York: Schocken, 1964), *Social Organization: A Study of the Larger Mind* (New York: Schocken, 1962), and *Social Process* (Carbondale: Southern Illinois Press, 1966). He lays down his optimistic, beginning-of-the-century sociology in this trilogy. Cooley displays his breadth and depth of interest in *Sociological Theory and Social Research* (New York: Kelley, 1969), which contains selected early papers. The best secondary source is Albert J. Reiss (ed.), *Cooley and Sociological Analysis* (Ann Arbor: University of Michigan Press, 1968), which is a recent collection of essays on Cooley's significance by contemporary theorists.

George H. Mead's primary contribution to social psychology is found in *Mind, Self, and Society*, Charles W. Morris (ed.) (Chicago: University of Chicago Press, 1934). *The Philosophy of the Act* (Chicago: University of Chicago Press, 1938) contains an analysis of the stages of the act, which is relevant to Mead's theory; *The Philosophy of the Present* (La Salle, Ill.: Open Court, 1959) includes important material on the self in relation to time; and *Movements of Thought in the Nineteenth Century* (Chicago: University of Chicago Press, 1936) presents a classic chapter on the problem of society, in addition to valuable work on the philosophic foundations of twentieth-century scientific sociology.

Worthwhile secondary sources are Jerome G. Manis and Bernard N. Meltzer, *Symbolic Interaction: A Reader in Social Psychology* (Boston: Allyn & Bacon, 1967), and Herbert Blumer, *Symbolic Interactionism: Perspective and Method* (Englewood Cliffs, N.J.: Prentice-Hall, 1969). The latter is the most exhaustive exposition of symbolic interactionism by Mead's foremost sociological pupil.

John Dewey, *Human Nature and Conduct* (New York: Modern Library, 1957), is his treatise on social psychology, and William James, *Psychology: Briefer Course* (New York: Collier, 1962), contains valuable material for understanding the development of self theory. See also John J. McDermott (ed.), *The Writings of William James* (New York: Random House, 1967).

CHAPTER NINE   The Discovery of the Ordinary World:
Thomas, Park, and the Chicago School

The history of the Chicago school is given in Robert E. L. Faris, *Chicago Sociology* (San Francisco: Chandler, 1967). The studies of Thomas and Znaniecki, Park, and their followers are described in John Madge, *The Rise of Scientific Sociology* (New York: Free Press, 1962). Representative writings may be sampled in Morris Janowitz (ed.), *W. I. Thomas on Social Organization and Social Personality* (Chicago: University of Chicago Press, 1967), Ralph H. Turner (ed.), *Robert E. Park on Social Control and Collective Behavior* (Chicago: University of Chicago Press, 1967), Otis Dudley Duncan (ed.), *William F. Ogburn on Culture and Social Change* (Chicago: University of Chicago Press, 1964), and Albert J. Reiss, Jr. (ed.), *Louis Wirth on Cities and Social Life* (Chicago: University of Chicago Press, 1966). Also of interest is the famous textbook by Robert E. Park and Ernest W. Burgess, *Introduction to the Science of Sociology* (Chicago: University of Chicago Press, 1921).

CHAPTER TEN   The Construction of the Social System:
Pareto and Parsons

Pareto's *The Mind and Society*, 5 vols. (New York: Harcourt, Brace, 1935), is best approached through the selections in Joseph Lopreato (ed.), *Vilfredo Pareto* (New York: Crowell, 1965). Talcott Parsons' first major work, *The Structure of Social Action* (New York: Free Press, 1968), contains an important interpretation of Pareto as well as of Alfred Marshall, Durkheim, and Weber. Parsons' other works include *The Social System* (New York: Free Press, 1951), *Essays in Sociological Theory* (New York: Free Press, 1954), *Toward a General Theory of Action* (with Edward Shils) (Cambridge: Harvard University Press, 1951), *Economy and Society* (with Neil J. Smelser) (New York: Free Press, 1956), *Societies: Comparative and Evolutionary Perspectives* (Englewood Cliffs, N.J.: Prentice-Hall, 1961), and the introductory essays in *Theories of Society* (edited with Edward Shils, Jesse R. Pitts, and Kaspar Naegele) (New York: Free Press, 1961). Commentaries are found in Max Black (ed.), *The Social Theories of Talcott Parsons* (Englewood Cliffs, N.J.: Prentice-Hall, 1961), and Alvin W. Gouldner, *The Coming Crisis in Western Sociology* (New York: Basic Books, 1970). Other varieties of functionalism are presented in Kingsley Davis, *Human Society* (New York: Macmillan, 1949), and Robert K. Merton, *Social Theory and Social Structure* (New York: Free Press, 1968), and are debated in the papers collected in N. J. Demerath III and Richard A. Peterson (eds.), *System, Change, and Conflict* (New York: Free Press, 1967). Representative works of modern functionalists include Neil J. Smelser, *Theory of Collective Behavior* (New York: Free Press, 1963); S. N. Eisenstadt, *The Political Systems of Empires* (New York: Free Press, 1963); and Robert N. Bellah, *Tokugawa Religion* (New York: Free Press, 1957).

CHAPTER ELEVEN   Hitler's Shadow: Michels, Mannheim, and Mills

Robert Michels' main work is *Political Parties* (New York: Collier, 1962); also available in English is his *Introductory Lectures on Political Sociology* (New York: Harper Torchbooks, 1966). Karl Mannheim's translated works include *Ideology and Utopia* (New York: Harcourt, Brace, 1936), *Man and Society in an Age of Reconstruction* (New York: Harcourt, Brace, 1940), *Diagnosis of Our Time* (London: Routledge & Kegan Paul, 1943), *Essays on the Sociology of Knowledge* (New York: Oxford University Press, 1952), and *Freedom, Power, and Democratic Planning* (New York: Oxford University Press, 1950). C. Wright Mills wrote *The New Men of Power* (New York: Harcourt, Brace, 1948), *The Puerto Rican Journey* (New York: Oxford University Press, 1950), *White Collar* (New York: Oxford University Press, 1951), *Character and Social Structure* (with Hans Gerth) (New York: Harcourt, Brace & World, 1953), *The Power Elite* (New York: Oxford University Press, 1956), *The Causes of World War Three* (New York: Simon and Schuster, 1958), and *The Sociological Imagination* (New York: Oxford University Press, 1959). His collected papers are edited by Irving Louis Horowitz under the title *Power, Politics, and People* (New York: Oxford University Press, 1963).

CHAPTER TWELVE   Erving Goffman and the Theater of Social Encounters

Erving Goffman's main works are *The Presentation of Self in Everyday Life* (Garden City, N.Y.: Doubleday, 1959), *Asylums* (Garden City, N.Y.: Doubleday, 1961), *Encounters* (Indianapolis: Bobbs-Merrill, 1961), *Behavior in Public Places* (New York: Free Press, 1963), and *Interaction Ritual* (Garden City, N.Y.: Doubleday, 1967). Harold Garfinkel's work is presented in *Studies in Ethnomethodology* (Englewood Cliffs, N.J.: Prentice-Hall, 1967). Important background for American ethnomethodology is Alfred Schutz, *Collected Papers* (The Hague: Nijhoff, 1962–1966). Schutz's work has also been developed in Peter Berger and Thomas Luckman, *The Social Construction of Reality* (Garden City, N.Y.: Doubleday, 1967).

INDEX